THE SAYINGS OF JESUS IN THE WRITINGS
OF JUSTIN MARTYR

SUPPLEMENTS
TO
NOVUM TESTAMENTUM

VOLUME XVII

LEIDEN
E. J. BRILL
1967

THE SAYINGS OF JESUS
IN THE WRITINGS
OF JUSTIN MARTYR

BY

A. J. BELLINZONI

LEIDEN
E. J. BRILL
1967

Library of Congress Catalog Card Number:
67-20358

TABLE OF CONTENTS

PREFACE

In the fall of 1958 Professor Helmut Köster offered at Harvard University a course in the development of gospel tradition in the second century. As a term project for this course, I prepared a paper on the relationship of Justin Martyr's *Dialogue* 35: 3 to the parallel gospel tradition. Unknowingly I had begun the preparation of this volume. Work on this paper excited in me an interest in second century Christianity and its relationship to the Christianity of the first generations. For my doctoral dissertation at Harvard, I, therefore, decided to pursue this interest and examine in detail the sayings of Jesus in the writings of Justin Martyr. The present volume is a revision of that dissertation.

For their helpful suggestions in the preparation of this manuscript at various stages, I should like to thank Professors Amos Wilder and Krister Stendahl of Harvard and Professor W. D. Davies of Union Theological Seminary. Only I can appreciate the unselfish contribution that Professor Helmut Köster of Harvard has made toward the preparation of this volume. He has read each word of the manuscript in various stages of preparation and has offered valuable suggestions concerning the organization and presentation of the material and countless detailed suggestions that I have incorporated into my argument. Without his assistance the final product would have been much inferior; yet I myself accept full responsibility for the shortcomings of this study.

I was helped in the reading of proofs by Mrs. Velma Van Buskirk, Director of Publications at Wells College, who made valuable criticisms and suggestions. To President L. J. Long of Wells College I am grateful for providing, with the help of an anonymous foundation, a grant to help defray part of the cost of the publication of this book. And, finally, what this modest volume owes to my parents must remain unexpressed. Its dedication to them serves as a small token of gratitude.

Arthur J. BELLINZONI, Jr.

Wells College, Aurora, New York.
December 9, 1966

CHAPTER ONE

INTRODUCTION

About the middle of the second century Justin Martyr engaged in an active defense of Christianity against paganism, Judaism, and heretical forms of Christianity for which work he can safely be called the first outstanding Christian apologist. As a young man Justin sought after the truth in the pagan philosophies of Stoicism, Aristotelianism, Pythagoreanism, and Platonism; but shortly after his conversion to Christianity in about 130 Justin opened in Rome a Christian school of philosophy from which he fearlessly defended Christianity until his martyrdom in about 165. In his role as a Christian apologist Justin wrote for those inside the church as well as for those outside to whom many of his writings were formally addressed. His work, therefore, certainly had a catechetical as well as an apologetic purpose.

Justin's writings frequently contain passages reminiscent of passages from the canonical gospels, and for the last two centuries many scholars have been trying to ascertain the exact literary relationship between the writings of Justin and the canonical gospels.[1] Justin's deviation from the text of the canonical gospels has been variously attributed in the nineteenth century and in the early part of the twentieth century to failure of memory,[2] to the use of one or more extra-canonical gospels,[3]

---

[1] It is beyond the scope of this work to recount the history of research concerning the problem of Justin's literary relationship to the canonical gospels, especially the older studies of the last century. A detailed account of this history can be found in the following works: Wilhelm Bousset, *Die Evangeliencitate Justins des Märtyrers in ihrem Wert für die Evangelienkritik* (Göttingen, 1891), pp. 1-12; Carl August Credner, *Beiträge zur Einleitung in die biblischen Schriften* (Halle, 1832), pp. 133-149; Adolf Hilgenfeld, *Kritische Untersuchungen über die Evangelien Justin's, der Clementinischen Homilien und Marcion's* (Halle, 1850), pp. 31-45; Karl Semisch, *Die apostolischen Denkwürdigkeiten des Märtyrers Justinus* (Hamburg, 1848), pp. 16-60.

[2] Semisch, see especially pp. 389 ff; Theodor Zahn, *Geschichte des neutestamentlichen Kanons*, I, 2 (Erlangen, 1888), pp. 463-585.

[3] Credner maintained that Justin used as his source the extra-canonical *Gospel according to Peter*, a document that Credner regarded as essentially identical to the *Diatessaron* of Tatian, and the *Gospel according to the Hebrews* (*Beiträge*, see especially p. 266; and *Geschichte des neutestamentlichen Kanons* [Berlin, 1860], see especially pp. 21 f.). The position that Justin used the *Gospel according to Peter* was defended again by Hilgenfeld, who also maintained that Justin used in addition the *Protoevangelium of James*. The thesis that Justin used a fourth synoptic gospel

to the use of pre-synoptic material,[1] and to the use of a post-synoptic harmony;[2] and it has sometimes been maintained that there is no way to prove the use of any source other than the canonical gospels.[3]

During this century, on the other hand, there have been fewer studies concerning Justin's dependence on gospel material. E. R. Buckley has proposed the thesis that Justin first became acquainted with many of the sayings of Jesus in a source in which these sayings "occurred in a somewhat different form and often in a different context from that in which they occur in the canonical Gospels," and that "this source may have been that to which Justin refers as 'the Gospel' in *Dialogue* 100." [4] Buckley believed that Justin later read the synoptic gospels but that his quotations were taken not from them but from this other gospel, which also probably provided "some account of the life and death of Christ as well as a collection of his sayings." [5]

In an unpublished doctoral thesis E. L. Titus acknowledged the possibility that Justin may have quoted from memory, [6] but his principal thesis was that there were dominant motivations that accounted for the textual variants in the writings of Justin, whether his sources were oral or written; and he has divided these motivations into the following categories: historical, harmonistic, ethical and practical, stylistic, explanatory, and dogmatic.[7]

Leon E. Wright maintained that Justin may have used the canonical gospels, but he has questioned the use of a harmony because of Justin's

---

was put forth by G. Volkmar (*Über Justin den Märtyrer und sein Verhältniss zu unsern Evangelien* [Zurich, 1853]), and A. Thoma argued that Justin knew a fifth canonical gospel ("Justins literarisches Verhältnis zu Paulus und zum Johannisevangelium," *Zeitschrift für wissenschaftliche Theologie*, XVIII [1875], pp. 383-412, 490-565).

[1] Bousset, see especially pp. 114 f.

[2] Moritz von Engelhardt, *Das Christenthum Justins des Märtyrers* (Erlangen, 1878), pp. 335 ff., especially p. 345; William Sanday, *The Gospels in the Second Century* (London, 1876), pp. 136 ff., note 1; Ernst Lippelt, *Quae Fuerint Justini Martyris* ΑΠΟΜΝΗΜΟΝΕΥΜΑΤΑ *Quaeque Ratione Cum Forma Syro-Latina Cohaeserint* (Halle, 1901), p. 35.

[3] Brooke Foss Westcott, *A General Survey of the History of the Canon of the New Testament* (London, 1870), pp. 133, 148; Aloys Baldus, *Das Verhältnis Justins des Märtyrers zu unsern synoptischen Evangelien* (Münster, 1895), pp. 98 ff.

[4] E. R. Buckley, "Justin Martyr's Quotations from the Synoptic Tradition," *Journal of Theological Studies*, XXXVI (1935), p. 175.

[5] *Ibid.*, pp. 175 f.

[6] Eric Lane Titus, "The Motivations of Changes Made in the New Testament by Justin Martyr and Clement of Alexandria: A Study in the Origin of New Testament Variation," Unpublished Ph. D. dissertation (University of Chicago, 1942), p. 7.

[7] *Ibid.*, p. 12.

inconsistent harmonization of parallel material.[1] But like Titus, Wright was concerned primarily with the motivations of alterations in the words of Jesus and classified these motivations under the following headings: ethical and practical, explanatory, stylistic, and dogmatic.[2]

Edouard Massaux has argued that Justin was dependent on only the canonical gospels, which he sometimes quoted exactly, sometimes harmonized, and sometimes modified for dogmatic or catechetical reasons.[3] And more recently Otto Piper has maintained that Justin's use of sources was not limited to the canonical gospels but extended to include any writings that were consistent with the *euangelion*, the saving work of God revealed in Jesus and still alive in the life of the early church, a thesis supported, according to Piper, by Justin's tendency to refer to his source or sources as "Memoirs of the Apostles" (ἀπομνημονεύματα τῶν ἀποστόλων) rather than as "Gospels" (εὐαγγέλια).[4]

But perhaps the most satisfactory approach to the question of Justin's dependence on gospel tradition has been made available by Form Criticism. One of the principal faults of the previous investigations is that they have tended to treat narrative and sayings material together, but the narrative tradition and the sayings tradition are not subject to the same laws of transmission.[5] First, the early church would not be expected to be so careful in preserving narrative material as it was in preserving the words of Jesus, to which a special oracular value was probably ascribed. Secondly, the sayings of Jesus were collected separately from the narrative material in documents such as Q and the *Gospel of Thomas*. Thirdly, it is almost certain that the early church used for proselytes oral and/or written catechetical material that embodied teachings based on sayings of Jesus and that these catechisms circulated apart from the rest of the gospel material.[6]

---

[1] Leon E. Wright, *Alterations of the Words of Jesus as Quoted in the Literature of the Second Century* (Cambridge, Massachusetss, 1952), p. 11.

[2] *Ibid.*, p. 14.

[3] Edouard Massaux, *Influence de l'Evangile de saint Matthieu sur la Litterature chrétienne avant Irénée* (Louvain, 1950), pp. 465-570; "Le Texte du Sermon sur la Montagne de Matthieu Utilisé par Saint Justin," *Ephemerides Theologicae Lovanienses*, XXVIII (1952), pp. 411-448.

[4] Otto A. Piper, "The Nature of the Gospel according to Justin Martyr," *The Journal of Religion*, XLI, 3 (July 1961), pp. 155-168.

[5] Martin Dibelius, *Die Formgeschichte des Evangeliums*, 3rd edition (Tübingen, 1959), p. 26; Rudolf Bultmann, *History of the Synoptic Tradition*, translated by John Marsh (New York, 1963).

[6] Philip Carrington, *The Primitive Christian Catechism* (Cambridge, 1940); Edward G. Selwyn, *The First Epistle of Peter* (London, 1946); Alfred Seeberg, *Der Katechismus der Urchristenheit* (Leipzig, 1903); Dibelius, pp. 25 f.

The question of the extent of the formative period of the gospel tradition has recently been treated by Helmut Köster, who found at the period of the Apostolic Fathers dependence on both written and oral tradition,[1] but who believed that Justin was probably dependent almost exclusively on the canonical gospels and that a study of the gospel citations of Justin is necessary to complete our understanding of the period of the Apostolic Fathers.[2] Such a study of Justin's gospel citations has already been begun by Köster himself in a still unpublished work limited to a study of the narrative material. There he concluded that Justin did not use the synoptic gospels in a systematic way but that he used them rather to interpret the Old Testament.[3] Köster argued that it did not occur to Justin to quote the exact text of a gospel narrative except when the gospels themselves were quoting from the Old Testament, and in such instances Justin quoted exactly.

Because of the different laws governing the transmission of the tradition of narrative material and the tradition of sayings material, it is necessary to treat a study of the quotations of the words of Jesus apart from a study of the narrative material; and it is such a study of the sayings of Jesus that I expect to undertake here. The importance of such a study is obvious when we realize that Justin wrote during the relatively short period of transition between the time when the Apostolic Fathers were still dependent, at least in part, on oral tradition and the time when Irenaeus assumed the authority of the Fourhold Gospel in about 180.[4]

It is also significant that since the end of the last century archaeologists have uncovered material that affects our understanding of the development of the sayings of Jesus in the second century. Parts of the *Gospel according to the Hebrews* and the *Gospel according to the Egyptians* had

---

[1] Helmut Köster, *Synoptische Überlieferung bei den Apostolischen Vätern* (Berlin, 1957). See also E. Basıl Redlich, *Form Criticism Its Value and Limitations* (London, 1939), p. 78, where it has been objected that Form Criticism has neglected to define the extent of the formative period; and Vincent Taylor, *The Formation of the Gospel Tradition* (London, 1957), p. 1, where it has been wrongly asserted that "in the Gospels the 'tradition' has attained a relatively fixed formation; it is no longer subject to change, except as it is altered by copyists or by the writers of the later Apocryphal Gospels."

[2] p. 267.

[3] Helmut Köster, *Septuaginta und Synoptischer Erzählungsstoff im Schriftbeweis Justins des Märtyrers* (Habilitationsschrift, Heidelberg 1956).

[4] *Against Heresies* III, 11, 8. Although his opinion was not, by any means, universally accepted by the early church, it is significant that Irenaeus assumed this position as early as about 180 (see also *Against Heresies* III, 1, 1). It should also be remembered that Justin's pupil Tatian harmonized all four of the canonical gospels in his *Diatessaron*.

already been known through quotations by Clement of Alexandria, and many other apocryphal gospels had long been known by name. But in 1886-87 Greek fragments of the *Gospel of Peter* were discovered,[1] and in 1897 the first volume of papyri found at Oxyrhynchus in Egypt was published.[2] A second century papyrus containing sayings of Jesus was discovered in 1935,[3] and about 1945 a wealth of material was found near Nag Hammadi among which was the *Gospel of Thomas*, a collection of sayings of Jesus.[4] From all this material we gain the assurance that during the period in which Justin wrote there were still circulating, at least among certain heretical circles in Egypt, sayings of Jesus different from the sayings that occur in the canonical gospels. There is, therefore, little doubt that there is need for a new investigation of the sayings of Jesus in the writings of Justin Martyr.

Although there are numerous works that have been attributed to Justin by both ancient and modern authors,[5] only three authentic works survive:[6] the *First Apology*, the *Second Apology*, and the *Dialogue with*

---

[1] Christian Maurer in Schneemelcher and Hennecke, *New Testament Apocrypha*, Volume I (Philadelphia, 1963), pp. 179 ff.

[2] B. P. Grenfell and A. S. Hunt, ΛΟΓΙΑ ΙΗΣΟΥ, *Sayings of our Lord* (New York, 1897); Grenfell and Hunt, *New Sayings of Jesus and Fragment of a Lost Gospel from Oxyrhynchus* (London, 1904); cf. also Hugh G. Evelyn White, *The Sayings of Jesus from Oxyrhynchus* (Cambridge, 1920).

[3] H. Idris Bell and T. C. Skeat, *Fragments of an Unknown Gospel and Other Early Christian Papyri* (London, 1935).

[4] Robert M. Grant, *The Secret Sayings of Jesus* (London, 1960; *The Gospel According to Thomas*, translated by A. Guillaumont, Henri-Charles Puech, Gilles Quispel, Walter Till, and Yassah 'Abd Al Masīḥ (New York, 1959).

[5] Eusebius listed eight works of Justin (*Eccl. Hist.* IV, 18): *Apology to Antoninus Pius, Apology to the Roman Senate, Discourse to the Greeks, A Confrontation, On the Sovereignty of God, Psaltes, On the Soul,* and *Dialogue with Trypho* (cf. also IV, 11, 11). He also mentioned that Irenaeus knew of a treatise *Against Marcion* (IV, 18, 9 and IV, 11, 8 f.). In addition, several other works have been preserved under the name of Justin, but they were certainly not written by him; see Edgar J. Goodspeed, *A History of Early Christian Literature* (Chicago, 1942), pp. 146 f.

[6] For a discussion of the genuineness of the writings of Justin, the reader is referred to the following: Edwin Preuschen, "Die Echtheit von Justin's Dialog gegen Trypho," *Zeitschrift für die neutestamentliche Wissenschaft* (1919-1920), pp. 102-127; Leopold Fonck, "Die Echtheit von Justins Dialog gegen Trypho," *Biblica*, II (1921), pp. 342-347; Gustav Krüger, "Zu Justin," *Zeitschrift für die neutestamentliche Wissenschaft*, VII (1906), pp. 138 f.; Wilhelm Arendt, "Kritische Untersuchungen über die Schriften Justins des Märtyrers," *Theologische Quartalschrift* (1834), pp. 256-295; Wilhelm von Christs, *Geschichte der griechischen Litteratur*, 5th ed., II, 2 (Munich, 1913), pp. 1028-1035; Johannes Dräseke, "Zu den unter des Justinus Namen überlieferten christologischen Bruchstücken," *Jahrbücher für protestantische Theologie*, X (1884), pp. 347-352; Adolf Harnack, *Geschichte der altchristlichen Litteratur* (Leipzig, 1893), pp. 99-114; Adolf Hilgenfeld, "Die Überlieferung über die griechischen Apologeten des Christenthums im

Trypho. In this study I shall, therefore, not consider any of the spurious works of Justin but rather only the *Dialogue* and the *First Apology*, the genuineness of which is well established.[1]

The *Apology* and the *Dialogue* are preserved in two manuscripts, one from 1364 and the other from 1541; and in addition there are a fifteenth century fragment and parts of two sixteenth century Latin manuscripts that preserve chapters 65-67 of the *Apology*.[2] It is generally agreed that these two complete manuscripts are either copies of a single prototype or that the latter is a copy of the former,[3] so the question of the reliability of the text of Justin's writings rests substantially upon the evidence of a single textual witness. There is, however, good reason to believe that we are dealing with a manuscript tradition that is not substantially different from Justin's own autograph manuscripts. (1) If the apparent references to the canonical gospels in the writings of Justin had been corrupted by the copyists in the course of the centuries of transmission, we would naturally expect this corruption to take the form of assimilation to the text of the canonical gospels; and such is not the case. Indeed, many of the sayings of Jesus in Justin's writings differ markedly from the text of the canonical gospels, and this deviation would seem to indicate that the text has not been deliberately altered by copyists. (2) In examining a fragment of a Greek text of Micah 4: 3-7 deposited in a cave of Judea after the revolt of Ben Kosebah, Barthélemy observed that it was substantially identical to a section of *Dialogue* 109, which quotes the same Old Testament text.[4] Barthélemy found that this manuscript agrees with Justin against the Septuagint more often than it disagrees with Justin, such variations being very few. Barthélemy,

---

zweiten Jahrhundert und ihr neuester Censor," *Zeitschrift für wissenschaftliche Theologie*, XXVI (1883), pp. 1-45; Hans Lietzmann, "Justinus der Märtyrer," *Pauly-Wissowa Real-Encyclopädie der classischen Altertumswissenschaft*, X (Stuttgart, 1919), cols. 1332-1337. Some scholars defend the authenticity of *De Resurrectione* as a genuine writing of Justin; although it is beyond the scope of this study to discuss this possibility, those sayings of Jesus from *De Resurrectione* that are parallel to sayings in either the *Apology* or the *Dialogue* will be carefully examined.

[1] For the sake of convenience the *Dialogue with Trypho* will be referred to throughout as the *Dialogue*, and the *First Apology* will be refered to as the *Apology*. The *Second Apology*, often referred to as the *Appendix*, does not contain any sayings of Jesus and is, therefore, not relevant to my study.

[2] Edgar J. Goodspeed, p. 142. cf. also Johannes Carl Theodor Eques de Otto, *Iustini Philosophi et Martyris Opera Quae Feruntur Omnia* (Jena, 1876), 3rd edition, pp. xx-xxxii.

[3] Goodspeed, p. 142.

[4] D. Barthélemy, "Redécouverte d'un chaînon manquant de l'histoire de la Septante," *Revue Biblique*, LX (1935), pp. 18-29.

consequently, suggested that Justin was quoting a real Jewish text that was in vogue at the time when he composed his *Dialogue*.[1] This work of Barthélemy also lends support to the belief that our manuscript witnesses are substantially reliable, and upon this supposition of the reliability of these manuscripts my thesis rests.[2]

My investigation will not duplicate previous studies and simply examine the question of Justin's dependence on the canonical gospels; this approach has led only to uncertainty and wide disagreement. My investigation will try rather to determine the place of Justin's quotations of the sayings of Jesus in the history of the development of early gospel tradition,[3] and I shall ask the question whether the variations of these sayings in Justin reflect certain form-critical motives. The study will assume the validity of the two-source hypothesis, namely that both Matthew and Luke were dependent on Mark and on a second source Q, which was primarily a sayings-collection.

---

[1] p. 21.

[2] It should be noted that P. Katz has questioned Barthélemy's dating of the manuscripts before A. D. 130, maintaining that this cave may have been a depository down to the period of the Arab conquests, a thesis beyond the interest of this investigation. But if Katz is correct, then Justin's Old Testament citations might be medieval corruptions rather than ancient readings (P. Katz, "Septuagintal Studies in the Mid-Century. Their links with the past and their present tendencies," *The Background of the New Testament and Its Eschatology*, edited by W. D. Davies and David Daube [Cambridge, 1956], pp. 176-208).

[3] I shall deal specifically with the explicit sayings of Jesus as they appear in the extant manuscripts of the *Apology* and the *Dialogue*. By the term "explicit saying" I mean a saying that is introduced in such a way as to indicate that Justin is attempting to quote the words of Jesus, such as those sayings introduced by various forms of the verbs εἶπον, διδάσκω, φημί, παρακαλέω, ἀποκρίνομαι, βοάω, λέγω, διαλέγομαι, and μαρτυρέω.

CHAPTER TWO

THE SAYINGS THAT OCCUR MORE THAN ONCE

Any hypothesis that attempts to explain the nature of the source or sources from which Justin Martyr drew his sayings of Jesus must confront the difficulties presented by those sayings which occur in Justin's writings more than once, often with different words. If a thesis cannot account for these variations within Justin's own writings, then it cannot successfully account for his divergences from the canonical gospels.

What appear to be duplicate versions of the same saying in Justin's writings may actually prove on careful examination to be quotations of the same saying from two different sources or quotations of the saying from the same source, which Justin himself chose to alter according to his own context or special need. But before it is possible to offer a comprehensive theory to account for the entire scope of the source or sources of Justin's sayings of Jesus, it is necessary first to examine separately each saying or group of sayings to try to determine its separate history of transmission until the time it reached the form found in Justin's *Apology* or *Dialogue*.

1. APOLOGY 15:13 AND DIALOGUE 96:3a

Apol. 15:13[1]	*Dial.* 96:3a
Γίνεσθε δὲ χρηστοὶ	Γίνεσθε χρηστοὶ
καὶ οἰκτίρμονες,	καὶ οἰκτίρμονες,
ὡς καὶ ὁ πατὴρ ὑμῶν	ὡς καὶ ὁ πατὴρ ὑμῶν
	ὁ οὐράνιος.
χρηστός ἐστι	
καὶ οἰκτίρμων,	
καὶ τὸν ἥλιον αὐτοῦ	
ἀνατέλλει ἐπὶ ἁρματωλοὺς	
καὶ δικαίους	
καὶ πονηρούς.	

Apology 15:13 and *Dialogue* 96:3a seem to be, at least in part, parallel

---

[1] Unless otherwise specified, all quotations from Justin's *Apology* and *Dialogue* are from the edition of Edgar J. Goodspeed, *Die ältesten Apologeten* (Göttingen, 1914).

versions of the same saying, the only differences between the two passages being (1) the presence of δὲ in *Apol.* 15:13,[1] (2) the presence of ὁ οὐράνιος in *Dial.* 96:3a, and (3) the obvious fact that *Dial.* 96:3a quotes only half as much as *Apol.* 15:13. *Dial.* 96:3a and *Apol.* 15:13 have no exact parallels in the canonical gospels; therefore, a comparison of these passages with their closest parallels in the gospels and in the patristic literature is necessary in order to determine whether or not the two sayings are actually dependent upon one source or upon two different sources.

Dial. 96:3a	*Mt.* 5:45, 48 [2]	*Lk.* 6:36
Γίνεσθε	[45] ὅπως γένησθε	Γίνεσθε
χρηστοὶ καὶ		
οἰκτίρμονες,	υἱοὶ	οἰκτίρμονες
ὡς καὶ		καθὼς
ὁ πατὴρ ὑμῶν	τοῦ πατρὸς ὑμῶν	ὁ πατὴρ ὑμῶν
ὁ οὐράνιος.	τοῦ ἐν οὐρανοῖς,	
		οἰκτίρμων ἐστίν.
	ὅτι τὸν ἥλιον	
	αὐτοῦ ἀνατέλλει	
	ἐπὶ πονηροὺς καὶ	
	ἀγαθοὺς καὶ βρέχει	
	ἐπὶ δικαίους	
	καὶ ἀδίκους	
	[48] Ἔσεσθε οὖν	
	ὑμεῖς τέλειοι	
	ὡς ὁ πατὴρ ὑμῶν	
	ὁ οὐράνιος	
	τέλειός ἐστιν.	

There are texts of Luke that can explain the reading of *Dial.* 96:3a: (1) the word χρηστός appears in Lk. 6:35 and may thereby have found its way into the text of *Dial.* 96:3a in combination with οἰκτίρμονες;[3] and (2) several manuscripts of Lk. 6:36 [4] have ὁ οὐράνιος after ὁ πατὴρ

---

[1] It will be shown later that this δὲ in *Apol.* 15:13 was not in Justin's source but that it was rather one of the devices by which Justin combined several citations (see below, p. 97).

[2] Unless otherwise specified, all quotations from the New Testament are from the edition of Eberhard Nestle, *Novum Testamentum Graece*, 25th edition (Stuttgart, 1963).

[3] So too Baldus, p. 96 and Wright, p. 50.

[4] Sinaiticus[a] (non item * nec[c]) 13. 69. al[5]. Aeth.

ὑμῶν in agreement with *Dial.* 96:3a. It is possible that the phrase ὁ οὐράνιος in these manuscripts of Lk. 6:36 and in *Dial.* 96:3a and the reading ὡς καὶ in *Dial.* 96:3a were originally the result of harmonization of Lk. 6:36 with Mt. 5:48, which reads ὡς ὁ πατὴρ ὑμῶν ὁ οὐράνιος.[1]

Although the quotation of Jesus in *Dial.* 96:3a ends with the words ὁ πατὴρ ὑμῶν ὁ οὐράνιος, Justin continues in the section that immediately follows the words of Jesus with a narrative section that parallels, more or less, Mt. 5:45b: [2]

Dial. 96:3b	Mt. 5:45b
καὶ γὰρ τὸν παντοκράτορα	
Θεὸν χρηστὸν καὶ	
οἰκτίρμονα ὁρῶμεν,	
τὸν ἥλιον αὐτοῦ	ὅτι τὸν ἥλιον αὐτοῦ
ἀνατέλλοντα ἐπὶ	ἀνατέλλει ἐπὶ
ἀχαρίστους καὶ δικαίους	πονηροὺς καὶ ἀγαθοὺς
καὶ βρέχοντα ἐπὶ	καὶ βρέχει ἐπὶ
ὁσίους καὶ πονηρούς,	δικαίους καὶ ἀδίκους.
οὓς πάντας ὅτι καὶ	
κρίνειν μέλλει ἐδίδαξε.	

Although *Dial.* 96:3 is part quotation material and part narrative, the verse as a whole reflects a harmonization of elements of Lk. 6:36 and Mt. 5:45b (and probably Lk. 6:35 and Mt. 5:48); and this same harmonization appears again in *Apol.* 15:13 to which I shall now turn.

Apol. 15:13	Mt. 5:45	Lk. 6:36
Γίνεσθε δὲ	ὅπως γένησθε	Γίνεσθε
χρηστοὶ καὶ		
οἰκτίρμονες,	υἱοὶ	οἰκτίρμονες
ὡς καὶ		καθὼς
ὁ πατὴρ ὑμῶν	τοῦ πατρὸς ὑμῶν	ὁ πατὴρ ὑμῶν
	τοῦ ἐν οὐρανοῖς	
χρηστός ἐστι		

---

[1] Manuscript 1241 of Mt. 5:48 actually reads ὡς καὶ ὁ πατὴρ ὑμῶν ὁ οὐράνιος, a reading identical to *Dial.* 96:3; however, this manuscript is a late minuscule and probably independent of the source underlying Justin's reading, the agreement of the two texts probably being completely accidental.

[2] The fact that Justin ends the quotation of Jesus in *Dial.* 96:3 where he does probably indicates that he is not trying to quote his source exactly in *Dial.* 96:3b; therefore, I shall not make any attempt to account for the peculiarities in this narrative section. They can most easily be attributed to Justin himself.

καὶ οἰκτίρμων,   οἰκτίρμων ἐστίν.
καὶ τὸν ἥλιον   ὅτι τὸν ἥλιον
αὐτοῦ ἀνατέλλει   αὐτοῦ ἀνατέλλει
ἐπὶ ἁρματωλοὺς   ἐπὶ πονηροὺς
καὶ   καὶ ἀγαθοὺς
                       καὶ βρέχει
δικαίους   ἐπὶ δικαίους
καὶ πονηρούς.   καὶ ἀδίκους.

From what I have already said concerning *Dial.* 96:3a, it is apparent with reference to *Apol.* 15:13 (1) that χρηστοί probably entered into the text of *Apol.* 15:13 either directly or indirectly from Lk. 6:35, (2) that δὲ is not an element of Justin's source but rather one of the devices by which he combined several citations, and (3) that the ὡς καὶ ὁ πατὴρ ὑμῶν is probably the result of harmonization with Mt. 5:48. Many of these same features of Justin's texts are found in the following patristic writings:

Clem. Alex., *Strom.* II, 19, 100 (Stählin, *GCS*, II, p. 168)
γίνεσθε ἐλεήμονες καὶ οἰκτίρμονες, ὡς ὁ πατὴρ ὑμῶν ὁ οὐράνιος οἰκτίρμων ἐστίν.

Ps. Athanasius, *Quaest. ad Antiochum* 89 (Migne, *PG*, XXVIII, 653)
Γίνεσθε οἰκτίρμονες καὶ ἀγαθοὶ ὡς ὁ Πατὴρ ὑμῶν ὁ ἐν τοῖς οὐρανοῖς.

Macarius of Egypt, *Hom.* 19, 2; *de custodia cordis* 13 (Migne, *PG*, XXXIV, 644, 836)
Γίνεσθε ἀγαθοὶ καὶ χρηστοί, καθὼς καὶ ὁ Πατὴρ ὑμῶν ὁ οὐράνιος οἰκτίρμων ἐστί.

Pseudoclementine *Homilies* III, 57 (Rehm, *GCS*, p. 77)
Γίνεσθε ἀγαθοὶ καὶ οἰκτίρμονες ὡς ὁ πατὴρ ὁ ἐν τοῖς οὐρανοῖς, ὃς ἀνατέλλει τὸν ἥλιον ἐπ' ἀγαθοῖς καὶ πονηροῖς καὶ φέρει τὸν ὑετὸν ἐπὶ δικαίοις καὶ ἀδίκοις.

Epiphanius, *Against Heresies* 66, 22, 4 (Holl, *GCS*, III, p. 50)
γίνεσθε ἀγαθοὶ ὡς ὁ πατὴρ ὑμῶν ὁ οὐράνιος, ὅτι ἀνατέλλει τὸν ἥλιον αὐτοῦ ἐπὶ δικαίους καὶ ἀδίκους, καὶ βρέχει αὐτοῦ τὸν ὑετὸν ἐπὶ πονηροὺς καὶ ἀγαθούς.

Epiphanius, *Against Heresies* 33, 10, 5 (Holl, *GCS*, I, p. 461)
ὅμοιοι γένεσθε τῷ πατρὶ ὑμῶν τῷ ἐν τοῖς οὐρανοῖς, ὅτι ἀνατέλλει αὐτοῦ

τὸν ἥλιον ἐπὶ ἀγαθοὺς καὶ πονηροὺς καὶ βρέχει ἐπὶ δικαίους καὶ ἀδίκους.

Hilarius, *Tractatus in CXVIII Psalm*, Lettera VIII, 18 (Migne, *PL*,
IX, 559)

Estote boni sicut Pater vester qui est in coelis, qui solem suum
oriri facit super bonos et malos, et pluit super justos et injustos.

Manichaeans according to Augustine, *Contra Adimantum* VII, 1
(Migne, *PL*, XLII, 137)

Estote benigni sicut Pater vester coelestis, qui solem suum oriri
facit super bonos et malos.

Augustine, *Contra Adimantum* VII, 3 (Migne, *PL*, XLII, 138)

Estote benigni quemadmodum Pater vester coelestis, qui solem
suum oriri facit super bonos et malos.

γίνεσθε ἐλεήμονες καὶ οἰκτίρμονες in Clem. Alex., γίνεσθε οἰκτίρμονες καὶ
ἀγαθοὶ in Ps. Athan., γίνεσθε ἀγαθοὶ καὶ χρηστοὶ in Macarius, and γίνεσθε
ἀγαθοὶ καὶ οἰκτίρμονες in Ps. Clem. reflect the form of *Apol.* 15:13 and
Dial. 96:3a by using two adjectives rather than the single adjective
of Lk. 6:36; however, all four fathers differ from Justin in their use of
these adjectives. Secondly, it should be noted that all of the fathers quoted
above have the ὁ οὐράνιος (ὁ ἐν τοῖς οὐρανοῖς or the equivalent) found in
Dial. 96:3a and, therefore, probably an element of Justin's source.
However, *Apol.* 15:13 and *Dial.* 96:3 have certain differences that must
be considered: (1) the absence of ὁ οὐράνιος in *Apol.* 15:13 is apparently
an intentional omission by Justin; (2) the phrase χρηστός ἐστι καὶ οἰκτίρμων
of *Apol.* 15:13 is not found in *Dial.* 96:3a but has an approximate parallel
in Lk. 6:36, Clem. Alex., and Macarius with the repetition of χρηστός
from the beginning of the saying in Justin's version. (3) But the most
striking feature about *Apol.* 15:13 is that it continues the saying of
Jesus with material parallel to Mt. 5:45b, a combination already apparent
from our analysis of *Dial.* 96:3b. *Apol.* 15:13b parallels Mt. 5:45b
exactly with the words τὸν ἥλιον αὐτοῦ ἀνατέλλει ἐπὶ, but thereafter the
two passages differ, the most significant differences being the absence
of the verb βρέχει in *Apol.* 15:13b and the variation in the use of the
nouns in *Apol.* 15:13b, *Dial.* 96:3b, and Mt. 5:45b.

That this harmonization of Lk. 6:36 and Mt. 5:45b was not peculiar
to Justin but was rather a written source in common circulation in the
early church appears evident not only because it is repeated in both
Apol. 15:13 and in *Dial.* 96:3 but more especially because Lk. 6:36 and
Mt. 5:45b occur together in six of the patristic passages already quoted

above (see p. 11). Although none of these passages agrees exactly with the text of *Apol.* 15:13 or *Dial.* 96:3, they reflect certain features that were probably peculiar to this harmony: (1) although Justin's source apparently read γίνεσθε χρηστοί, another version was known that read γίνεσθε ἀγαθοί; (2) Justin's καὶ οἰκτίρμονες was probably an element of his written source, because it is supported by Ps. Clem.; (3) the phrase ὁ οὐράνιος of *Dial.* 96:3, although not found in *Apol.* 15:13, was probably part of Justin's source, because it is found in one form or another in all of the patristic parallels quoted above; (4) the presence of both ἀνατέλλοντα and βρέχοντα in *Dial.* 96:3b and in some form in Ps. Clem., Hilarius, and Epiphanius [1] indicates that both words were probably in Justin's source and that in *Apol.* 15:13 Justin chose to modify his source by omitting βρέχει; and (5) the consensus of the above passages is that this written harmony had the nouns ἀγαθοὺς καὶ πονηρούς and δικαίους καὶ ἀδίκους, and Justin's inconsistency in quoting ἁρματωλοὺς καὶ δικαίους καὶ πονηρούς in *Apol.* 15:13 and ἀχαρίστους καὶ δικαίους and ὁσίους καὶ πονηρούς in *Dial.* 96:3b perhaps indicates that he both times modified a source that contained the reading found in many of these other fathers.

Baldus,[2] Credner,[3] and Semisch [4] attribute these divergences in *Apol.* 15:13 from the canonical gospels to a failure of memory; and Lippelt [5] recognizes the use of a harmony here. Massaux [6] sees a literary contact with Matthew and Luke, maintaining that Justin combined this material himself; and Bousset [7] suggests the possibility of a precanonical source. However, the overwhelming evidence of our present discussion points, as Lippelt suggests, to a harmony of Lk. 6:36 and Mt. 5:45b (with elements from Lk. 6:35 and Mt. 5:48), a harmony in wide circulation in the early church and used by several of the fathers. It is possible that this harmony was known to Justin in two different forms, one of which he used as his source for *Apol.* 15:13 and the other as his source for *Dial.* 96:3; but it is more likely that this saying was known to Justin in a single form which he altered slightly in both *Apol.* 15:13 and *Dial.* 96:3, a text which may have read:

---

[1] So too Naasenes according to Hippolytus, *Philos.* V, 7, 26 (Wendland, *GCS*, III, p. 85) ὃς ἀνατέλλει τὸν ἥλιον αὐτοῦ ἐπὶ δικαίους καὶ ἀδίκους καὶ βρέχει ἐπὶ ὁσίους καὶ ἁμαρτωλούς.

[2] p. 39.

[3] *Beiträge*, p. 241.

[4] pp. 274-276.

[5] p. 29.

[6] *Influence de l'Evangile*, p. 476; "Le Texte du Sermon," pp. 433 f.

[7] p. 82.

γίνεσθε χρηστοί καὶ οἰκτίρμονες, ὡς καὶ ὁ πατὴρ ὑμῶν ὁ οὐράνιος χρηστός
ἐστι καὶ οἰκτίρμων, καὶ τὸν ἥλοιν αὐτοῦ ἀνατέλλει ἐπὶ ἀγαθοὺς καὶ πονηροὺς
καὶ βρέχει ἐπὶ δικαίους καὶ ἀδίκους.

2. APOLOGY 15:14 AND APOLOGY 15:15

Apol. 15:14 μὴ μεριμνᾶτε δὲ τί φάγητε ἢ τί ἐνδύσησθε. οὐχ ὑμεῖς τῶν πετεινῶν καὶ τῶν θηρίων διαφέρετε; καὶ ὁ θεὸς τρέφει αὐτά.

Apol. 15:15 μὴ οὖν μεριμνήσητε τί φάγητε ἢ τί ἐνδύσησθε· οἶδε γὰρ ὁ πατὴρ
ὑμῶν ὁ οὐράνιος ὅτι τούτων χρείαν ἔχετε.

Although both quotations start with a similar sentence, the only
difference being that where 15:14 has μεριμνᾶτε δὲ, 15:15 has οὖν μεριμνήσητε, the second half of the passages indicates that *Apol.* 15:14 and
Apol. 15:15 are almost certainly different sayings. Furthermore, we
would not expect Justin to have two versions of the same saying in
consecutive sentences, and yet *Apol.* 15:14 and *Apol.* 15:15 follow
immediately one upon the other. I shall, therefore, examine separately
each of the two passages with its closest gospel parallels and then discuss
the relationship, if any, between the two verses in Apol. 15.

Apol. 15:14	Mt. 6:25, 26	Lk. 12:22-24
		[22]Εἶπεν δὲ πρὸς τοὺς μαθητὰς (αὐτοῦ).
	[25]Διὰ τοῦτο λέγω ὑμῖν·	διὰ τοῦτο λέγω ὑμῖν·
μὴ μεριμνᾶτε δὲ	μὴ μεριμνᾶτε τῇ ψυχῇ ὑμῶν	μὴ μεριμνᾶτε τῇ ψυχῇ
τί φάγητε	τί φάγητε, (ἢ τί πίητε), μηδὲ τῷ σώματι ὑμῶν	τί φάγητε, μηδὲ τῷ σώματι (ὑμῶν)
ἢ τί ἐνδύσησθε.	τί ἐνδύσησθε. οὐχὶ ἡ ψυχὴ πλεῖόν ἐστιν τῆς τροφῆς καὶ τὸ σῶμα τοῦ ἐνδύματος; [26]ἐμβλέψατε εἰς τὰ πετεινὰ	τί ἐνδύσησθε. [23]ἡ γὰρ ψυχὴ πλεῖόν ἐστιν τῆς τροφῆς καὶ τὸ σῶμα τοῦ ἐνδύματος. [24]κατανοήσατε τοὺς κόρακας

τοῦ οὐρανοῦ,

ὅτι οὐ σπείρουσιν   ὅτι οὔτε σπείρουσιν

οὐδὲ θερίζουσιν   οὔτε θερίζουσιν,

   οἷς οὐκ

οὐδὲ συνάγουσιν   ἔστιν ταμιεῖον

εἰς ἀποθήκας,   οὐδὲ ἀποθήκη,

οὐχ ὑμεῖς   καὶ ὁ πατὴρ ὑμῶν   καὶ ὁ θεὸς

τῶν πετεινῶν   ὁ οὐράνιος

καὶ τῶν θηρίων   τρέφει αὐτά·   τρέφει αὐτούς·

διαφέρετε;   οὐχ ὑμεῖς μᾶλλον   πόσῳ μᾶλλον ὑμεῖς

καὶ ὁ θεὸς   διαφέρετε   διαφέρετε

τρέφει αὐτά.   αὐτῶν;   τῶν πετεινῶν.

The first part of *Apol.* 15:14 μὴ μεριμνᾶτε δὲ τί φάγητε ἢ τί ἐνδύσησθε has parallel material in both Mt. 6:25 and in Lk. 12:22, because Mt. 6:25 and Lk. 12:22 are almost identical, both following closely their common source Q in this section. It is with the rest of the verse that I shall be most concerned, and here the situation is complicated by the fact that the order of the text of *Apol.* 15:14 is the exact opposite of the order in both the Matthaean and the Lukan parallels. The words καὶ ὁ θεὸς τρέφει αὐτά are identical to Lk. 12:24 except for the fact that Lk. 12:24 reads αὐτούς where Justin has αὐτά; however, τὰ πετεινά and τὰ θηρία in *Apol.* 15:14 are both neuter gender and require the pronoun αὐτά in place of Luke's αὐτούς, which has for its antecedent the masculine form τοὺς κόρακας.[1] Mt. 6:26, on the other hand, reads καὶ ὁ πατὴρ ὑμῶν ὁ οὐράνιος τρέφει αὐτά with the parallel to the αὐτά of *Apol.* 15:14, but it is much more likely that either Justin or his source has the reading αὐτά not because of Matthew with whose text *Apol.* 15:14 is otherwise not parallel in this section but rather because of the need for Justin's pronoun to agree with its antecedent. The phrase οὐχ ὑμεῖς τῶν πετεινῶν καὶ τῶν θηρίων διαφέρετε is in the form of a question as is the parallel in Matthew; whereas Luke, on the other hand, is in the form of an exclamation. Further, the words οὐχ ὑμεῖς are also paralleled in Matthew and not in Luke. Different from Matthew, however, *Apol.* 15:14 has the noun τῶν πετεινῶν in the genitive in parallel with Luke and, therefore, had no use for Matthew's αὐτῶν here, a pronoun referring back to Mt. 6:26a, which is not quoted by Justin.

---

[1] Lk. 12:24 D 69. 253. 346 reads αὐτά; however, this reading is probably an assimilation to the Matthaean parallel and is certainly incorrect Greek. That Justin knew such a text of Luke here is unlikely; it is more probable that the αὐτά in *Apol.* 15:14 is the result of the neuter antecedents in Justin's text.

Apol. 15:14 also has καὶ τῶν θηρίων, which occurs in neither Matthew nor Luke and which is certainly an addition of either Justin or his source, which was apparently a harmony that condensed and paraphrased Matthew and Luke.[1] The following table summarizes my conclusions regarding this verse:

μὴ μεριμνᾶτε δὲ τί	could be related to either
φάγητε ἢ τί ἐνδύσησθε.	Matthew or Luke
οὐχ ὑμεῖς τῶν πετεινῶν καὶ	has the form of Matthew (question)
τῶν θηρίων διαφέρετε;	and is closer to Matthew
καὶ ὁ θεὸς τρέφει αὐτά.	closer to Luke

This analysis would indicate that either Justin himself combined and edited Mt. 6:25f. and Lk. 12:22ff. or that he used a harmony that had already harmonized these texts. In either case, elements of both Matthew and Luke appear in *Apol.* 15:14.[2]

Let us now turn our attention to *Apol.* 15:15 and its gospel parallels:

Apol. 15:15	Mt. 6:31, 32	Lk. 12:30
μὴ οὖν	[31]μὴ οὖν	
μεριμνήσητε	μεριμνήσητε	
	λέγοντες·	
τί φάγητε	τί φάγωμεν;	
	ἤ· τί πίωμεν;	
ἢ τί	ἤ· τί	
ἐνδύσησθε·	περιβαλώμεθα;	
	[32]πάντα γὰρ	ταῦτα γὰρ πάντα
	ταῦτα τὰ ἔθνη	τὰ ἔθνη τοῦ κόσμου
	ἐπιζητοῦσιν·	ἐπιζητοῦσιν·
οἶδε γὰρ	οἶδεν γὰρ	ὑμῶν δὲ
ὁ πατὴρ ὑμῶν	ὁ πατὴρ ὑμῶν	ὁ πατὴρ
ὁ οὐράνιος	ὁ οὐράνιος	οἶδεν
ὅτι τούτων	ὅτι χρῄζετε	ὅτι χρῄζετε
χρείαν ἔχετε.	τούτων ἁπάντων.	τούτων·

---

[1] Massaux ("Le Texte du Sermon," p. 435) suggests that the addition of τῶν θηρίων should be attributed to Justin's tendency to give a more general sense to Matthew's sentences; but it is possible that Justin's source, if a text other than the canonical gospels, itself had this tendency.

[2] Massaux (*Influence de l'Evangile*, p. 471) argues that Justin follows Matthew here to the preference of Luke, but this conclusion is impossible because of Justin's use of the phrase καὶ ὁ θεὸς τρέφει αὐτά, which does not appear in any manuscripts of Matthew at this point.

In the first part of *Apol.* 15:15 Justin differs considerably from the text of Mt. 6:31. He has μὴ οὖν μεριμνήσητε in common with Mt. 6:31; but he has τί φάγητε where Matthew has τί φάγωμεν and τί πίωμεν, and τί ἐνδύσησθε where Matthew has τί περιβαλώμεθα. This first part of *Apol.* 15:15 is parallel to *Apol.* 15:14 and to the Matthaean and Lukan parallels to that passage except for the fact that *Apol.* 15:15 has μεριμνήσητε in agreement with its gospel parallel, Mt. 6:31. Mt. 6:32a is absent from *Apol.* 15:15, probably because it was not suitable for Justin's heathen audience.[1] But the text of *Apol.* 15:15 reproduces almost exactly Mt. 6:32b, and there is no influence from Luke evident. From these observations we can conclude that Justin used either Mt. 6:31, 32 with modifications and assimilation to *Apol.* 15:14 or a source that contained these same elements. And further, we can be certain that *Apol.* 15:14 and *Apol.* 15:15 are not parallel versions of the same text but that both verses probably appeared in Justin's source as adaptations of Mt. 6:25, 26 // Lk. 12:22-24 (= *Apol.* 15:14) and Mt. 6:31, 32 (= *Apol.* 15:15).

3. APOLOGY 16:7 AND DIALOGUE 101:2

Apol. 16:7	*Dial.* 101:2	Mt. 19:16f.	Mk. 10:17f.	Lk. 18:18f.
			¹⁷Καὶ ἐκπορευομένου αὐτοῦ εἰς ὁδὸν προσδραμὼν εἷς	
καὶ προσελθόντος αὐτῷ τινος καὶ εἰπόντος·	καὶ γὰρ ἐπὶ γῆς τὸ αὐτὸ ἔπραξε· λέγοντος αὐτῷ τινος·	¹⁶Καὶ ἰδοὺ εἷς προσελθὼν αὐτῷ εἶπεν·	καὶ γονυπετήσας αὐτὸν ἐπηρώτα αὐτόν·	¹⁸Καὶ ἐπηρώτησέν τις αὐτὸν ἄρχων λέγων·
Διδάσκαλε ἀγαθέ,	Διδάσκαλε ἀγαθέ,	διδάσκαλε,	διδάσκαλε ἀγαθέ,	διδάσκαλε ἀγαθέ,
		τί ἀγαθὸν ποιήσω ἵνα σχῶ ζωὴν αἰώνιον;	τί ποιήσω ἵνα ζωὴν αἰώνιον κληρονομήσω;	τί ποιήσας ζωὴν αἰώνιον κληρονομήσω;
ἀπεκρίνατο λέγων·	ἀπεκρίνατο·	¹⁷ὁ δὲ εἶπεν	¹⁸ὁ δὲ Ἰησοῦς	¹⁹εἶπεν δὲ αὐτῷ

---

[1] So too Baldus, pp. 69 f. and Massaux, "Le Texte du Sermon," p. 435.

	αὐτῷ·	εἶπεν αὐτῷ·	ὁ Ἰησοῦς·
Τί με	τί με	τί με	τί με
λέγεις	ἐρωτᾷς	λέγεις	λέγεις
	περὶ τοῦ		
ἀγαθόν;	ἀγαθοῦ;	ἀγαθόν;	ἀγαθόν;
Οὐδεὶς	εἷς ἐστιν	εἷς ἐστιν	οὐδεὶς
ἀγαθὸς	ἀγαθός,	ὁ ἀγαθός·	ἀγαθὸς
εἰ μὴ μόνος		οὐδεὶς	οὐδεὶς
ὁ θεός,	ὁ πατήρ μου	ἀγαθὸς	ἀγαθὸς
ὁ ποιήσας	ὁ ἐν τοῖς	εἰ μὴ εἷς	εἰ μὴ εἷς
τὰ πάντα.	οὐρανοῖς.	ὁ θεός.	(ὁ) θεός.

By comparing the introductions to this saying in *Apol.* 16:7 and *Dial.* 101:2 with their gospel parallels, we discover that (1) προσελθόντος αὐτῷ and εἰπόντος in *Apol.* 16:7 reflect προσελθὼν αὐτῷ and εἶπεν in Mt. 19:16 and are quite different from the parallel sections in Mark and Luke and (2) the introduction to *Dial.* 101:2 has no gospel parallel and is probably Justin's own composition. The address to Jesus in both of Justin's texts, Διδάσκαλε ἀγαθέ, has an exact parallel in Mk. 10:17, in Lk. 18:18, and in many manuscripts of Mt. 19:16.[1]

At this point both *Apol.* 16:7 and *Dial.* 101:2 depart from the reading of the synoptic gospels (1) by omitting the question addressed to Jesus and (2) by continuing with the verb ἀπεκρίνατο, a verb found in none of the synoptic parallels; but thereafter *Apol.* 16:7 and *Dial.* 101:2 differ in their readings. *Apol.* 16:7 agrees almost exactly with Mk. 10:18 and Lk. 18:19 except for the fact that *Apol.* 16:7 has μόνος where both Mark and Luke have εἷς [2] and *Apol.* 16:7 has the additional phrase ὁ ποιήσας τὰ πάντα not found in any of the synoptic parallels. These two variations find little support among the manuscript variants and patristic witnesses; therefore, it is impossible to determine at this point whether this reading

---

[1] The best manuscripts of Matthew do not have ἀγαθέ; however, there is such strong manuscript evidence for διδάσκαλε ἀγαθέ in Mt. 19:16 (CEFGHKMSUVΓΔ minusc. pler. b c f ff² g¹·²· h l m q [r¹] aur. vg. Syr.omn. Cop. sa·bo· (aliq·) Arm. Geo.²) that this reading may very well have existed in manuscripts of Matthew extant at the time when Justin composed his writings.

[2] It is impossible to determine with any certainty whether μόνος was an element of Justin's source or a change made by Justin himself; however, there is some manuscript evidence that supports the reading μόνος ὁ θεός in Mk 10:18 (D *item* solus unus deus d, unus solus deus ff, *similiter* Cop. sa·bo·, cf. unus ac solus deus b; solus deus c vg. [gat.] Geo.). See also Dionysius the Areopagate I, 315 (Migne *PG*, III, 636) οὐδεὶς ἀγαθὸς, εἰ μὴ μόνος ὁ Θεός.

of *Apol.* 16:7 should be attributed to Justin himself or whether he found it in his source.[1]

Dial. 101:2, on the other hand, shows evidence of harmonization at this point. τί με λέγεις ἀγαθόν of *Dial.* 101:2 is identical to the Markan and Lukan parallels; however, εἷς ἐστιν ἀγαθός of *Dial.* 101:2 finds its only parallel in Mt. 19:17 (εἷς ἐστιν ὁ ἀγαθός). That this harmonization of Mk. 10:18 and/or Lk. 18:19 with Mt. 19:17 was not peculiar to Justin but was widespread in the early church is supported by the following patristic evidence, all of which has τί με λέγεις ἀγαθόν (Mark and/or Luke) and εἷς ἐστιν ἀγαθός (Matthew) or equivalent elements:

Epiphanius, *Adversus Haereses* 69, 19 (Holl, III, *GCS*, p. 168)
Εἶτα πάλιν φησὶν ὁ μανιώδης ῎Αρειος· πῶς εἶπεν ὁ κύριος, τί με λέγεις ἀγαθόν; εἷς ἐστιν ἀγαθὸς ὁ θεός.

Irenaeus, *Contra Haereses* I, 20, 2 (Migne, *PG*, VII, 653)
Τί με λέγεις ἀγαθόν; εἷς ἐστιν ἀγαθὸς, ὁ Πατὴρ ἐν τοῖς οὐρανοῖς.

Origen, *Contra Haereses* 5, 7 (Migne, *PG*, XVI³, 3134)
τί με λέγεις ἀγαθόν; Εἷς ἐστιν ἀγαθὸς, ὁ Πατήρ μου ὁ ἐν τοῖς οὐρανοῖς.

Pseudoclementine *Homilies* XVIII, 3 (Rehm, *GCS*, p. 242)
Μή με λέγε ἀγαθόν· ὁ γὰρ ἀγαθὸς εἷς ἐστιν, ὁ πατὴρ ὁ ἐν τοῖς οὐρανοῖς.

It should also be noted that in each of the above quotations as in the text of *Dial.* 101:2 there are endings added to the Matthaean phrase εἷς ἐστιν ἀγαθὸς, a phrase that seems to be incomplete in itself. Arius (according to Epiphanius) adds ὁ θεός (perhaps from Mark or Luke), but all the other fathers, including Justin, add ὁ πατὴρ ὁ ἐν τοῖς οὐρανοῖς or some similar phrase.[2] This agreement indicates that Justin shared with several other fathers a text that harmonized Mk. 10:18 and/or Lk. 18:19 with Mt. 19:17 and that contained the phrase ὁ πατήρ μου ὁ ἐν τοῖς οὐρανοῖς or its equivalent.[3]

The results of this analysis of *Apol.* 16:7 and *Dial.* 101:2 can be seen and compared in the following table:

---

[1] Bousset (p. 105) regards the phrase ὁ ποιήσας τὰ πάντα as an anti-Gnostic addition by Justin, but it is possible that this phrase was an element of Justin's source.

[2] Ireaneus has ὁ Πατὴρ ἐν τοῖς οὐρανοῖς; Origen has ὁ Πατήρ μου ὁ ἐν τοῖς οὐρανοῖς; *Homilies* has ὁ πατὴρ ὁ ἐν τοῖς οὐρανοῖς; and *Dial.* 101: 2 has ὁ πατὴρ μου ὁ ἐν τοῖς οὐρανοῖς.

[3] Further evidence of harmonization of Mt. 19: 17 with its synoptic parallels is indicated by the large number of manuscripts of Mt. 19: 17 that read τί με λέγεις ἀγαθόν; οὐδεὶς ἀγαθὸς εἰ μὴ εἷς ὁ θεός (CWΔΣΦ⁵ minusc. pler. f q Syr.^pesh·hl· Cop.^sa.).

	Apol. 16:7	*Dial.* 101:2
Introduction	reflects Mt. 19:16	free composition
Address to Jesus	Mk. or Lk. (or Mt.)	Mk. or Lk. (or Mt.)
Question to Jesus	- - - - - - - -	- - - - - - - -
Introductory verb to Jesus' reply	ἀπεκρίνατο	ἀπεκρίνατο
Jesus' answer	- - - - - - - -	Mk. 10:18 and/or Lk. 18:19 in harmony with Mt. 19:17 (a harmony known to other fathers)
	Mk. 10:18 and/or Lk. 18:19	
	+	+
	ὁ ποιήσας τὰ πάντα	ending known to other fathers

In only one section do *Apol.* 16:7 and *Dial.* 101:2 contradict each
other in such a way as to indicate that Justin did not use a single source
for the two versions of this saying, and that is in the last section, Jesus'
answer, where *Apol.* 16:7 (Οὐδεὶς ἀγαθὸς εἰ μὴ μόνος ὁ θεός, ὁ ποιήσας τὰ
πάντα.) parallels Mk. 10:18 and/or Lk. 18:19 whereas *Dial.* 101:2
(Τί με λέγεις ἀγαθόν; εἷς ἐστιν ἀγαθός, ὁ πατήρ μου ὁ ἐν τοῖς οὐρανοῖς.)
parallels Mk. 10:18 and/or Lk. 18:19 in harmony with Mt. 19:17; and
this point of disagreement suggests that Justin probably quoted these
two versions of the saying from different sources (see below pp. 95-100
and 118-121).

4. APOLOGY 16:10 AND APOLOGY 63:5

Apol. 16:10	*Apol.* 63:5	Mt. 10:40	Lk. 10:16
ὃς γὰρ ἀκούει μου καὶ ποιεῖ ἃ λέγω	Ὁ ἐμοῦ ἀκούων	Ὁ δεχόμενος ὑμᾶς ἐμὲ δέχεται, καὶ ὁ ἐμὲ δεχόμενος	Ὁ ἀκούων ὑμῶν ἐμοῦ ἀκούει, καὶ ὁ ἀθετῶν ὑμᾶς ἐμὲ ἀθετεῖ· ὁ δὲ ἐμὲ ἀθετῶν
ἀκούει τοῦ ἀποστείλαντός με.	ἀκούει τοῦ ἀποστείλαντός με.	δέχεται τὸν ἀποστείλαντά με.	ἀθετεῖ τὸν ἀποστείλαντά με.

From the above chart it does not appear that either of Justin's passages
is very closely related to either Mt. 10:40 or to Lk. 10:16, but the textual

additions to Lk. 10:16 are especially significant for a study of this passage:

W^a adds καὶ ὁ ἐμοῦ ἀκούων ἀκούει τοῦ πέμψαντός με

D a b i l add ὁ δὲ (i om.) ἐμοῦ ἀκούων ἀκούει τοῦ ἀποστείλαντός με

E^{mg} 13. 124. 346. Syr. ^{cu. p. hr.} Arm. Aeth. add καὶ ὁ ἀκούων ἐμοῦ (E ἐμοῦ ἀκούων) ἀκούει τοῦ ἀποστείλαντός με

From this textual evidence it is apparent that many manuscripts and versions of Lk. 10:16 added a fourth line to this verse, [1] and the testimony of many of the fathers also attests to this later addition to the text of Luke:

Apostolic Constitutions 8, 46, 1 (Migne, *PG*, I, 1149)
'Ο ὑμῶν γὰρ, φησὶν ὁ Κύριος, ἀκούων, ἐμοῦ ἀκούει· καὶ ὁ ἐμοῦ ἀκούων, ἀκούει τοῦ ἀποστείλαντός με· καὶ ὁ ὑμᾶς ἀθετῶν, ἐμὲ ἀθετεῖ· ὁ δὲ ἐμὲ ἀθετῶν, ἀθετεῖ τὸν ἀποστείλαντά με.

Pseudo-Ignatius, *To the Ephesians* 5 (Migne, *PG*, V, 737)
'Ο ὑμῶν ἀκούων, ἐμοῦ ἀκούει· καὶ ὁ ἐμοῦ ἀκούων, ἀκούει τοῦ πέμψαντός με Πατρός· ὁ ὑμᾶς ἀθετῶν, ἐμὲ ἀθετεῖ· ὁ δὲ ἐμὲ ἀθετῶν, ἀθετεῖ τὸν πέμψαντά με.

Cyprian, *Epistulae* 59, 4 (Hartel, p. 671)
qui audit vos me audit et eum qui me misit, et qui rejicit vos me rejicit et eum qui me misit.

Cyprian, *Epistulae* 66, 4 (Hartel, pp. 729f.)
qui audit vos, me audit: et qui me audit, audit eum qui me misit. et qui rejicit vos, me rejicit et eum qui me misit.

Evangeliarum Hieros. p. 464 (quoted from Resch, *Agrapha*, p. 49)
et ille qui audit me, audit illum, qui me misit.

From this investigation it appears probable that *Apol.* 63:5 shared with many other fathers and many manuscripts of Lk. 10:16 a text that added a fourth line to Lk. 10:16; but because Justin is the earliest of these witnesses, it is impossible to conclude whether this variant existed before Justin or whether he himself is its author. *Apol.* 16:10

---

[1] So too Joachim Jeremias, *Unknown Sayings of Jesus*, trans. by Reginald Fuller (London, 1957), pp. 5 f., who regards the addition as "a pedantic expression of the *parallelismus membrorum*." Jeremias argues convincingly that this line is an addition to the text of Lk. 10: 16, because it spoils the structure of step parallelism otherwise preserved in the original Lukan form. This position overthrows both Resch's argument that this line is original in Jesus' saying and through a shortening of the text by Luke fell from the gospel text (*Agrapha*, p. 49) and Bousset's argument that Justin is quoting from a pre-synoptic source (p. 87).

reproduces this same variant reading with the addition of καὶ ποιεῖ ἃ λέγω, an addition perhaps influenced by Mt. 7:24 and/or Lk. 6:46f.[1]

5. APOLOGY 16:11 AND DIALOGUE 76:5

Apol. 16:11	Dial. 76:5	Mt. 7:22, 23	Lk. 13:26, 27
πολλοὶ δὲ	Πολλοὶ	[22]πολλοὶ	[26]τότε
ἐροῦσί μοι·	ἐροῦσί μοι	ἐροῦσίν μοι	ἄρξεσθε λέγειν·
	τῇ ἡμέρᾳ	ἐν ἐκείνῃ	
	ἐκείνῃ·	τῇ ἡμέρᾳ·	
Κύριε κύριε,	Κύριε, κύριε	κύριε κύριε,	
οὐ τῷ σῷ	οὐ τῷ σῷ	οὐ τῷ σῷ	
ὀνόματι	ὀνόματι	ὀνόματι	
ἐφάγομεν καὶ	ἐφάγομεν καὶ		ἐφάγομεν ἐνώπιόν
			σου καὶ
ἐπίομεν καὶ	ἐπίομεν καὶ		ἐπίομεν, καὶ
	προεφη-	ἐπροφη-	
	τεύσαμεν	τεύσαμεν,	ἐν
	καὶ	καὶ τῷ σῷ	ταῖς
		ὀνόματι	
	δαιμόνια	δαιμόνια	πλατείαις
	ἐξεβάλομεν;	ἐξεβάλομεν,	ἡμῶν
		καὶ τῷ σῷ	ἐδίδαξας·
		ὀνόματι	
δυνάμεις		δυνάμεις πολλὰς	
ἐποιήσαμεν;		ἐποιήσαμεν;	
καὶ τότε	καὶ	[23]καὶ τότε	[27]καὶ
ἐρῶ αὐτοῖς·	ἐρῶ αὐτοῖς·	ὁμολογήσω	ἐρεῖ λέγων
		αὐτοῖς	ὑμῖν·
		ὅτι οὐδέποτε	οὐκ οἶδα
		ἔγνων ὑμᾶς·	πόθεν ἐστέ·
Ἀποχωρεῖτε	Ἀναχωρεῖτε	ἀποχωρεῖτε	ἀπόστητε
ἀπ' ἐμοῦ,	ἀπ' ἐμοῦ.	ἀπ' ἐμοῦ	ἀπ' ἐμοῦ
ἐργάται		οἱ ἐργαζόμενοι	πάντες ἐργάται
τῆς ἀνομίας		τὴν ἀνομίαν.	ἀδικίας.

---

[1] Mt. 7:24 Πᾶς οὖν ὅστις ἀκούει μου τοὺς λόγους τούτους καὶ ποιεῖ αὐτούς, ὁμοιωθή-σεται ἀνδρὶ φρονίμῳ, ὅστις ᾠκοδόμησεν αὐτοῦ τὴν οἰκίαν ἐπὶ τὴν πέτραν.
Lk. 6:46 f. Τί δέ με καλεῖτε· κύριε κύριε, καὶ οὐ ποιεῖτε ἃ λέγω; Πᾶς ὁ ἐρχόμενος πρός με καὶ ἀκούων μου τῶν λόγων καὶ ποιῶν αὐτούς, ὑποδείξω ὑμῖν τίνι ἐστὶν ὅμοιος. I shall demonstrate later (see p. 99) that there is underlying *Apol.* 16: 10 a written text that combined, among other elements, this fourth line of Lk. 10: 16 with the

A comparison of *Apol.* 16:11 and *Dial.* 76:5 indicates that wherever the two passages are parallel they agree with each other, often against their synoptic parallels, except that (1) δὲ appears in *Apol.* 16:11 but not in *Dial.* 76:5, [1] (2) τότε appears in *Apol.* 16:11 but not in *Dial.* 76:5, and (3) *Apol.* 16:11 has ἀποχωρεῖτε where *Dial.* 76:5 has ἀναχωρεῖτε; however, all of these differences are minor and can probably be regarded as stylistic changes. This observation permits us to conclude that Justin used as his source for *Apol.* 16:11 and *Dial.* 76:5 a single written text that can be recovered by conflating the two texts from Justin, and at the same time such a hypothesis naturally implies that Justin drew from this source only certain sections for both *Apol.* 16:11 and *Dial.* 76:5.[2] But now let us compare this material from *Apol.* 16:11 and *Dial.* 76:5 with its closest gospel parallels, Mt. 7:22f. and Lk. 13:26f. From an examination of the above table it is observed that the texts of Mt. 7:22f. and Lk. 13:26f. are hardly parallel, especially Mt. 7:22 and Lk. 13:26; however, Justin's source reveals certain features of harmonization of these texts of Matthew and Luke: (1) πολλοὶ ἐροῦσί μοι τῇ ἡμέρᾳ ἐκείνῃ· Κύριε κύριε, οὐ τῷ σῷ ὀνόματι of Justin's source is parallel to Mt. 7:22; (2) ἐφάγομεν καὶ ἐπίομεν from Justin's source is parallel to Lk. 13:26; (3) προεφητεύσαμεν[3] καὶ δαιμόνια ἐξεβάλομεν; δυνάμεις ἐποιήσαμεν; from Justin's source is parallel to Mt. 7:22; (4) Justin's καὶ has a parallel in both Mt. 7:23 and Lk. 13:27, but τότε of *Apol.* 16:11 finds a parallel in only Mt. 7:23; (5) ἐρῶ in Justin finds its closest parallel in Lk. 13:27 (ἐρεῖ), but αὐτοῖς in Justin is found in only Mt. 7:23; (6) ἀποχωρεῖτε[4]

text of Lk. 6:46; therefore, I shall suspend final judgment about this passage until later in this study when I shall discuss *Apol.* 16:10 in its full context. See also Köster, *Synoptische Überlieferung*, pp. 87 ff.

[1] It will be shown below in the section on *Apol.* 16:9-13 that this δὲ in *Apol.* 16:11 was not in Justin's source but that it was rather one of the devices by which Justin combined several citations (see below, p. 98-100).

[2] It is possible that Justin chose to omit certain material of his source from both *Apol.* 16:11 and *Dial.* 76:5, and such sections naturally cannot be reconstructed merely by conflating *Apol.* 16:11 and *Dial.* 76:5; however, such a consideration is beyond the immediate concern of this study.

[3] The difference between ἐπροφητεύσαμεν in Mt. 7:22 and προεφητεύσαμεν in *Dial.* 76:5 is of only linguistic interest and reveals nothing about the reading of Justin's source. In Mt. 7:22 the prefix προ is considered part of the verb; therefore, the augment ἐ is placed before προ. In *Dial.* 76:5, however, Justin does not regard the prefix as a part of the verb; therefore, the augment is placed between the prefix and the rest of the verb. See also F. Blass and A. Debrunner, *A Greek Grammar of the New Testament and Other Early Christian Literature*, translated and revised by Robert Funk (Chicago, 1961), 69 (4).

[4] ἀποχωρεῖτε is probably the reading of Justin's source in agreement with Mt. 7:23; however, it is not significant which verb is original, because the difference between the two verbs in Justin is probably the result of stylistic alteration.

in *Apol.* 16:11 is parallel to Mt. 7:22, but ἀπ' ἐμοῦ in Justin's texts finds a parallel in both Matthew and Luke; (7) ἐργάται of *Apol.* 16:11 is parallel to Lk. 13:27, but τῆς ἀνομίας is closest to Mt. 7:23 (τὴν ἀνομίαν). These consistent features of harmonization found in *Apol.* 16:11 and *Dial.* 76:5 leave little doubt that Justin used as his source for these passages a written harmony of Mt. 7:22f. and Lk. 13:26f., and this harmonization of Matthew and Luke is further evident in several of the early fathers quoted in the texts below, where I have indicated material parallel to Matthew by single underlining and material parallel to Luke by double underlining:

Origen, *Contra Celsum* II, 49 (Koetschau, I, *GCS*, p. 171)

πολλοὶ ἐροῦσί μοι ἐν ἐκείνῃ τῇ ἡμέρᾳ· κύριε, κύριε, οὐ τῷ ὀνόματί σου ἐφάγομεν καὶ τῷ ὀνόματί σου ἐπίομεν καὶ τῷ ὀνόματί σου δαιμόνια ἐξεβάλομεν καὶ δυνάμεις πολλὰς ἐποιήσαμεν; καὶ ἐρῶ αὐτοῖς· ἀποχωρεῖτε ἀπ' ἐμου, ὅτι ἐστὲ ἐργάται ἀδικίας.

Origen, *In Evangelium Joannis* XXXII, 11 (Preuschen, IV, *GCS*, p. 443)

Κύριε, κύριε, οὐκ ἐν τῷ ὀνόματί σου ἐφάγομεν, καὶ ἐν τῷ ὀνόματί σου ἐπίομεν, καὶ ἐν τῷ ὀνόματί σου δαιμόνια ἐξεβάλομεν, καὶ δυνάμεις πεποιή-καμεν; φήσει γοῦν αὐτοῖς ὁ Ἰησοῦς· Ἀποχωρεῖτε ἀπ' ἐμοῦ. οὐδέποτε ἔγνων ὑμᾶς, ὅτι ἐργάται ἐστὲ ἀδικίας.

Origen, *In Evangelium Joannis* XXXII, 8 (Preuschen, IV, *GCS*, p. 447)

φησί που ὁ σωτὴρ ἐρεῖν τοῖς λέξουσι· "Τῷ ὀνόματί σου ἐφάγομεν, καὶ ἐπίομεν, καὶ δαιμόνια ἐξεβάλομεν·" τό· "Οὐδέποτε ἔγνων ὑμᾶς·" καὶ τό· "Οὐκ οἶδα ὑμᾶς, πόθεν ἐστέ·"

Pamphilius, *Apologia pro Origene* V (Migne, *PG*, XVII, 572f.)

Πολλοὶ ἐροῦσί μοι ἐν ἐκείνῃ τῇ ἡμέρᾳ. Κύριε, Κύριε, οὐ τῷ ὀνόματί σου ἐφάγομεν, καὶ τῷ ὀνόματί σου ἐπίομεν, καὶ τῷ ὀνόματί σου δαιμόνια ἐξεβάλομεν; καὶ ἐρῶ αὐτοῖς· Ἀποχωρεῖτε ἀπ' ἐμοῦ, οἱ ἐργαζόμενοι τὴν ἀνομίαν, οὐδέποτε ἔγνων ὑμᾶς.

2 Clement 4:5 (Lake, I, p. 134)

καὶ ἐρῶ ὑμῖν· Ὑπάγατε ἀπ᾽ ἐμοῦ, οὐκ οἶδα ὑμᾶς, πόθεν ἐστέ, ἐργάται ἀνομίας.

A comparison of this harmonization of Matthew and Luke in the patristic quotations with the analysis of *Apol.* 16:11 and *Dial.* 76:5 leaves little doubt that Justin used a harmony of Mt. 7:22f. and Lk. 13:26f. and that this harmony was known to other fathers in substantially the same form as that used by Justin.[1] Further, the witness of *2 Clement* here proves the existence of this harmonization of Matthew and Luke previous to Justin.[2]

6. APOLOGY 63:3, APOLOGY 63:13, AND DIALOGUE 100:1

Apol. 63:3	*Apol.* 63:13	*Dial.* 100:1	Mt. 11:27	Lk. 10:22
		Πάντα μοι	Πάντα μοι	πάντα μοι
		παραδέδοται	παρεδόθη	παρεδόθη
		ὑπὸ τοῦ	ὑπὸ τοῦ	ὑπὸ τοῦ
		πατρός,	πατρός μου,	πατρός μου,
Οὐδείς	Οὐδείς	καὶ οὐδεὶς	καὶ οὐδεὶς	καὶ οὐδεὶς
ἔγνω	ἔγνω	γινώσκει	ἐπιγινώσκει	γινώσκει
τὸν πατέρα	τὸν πατέρα	τὸν πατέρα	τὸν υἱὸν	τίς ἐστιν
				ὁ υἱὸς
εἰ μὴ ὁ	εἰ μὴ ὁ	εἰ μὴ ὁ	εἰ μὴ ὁ	εἰ μὴ ὁ
υἱός,	υἱός,	υἱός,	πατήρ,	πατήρ,
οὐδὲ	οὐδὲ	οὐδὲ	οὐδὲ	καὶ τις ἐστιν
τὸν υἱὸν	τὸν υἱὸν	τὸν υἱὸν	τὸν πατέρα	ὁ πατὴρ
			τις	
			ἐπιγινώσκει	
εἰ μὴ ὁ	εἰ μὴ ὁ	εἰ μὴ ὁ	εἰ μὴ ὁ	εἰ μὴ ὁ
πατὴρ καὶ	πατὴρ καὶ	πατὴρ καὶ	υἱὸς καὶ	υἱὸς καὶ
οἷς ἂν	οἷς ἂν	οἷς ἂν	ᾧ ἐὰν	ᾧ ἐὰν
			βούληται	βούληται
ἀποκαλύψη	ὁ υἱὸς	ὁ υἱὸς	ὁ υἱὸς	ὁ υἱὸς
ὁ υἱός.	ἀποκαλύψη.	ἀποκαλύψη.	ἀποκαλύψαι.	ἀποκαλύψαι.

[1] Baldus (p. 38) suggests that Justin's readings are the result of a failure of memory in an attempt to quote Matthew, but it would be incredible to assume that these other patristic witnesses could have suffered the same memory failure. And Bousset (p. 92) sees the use of a pre-synoptic text, but the consistent features of harmonization in Justin and the other fathers refute this theory.

[2] See also Köster (*Synoptische Überlieferung*), who reaches the same conclusion in his analysis of 2 *Clem.* 4:2, 5.

We notice from the above table that the three versions of this saying in Justin are almost identical, there being only three minor differences among Justin's versions. (1) Only *Dial.* 100:1 has the opening phrase πάντα μοι παραδέδοται ὑπὸ τοῦ πατρός paralleled in both Matthew and Luke;[1] but this addition is not significant, because Justin may have chosen to quote this saying without this preface in *Apol.* 63:3 and *Apol.* 63:13. (2) γινώσκει is used in *Dial.* 100:1, whereas *Apol.* 63:3 and *Apol.* 63:13 both use ἔγνω. The reading γινώσκει has its parallel in Lk. 10:22 (Matthew has the composite verb ἐπιγινώσκει), but the aorist ἔγνω, although found in neither Matthew nor Luke, has the support of many of the early fathers. (3) *Apol.* 63:3 has the word order ἀποκαλύψῃ ὁ υἱός, whereas both *Apol.* 63:13 and *Dial.* 100:1 have the order ὁ υἱὸς ἀποκαλύψῃ; however, this variant is not significant, because it is unlikely that Justin would have used two different sources for *Apol* 63:3 and *Apol.* 63:13 in such close proximity. Rather this variant probably indicates that Justin felt free to alter his source in adapting it to his usage. Indeed, none of these three differences among *Apol.* 63:3, *Apol.* 63:13, and *Dial.* 100:1 are serious enough to indicate that Justin used more than a single source for this saying.

The most significant difference between the texts of Justin and the gospel parallels is the consistent inversion of the father and the son in all three passages of Justin as compared with the order in Matthew and Luke, a variant found in none of the manuscript evidence [2] but known to many early fathers. Further, all three texts of Justin agree in reading οἷς ἂν ὁ υἱὸς ἀποκαλύψῃ (ἀποκαλύψῃ ὁ υἱός in *Apol.* 63:3) against the Matthaean and Lukan reading (ᾧ ἐὰν βούληται ὁ υἱὸς ἀποκαλύψαι), a variant that, together with the consistent inversion of the father and the son, probably indicates that Justin's source was not our synoptic gospels. The evidence of many of the fathers also reflects these peculiarities of Justin's text, although never in exactly the same words that we find in Justin:

Pseudoclementine *Homilies* 17, 4 and 18, 4 (Rehm, *GCS*, pp. 230, 243)

Οὐδεὶς ἔγνω τὸν πατέρα, εἰ μὴ ὁ υἱός, ὡς οὐδὲ τὸν υἱόν τις οἶδεν εἰ μὴ ὁ πατὴρ καὶ οἷς ἂν βούληται ὁ υἱὸς ἀποκαλύψαι.

---

[1] *Dial.* 100:1 reads παραδέδοται where Mt. 11:27 and Lk. 10:22 both read παρέδοθη. Although some manuscripts of Lk. 10:22 read παραδέδοται (KΠ al. pauc.), this evidence is of little significance and does not lead to the conclusion that Justin was here dependent on a text of Luke for this introduction.

[2] U and b of Lk. 10:22 have the inversion of the father and the son but in the Lukan form, which is unlike the form found in Justin and in Matthew in the inverse word order, but this Lukan variant has not influenced the text of Justin.

Pseudoclementine *Homilies* 18, 13 (Rehm, *GCS*, p. 247)

διὸ καὶ οἰκείως εἴρηται· "Οὐδεὶς ἔγνω τὸν πατέρα," ἐπεὶ ἀντὶ τοῦ θεοῦ τὸν Δαυὶδ πάντες ἔλεγον. τὸ δὲ ἐπάξαντα εἰπεῖν ὡς "οὐδὲ τὸν υἱόν τις οἶδεν," ἐπεὶ αὐτὸν υἱὸν ὄντα οὐκ ᾔδεισαν. καὶ τὸ εἰπεῖν "οἷς ἂν βούληται ὁ υἱὸς ἀποκαλύψαι" ὀρθῶς εἴρηται·

Pseudoclementine *Homilies* 18, 20 (Rehm, *GCS*, p. 250)

Οὐδεὶς ἔγνω τὸν πατέρα, εἰ μὴ ὁ υἱός, ὡς οὐδὲ τὸν υἱόν τις οἶδεν, εἰ μὴ ὁ πατήρ.

Clem. Alex., *Paed.* I, 5, 20 (Stählin, I, *GCS*, p. 101)

θεὸν γὰρ οὐδεὶς ἔγνω, εἰ μὴ ὁ υἱός, καὶ ᾧ ἂν ὁ υἱὸς ἀποκαλύψῃ.

Clem. Alex., *Paed.* I, 9, 88 (Stählin, I, *GCS*, p. 142)

"οὐδεὶς ἔγνω τὸν υἱὸν εἰ μὴ ὁ πατήρ," λέγων, "οὐδὲ τὸν πατέρα εἰ μὴ ὁ υἱός."

Clem. Alex., *Strom.* VII, 10, 58 (Stählin, III, *GCS*, p. 43)

ὃν οὐδεὶς ἔγνω εἰ μὴ ὁ υἱός, καὶ ᾧ ἐὰν ὁ υἱὸς ἀποκαλύψῃ.

Clem. Alex., *Strom.* VII, 18, 4 (Stählin, III, *GCS*, p. 78)

"οὐδεὶς γάρ," φησί, "γινώσκει τὸν πατέρα εἰ μὴ ὁ υἱὸς καὶ ᾧ ἂν ὁ υἱὸς ἀποκαλύψῃ."

Tertullian, *Adversus Marcionem* II, 27 (Migne, *PL*, II, 317)

Nemo cognovit Patrem nisi Filius.

Irenaeus, *Contra Haereses* II, 14, 7 (Migne, *PG*, VII, 775)

Nemo cognovit Patrem, nisi Filius.

Irenaeus, *Contra Haereses* IV, 6, 1 (Migne, *PG*, VII, 987)

Nemo cognoscit Patrem nisi Filius, nec Filium nisi Pater, et cui voluerit Filius revelare.

Irenaeus, *Contra Haereses* IV, 6, 3 (Migne, *PG*, VII, 988)

Nemo cognoscit Patrem nisi Filius, neque Filium nisi Pater et quibuscunque Filius revelaverit.

These patristic witnesses reveal certain features in common with Justin's reading against the synoptic gospels:

1) ἔγνω Ps. Clem. *Hom.* 17, 4; 18, 4; 18, 13; 18, 20; Clem. Alex., *Paed.* I, 5, 20; I, 9, 88; *Strom.* VII, 10, 58

2) Inversion of the father and the son
   Ps. Clem. *Hom.* 17, 4; 18, 4; 18, 13; 18, 20; Clem. Alex. *Paed.* I, 5, 20;
   Strom. VII, 10, 58; *Strom.* VII, 18, 4; Tert. *Adv. Marcion.* II, 27;
   Iren. *Contra Haer.* II, 14, 7; IV, 6, 1; IV, 6, 3[1]

3) οἷς Ps. Clem. *Hom.* 17, 4; 18, 4; 18, 13

4) ἄν (ἐάν) ὁ υἱὸς ἀποκαλύψῃ Clem. Alex. *Paed.* I, 5, 20; *Strom.* VII, 10,
   58; VII, 18, 4

It is difficult to believe that so many fathers have so often misquoted
the text of either Mt. 11:27 or Lk. 10:22 in a way that duplicates many
of the peculiarities of Justin's text.[2] Rather, it seems certain that Justin,
Clement of Alexandria, Tertullian, Irenaeus, and the author of the
Pseudoclementine *Homilies* all knew and used a similar source for this
saying of Jesus, but at this point it is impossible to say whether this
source was a variant text of Matthew or Luke or whether it was a text
based on one of these gospels.[3]

7. Dialogue 76:4, Dialogue 120:6, and Dialogue 140:4

Dial. 76:4	Dial. 120:6	Dial. 140:4	Mt. 8:11f.	Lk. 13:28f.
			[11]λέγω δὲ	[28]ἐκεῖ ἔσται
			ὑμῖν ὅτι	ὁ κλαυθμὸς

---

[1] It should also be pointed out that in close proximity to passages where Irenaeus
quotes the saying of Jesus about the father and the son in the inverted order
similar to Justin, he also quotes the passage with the order found in Matthew:
Contra Haereses IV, 6, 1 (Migne, *PG*, VII, 986) Nemo cognoscit Filium nisi Pater,
neque Patrem quis cognoscit nisi Filium, et cui voluerit Filius revelare; *Contra
Haereses* IV, 6, 7 (Migne, *PG*, VII, 990) Nemo cognoscit Filium, nisi Pater: neque
Patrem, nisi Filius, et quibuscunque Filius revelaverit. Perhaps this freedom of
quoting in Irenaeus is indicative of a tendency among the early fathers to quote
their sources freely.

[2] So too Leon E. Wright (pp. 63 f.), who argues that the evidence points to the
use of "some kind of documentary authority."

[3] It is impossible to agree with Baldus (p. 39) that these variants of Justin can
best be accounted for as the result of a failure of memory because of the recurring
testimony of so many patristic witnesses. Bousset argues that it is easiest to
explain this agreement of the texts of the early church fathers by appealing to the
use of an extra-canonical source, and with this position I basically agree. However,
it is difficult to understand how Bousset can regard this source as a pre-synoptic
text, which Matthew and Luke both used and altered for dogmatic anti-Gnostic
reasons but which the early church fathers were able to preserve in an unmodified
form (p. 103). It is certainly more reasonable to propose that this extra-canonical
source, used by Justin and many other fathers, was a text later than our synoptic
gospels and based on them. The principal weakness of Bousset's suggestion here
is that he fails to explain how or why this pre-synoptic source should suddenly
reappear after having been supplanted by the canonical gospels.

Ἥξουσιν	Ἥξουσι γὰρ	Ἥξουσιν	πολλοὶ	καὶ
ἀπὸ	ἀπὸ	ἀπὸ	ἀπὸ	ὁ
ἀνατολῶν	δυσμῶν	δυσμῶν	ἀνατολῶν	βρυγμὸς
καὶ	καὶ	καὶ	καὶ	τῶν
δυσμῶν,	ἀνατολῶν,	ἀνατολῶν,	δυσμῶν	ὀδόντων,
			ἥξουσιν	
καὶ	καὶ	καὶ	καὶ	ὅταν
ἀνακλιθή-	ἀνακλιθή-	ἀνακλιθή-	ἀνακλιθή-	ὄψησθε
σονται	σονται	σονται	σονται	
μετὰ	μετὰ	μετὰ	μετὰ	
Ἀβραὰμ	Ἀβραὰμ	Ἀβραὰμ	Ἀβραὰμ	Ἀβραὰμ
καὶ Ἰσαὰκ	καὶ Ἰσαὰκ	καὶ Ἰσαὰκ	καὶ Ἰσαὰκ	καὶ Ἰσαὰκ
καὶ Ἰακὼβ	καὶ Ἰακὼβ	καὶ Ἰακὼβ	καὶ Ἰακὼβ	καὶ Ἰακὼβ
				καὶ πάντας
				τοὺς προφήτας
ἐν τῇ	ἐν τῇ	ἐν τῇ	ἐν τῇ	ἐν τῇ
βασιλείᾳ	βασιλείᾳ	βασιλείᾳ	βασιλείᾳ	βασιλείᾳ
τῶν	τῶν	τῶν	τῶν	τοῦ
οὐρανῶν·	οὐρανῶν·	οὐρανῶν·	οὐρανῶν·	θεοῦ,
οἱ δὲ υἱοὶ	οἱ δὲ υἱοὶ	οἱ δὲ υἱοὶ	12οἱ δὲ υἱοὶ	ὑμᾶς δὲ
τῆς	τῆς	τῆς	τῆς	ἐκβαλλομένους
βασιλείας	βασιλείας	βασιλείας	βασιλείας	ἔξω.
ἐκβληθή-	ἐκβληθή-	ἐκβληθή-	ἐκβληθή-	29καὶ ἥξουσιν
σονται	σονται	σονται	σονται	ἀπὸ ἀνατολῶν
εἰς τὸ	εἰς τὸ	εἰς τὸ	εἰς τὸ	καὶ δυσμῶν
σκότος τὸ	σκότος τὸ	σκότος τὸ	σκότος τὸ	καὶ ἀπὸ
ἐξώτερον.	ἐξώτερον.	ἐξώτερον.	ἐξώτερον.	βορρᾶ καὶ
				νότου, καὶ
				ἀνακλιθή-
				σονται
				ἐν τῇ
				βασιλείᾳ
				τοῦ θεοῦ.

The texts of *Dial.* 76:4, *Dial.* 120:6, and *Dial.* 140:4 are substantially identical with only a few minor variations: (1) ἤξουσιν in *Dial.* 76:4 and *Dial.* 140:4 but ἤξουσι in *Dial.* 120:6;[1] (12) the addition of γὰρ

---

[1] This can hardly be regarded as a textual difference. It shows rather a different way of writing and may be a scribal modification rather than a change made by Justin.

in *Dial.* 120:6, a stylistic change made by Justin to connect this saying more closely with the preceding material; and (3) ἀπὸ ἀνατολῶν καὶ δυσμῶν in *Dial.* 76:4 but ἀπὸ δυσμῶν καὶ ἀνατολῶν in *Dial.* 120:6 and *Dial.* 140:4.[1] These variations are all minor and can easily be attributed to a stylistic change made by Justin himself. It is, therefore, quite probable that a single source underlies the three texts of this saying, because they are identical except for these minor variants already noted.

A careful examination of the chart above indicates that the text of Justin is identical to Mt. 8:11, 12 except for the opening words ἥξουσιν ἀπὸ δυσμῶν καὶ ἀνατολῶν (or ἥξουσιν ἀπὸ ἀνατολῶν καὶ δυσμῶν as in *Dial.* 76:4) where Mt. 8:11 reads πολλοὶ ἀπὸ ἀνατολῶν καὶ δυσμῶν ἥξουσιν. Baldus[2] believes that Justin's divergence from Matthew here can be explained as a memory failure, and Massaux[3] argues that Justin is clearly in literary contact with the text of Matthew, which he adopts literally; however, it seems unlikely that Justin would three times have accidentally reversed this Matthaean word order in almost exactly the same way. Rather it is more probable that Justin used a source that was based on Mt. 8:11, 12 harmonized with Lk. 13:29, which starts with the words ἥξουσιν ἀπὸ ἀνατολῶν καὶ δυσμῶν as Justin does.

8. Dialogue 76:7, Dialogue 100:3, and Dialogue 51:2

Dial. 76:7	*Dial.* 100:3	*Dial.* 51:2	Mt. 16:21	Mk. 8:31	Lk. 9:22
			Ἀπὸ τότε	Καὶ	
			ἤρξατο	ἤρξατο	
			Ἰησοῦς		
			Χριστὸς		
			δεικνύειν	διδάσκειν	
			τοῖς		εἰπὼν
			μαθηταῖς	αὐτοὺς	
			αὐτοῦ		
Δεῖ	Δεῖ	ὅτι δεῖ	ὅτι δεῖ	ὅτι δεῖ	ὅτι δεῖ
τὸν υἱὸν	τὸν υἱὸν	αὐτὸν	αὐτὸν εἰς	τὸν υἱὸν	τὸν υἱὸν
τοῦ	τοῦ		Ἱεροσό-	τοῦ	τοῦ
ἀνθρώπου	ἀνθρώπου		λυμα	ἀνθρώπου	ἀνθρώπου

---

[1] This variation is reminiscent of the variation between ἀποκαλύψη ὁ υἱός in *Apol.* 63:3 and ὁ υἱὸς ἀποκαλύψη in *Apol.* 63:13 and *Dial.* 100:1 (see above, p. 26) and can probably, in similar manner, be regarded as a stylistic variant made by Justin.

[2] Baldus, pp. 46 f.

[3] Massaux, *Influence de l'Evangile*, p. 522.

			ἀπελθεῖν καὶ		
πολλά	πολλά	πολλά	πολλά	πολλά	πολλά
παθεῖν	παθεῖν	παθεῖν	παθεῖν	παθεῖν,	παθεῖν
καὶ	καὶ		ἀπὸ τῶν	καὶ	καὶ
ἀποδοκι-	ἀποδοκι-		πρεσβυ-	ἀποδοκι-	ἀποδοκι-
μασθῆναι	μασθῆναι		τέρων	μασθῆναι	μασθῆναι
ὑπὸ τῶν	ὑπὸ τῶν	ἀπὸ τῶν	καὶ	ὑπὸ τῶν	ἀπὸ τῶν
γραμμα-	Φαρι-	γραμμα-	ἀρχιε-	πρεσβυ-	πρεσβυ-
τέων	σαίων	τέων	ρέων	τέρων	τέρων
				καὶ τῶν	καὶ
				ἀρχιερέων	ἀρχιερέων
καὶ	καὶ	καὶ	καὶ	καὶ τῶν	καὶ
Φαρι-	γραμμα-	Φαρι-	γραμμα-	γραμμα-	γραμμα-
σαίων,	τέων,	σαίων,	τέων	τέων	τέων
καὶ	καὶ	καὶ	καὶ	καὶ	καὶ
σταυρω-	σταυρω-	σταυρω-	ἀποκταν-	ἀποκταν-	ἀποκταν-
θῆναι	θῆναι	θῆναι	θῆναι	θῆναι	θῆναι
καὶ τῇ	καὶ τῇ	καὶ τῇ	καὶ τῇ	καὶ μετὰ	καὶ τῇ
τρίτη	τρίτη	τρίτη	τρίτη	τρεῖς	τρίτη
ἡμέρα	ἡμέρα	ἡμέρα	ἡμέρα	ἡμέρας	ἡμέρα
ἀνα-	ἀνα-	ἀνα-	ἐγερ-	ἀνα-	ἐγερ-
στῆναι.	στῆναι.	στῆναι.	θῆναι.	στῆναι.	θῆναι.

The texts of *Dial.* 76:7 and *Dial.* 100:3 are identical except for their inversion of γραμματέων and Φαρισαίων;[1] and even the text of *Dial.* 51:2, although not a direct quotation, confirms this basic text of Justin with its differences from the gospel material. All three texts of Justin share two characteristics that distinguish them from the gospel material: (1) in each instance Justin has τῶν γραμματέων καὶ Φαρισαίων (reversed in *Dial.* 100:3), a combination found in none of the gospels nor in any of the early fathers; and (2) in each instance Justin has σταυρωθῆναι, although this variant occurs in none of the gospel parallels.[2]

Aside from these variants Justin's source seems to follow the text of either Mk. 8:31 or Lk. 9:22 with one difference. Whereas in each case Justin's text reads καὶ τῇ τρίτη ἡμέρα ἀναστῆναι, Mk. 8:31 reads καὶ μετὰ

---

[1] This kind of stylistic inversion has been noted twice before (see above, pp. 26 and 30).

[2] Bousset (p. 109) argues that these two variants point to a special text used by Justin, but he feels that there is too little evidence to trace the nature of this source.

τρεῖς ἡμέρας ἀναστῆναι, and Lk. 9:22 reads καὶ τῇ τρίτῃ ἡμέρᾳ ἐγερθῆναι. However, if we examine the text of Lk. 24:7, we see that Justin's text is very possibly a combination of Lk. 9:22 (or Mk. 8:31) and this text of Lk. 24:7, which, although not a gospel parallel to the passage under discussion, has a similar context:

Lk. 24:7

λέγων τὸν υἱὸν τοῦ ἀνθρώπου ὅτι δεῖ παραδοθῆναι εἰς χεῖρας ἀνθρώπων ἁμαρτωλῶν καὶ σταυρωθῆναι καὶ τῇ τρίτῃ ἡμέρᾳ ἀναστῆναι.

By such a harmonization of Lk. 9:22 (or Mk. 8:31) with Lk. 24:7,[1] we can account for the appearance of καὶ σταυρωθῆναι καὶ τῇ τρίτῃ ἡμέρᾳ ἀναστῆναι in the text of Justin.[2] Thus we again conclude that Justin here used an extracanonical source later than our synoptic gospels and combining two elements from the gospel material, Lk. 9:22 (or Mk. 8:31) and Lk. 24:7.

9. DIALOGUE 99:2 AND DIALOGUE 103:8

Dial. 99:2	*Dial.* 103:8	Mt. 26:39	Mk. 14:36	Lk. 22:42
		καὶ λέγων·	καὶ ἔλεγεν·	λέγων·
Πάτερ,		πάτερ μου,	ἀββὰ ὁ πατήρ,	πάτερ,
εἰ δυνατόν ἐστι,		εἰ δυνατόν ἐστιν,	πάντα δυνατά σοι·	εἰ βούλει
παρελθέτω τὸ ποτήριον τοῦτο ἀπ' ἐμοῦ καὶ μετὰ τοῦτο εὐχόμενος λέγει·	Παρελθέτω, εἰ δυνατόν, τὸ ποτήριον τοῦτο·	παρελθάτω ἀπ' ἐμοῦ τὸ ποτήριον τοῦτο·	παρένεγκε τὸ ποτήριον τοῦτο ἀπ' ἐμοῦ·	παρένεγκε τοῦτο τὸ ποτήριον ἀπ' ἐμοῦ·

---

[1] Lk. 24:7 has no gospel parallels and is certainly a Lukan formulation made by the gospel writer on the basis of Lk. 9:22 (and parallels), Lk. 9:43b-45 (and parallels), and Lk. 18:31-34 (and parallels) to replace Mk 16:7. This use of peculiarly Lukan material excludes the possibility of the use of a pre-synoptic source here.

[2] ἀναστῆναι also occurs in Lk. 9:22 in ACDFW* KΠ 1. 69*. 118. 131. 157 and may have entered into the text of Luke by assimilation to Mk. 8:31. Mk. 8:31 does not have σταυρωθῆναι; therefore, it is more probable that both of these readings entered the text of Justin's source from an assimilation of Lk. 9:22 (or Mk. 8:31) with Lk. 24:7.

Μὴ	πλὴν οὐχ	ἀλλ' οὐ	πλὴν μὴ
ὡς ἐγὼ	ὡς ἐγὼ	τί ἐγὼ	τὸ θέλημά
βούλομαι,	θέλω	θέλω	μου
ἀλλ' ὡς	ἀλλ' ὡς	ἀλλὰ	ἀλλὰ τὸ σὸν
σὺ θέλεις·	σύ.	τί σύ.	γινέσθω.

The text of *Dial.* 99:2 most closely parallels Mt. 26:39. The opening words of *Dial.* 99:2 (Πάτερ, εἰ δυνατόν ἐστι) are closest to Mt. 26:39 (πάτερ μου, εἰ δυνατόν ἐστιν). The following phrase, however, shows a tendency to harmonize Mt. 26:39 with Mk. 14:36: whereas παρελθέτω (*Dial.* 99:2) is closest to Mt. 26:39 (παρελθάτω),[1] the word order of τὸ ποτήριον τοῦτο ἀπ' ἐμοῦ (*Dial.* 99:2) is identical to Mk. 14:36 but different in this instance from Mt. 26:39 (ἀπ' ἐμοῦ τὸ ποτήριον τοῦτο).

In the second part of the saying in *Dial.* 99:2 the text shows less resemblance to the synoptic parallels; however, Justin's reading (μὴ ὡς ἐγὼ βούλομαι, ἀλλ' ὡς σὺ θέλεις) is closest to Mt. 26:39 (πλὴν οὐχ ὡς ἐγὼ θέλω ἀλλ' ὡς σύ). Therefore, we can conclude that Justin's source for *Dial.* 99:2 was probably based on Mt. 26:39 with influence perhaps from Mk. 14:36 for the word order.

The text of *Dial.* 103:8 is too short to enable us to draw any certain conclusions. Its only difference from *Dial.* 99:2 is in the placement of εἰ δυνατόν in the middle of the sentence, but we have already observed this tendency in Justin.[2] It is also possible that for such a short quotation Justin might have quoted from memory, but in any case it is certain that there is no need to conclude that Justin used separate sources for *Dial.* 99:2 and *Dial.* 103:8.

10. DIALOGUE 17:4 AND DIALOGUE 112:4

Dial. 17:4	*Dial.* 112:4	Mt. 23:13, 16, 23, 24, 27	Lk. 11:52, 42
γ) καὶ τοῖς γραμματεῦσιν·			
Οὐαὶ		[13]Οὐαὶ δὲ	[52]οὐαὶ
ὑμῖν		ὑμῖν,	ὑμῖν

---

[1] That Justin's source read παρελθέτω here is supported by the text of *Dial.* 103:8, which also has παρελθέτω. Although the best manuscripts of Mt. 26:39 read παρελθάτω, it should be noted that παρελθέτω is supported by good manuscript witnesses (BHKMSUVWYΓΠΦ 067 pap. ^Mich. 6652 fam. 1 1582. 22. 69. 157. 565. 892. 1241. al. pler.) and may have been the reading of some manuscripts of Matthew from Justin's time.

[2] See above, pp. 26, 30, and 31.

Dial. 17:4	*Dial.* 112:4	Mt. 23:13, 16, 23, 24, 27	Lk. 11:52, 42
γραμματεῖς,		γραμματεῖς καὶ Φαρισαῖοι ὑποκριταί,	τοῖς νομικοῖς ὅτι ἤρατε
ὅτι τὰς κλεῖς ἔχετε		ὅτι κλείετε τὴν βασιλείαν τῶν οὐρανῶν ἔμπροσθεν τῶν ἀνθρώπων·	τὴν κλεῖδα τῆς γνώσεως·
καὶ αὐτοὶ οὐκ εἰσέρχεσθε καὶ τοὺς εἰσερχομένους κωλύετε		ὑμεῖς γὰρ οὐκ εἰσέρχεσθε, οὐδὲ τοὺς εἰσερχομένους ἀφίετε εἰσελθεῖν.	αὐτοὶ οὐκ εἰσήλθατε καὶ τοὺς εἰσερχομένους ἐκωλύσατε
ὁδηγοὶ τυφλοί.		¹⁶Οὐαὶ ὑμῖν, ὁδηγοὶ τυφλοὶ . . .	
α) Οὐαὶ ὑμῖν, γραμματεῖς καὶ Φαρισαῖοι, ὑποκριταί,		²³Οὐαὶ ὑμῖν, γραμματεῖς καὶ Φαρισαῖοι ὑποκριταί,	⁴²ἀλλὰ οὐαὶ ὑμῖν τοῖς Φαρισαίοις,
ὅτι ἀποδεκατοῦτε τὸ ἡδύοσμον καὶ τὸ πήγανον,	β) τὸ ἡδύοσμον ἀποδεκα- τοῦντες,	ὅτι ἀποδεκατοῦτε τὸ ἡδύοσμον καὶ τὸ ἄνηθον καὶ τὸ κύμινον, καὶ ἀφήκατε τὰ βαρύτερα τοῦ νόμου,	ὅτι ἀποδεκατοῦτε τὸ ἡδύοσμον καὶ τὸ πήγανον καὶ πᾶν λάχανον, καὶ παρέρχεσθε
τὴν δὲ ἀγάπην τοῦ θεοῦ καὶ τὴν κρίσιν		τὴν κρίσιν καὶ τὸ ἔλεος καὶ τὴν πίστιν·	τὴν κρίσιν καὶ τὴν ἀγάπην τοῦ θεοῦ·
οὐ κατανοεῖτε·		ταῦτα δὲ	ταῦτα δὲ

		ἔδει ποιῆσαι κἀκεῖνα μὴ ἀφεῖναι.	ἔδει ποιῆσαι κἀκεῖνα μὴ παρεῖναι·
	τὴν δὲ κάμηλον καταπίνοντες, τυφλοὶ ὁδηγοί;	²⁴ὁδηγοὶ τυφλοί, οἱ διϋλίζοντες τὸν κώνωπα, τὴν δὲ κάμηλον καταπίνοντες. ²⁷Οὐαὶ ὑμῖν, γραμματεῖς καὶ Φαρισαῖοι ὑποκριταί, ὅτι παρομοιάζετε	
β) τάφοι κεκονιαμένοι, ἔξωθεν φαινόμενοι ὡραῖοι, ἔσωθεν δὲ γέμοντες ὀστέων νεκρῶν.	α) Τάφοι κεκονιαμένοι, ἔξωθεν φαινόμενοι ὡραῖοι καὶ ἔσωθεν γεμοντες ὀστέων νεκρῶν,	τάφοις κεκονιαμένοις, οἵτινες ἔξωθεν μὲν φαίνονται ὡραῖοι, ἔσωθεν δὲ γέμουσιν ὀστέων νεκρῶν καὶ πάσης ἀκαθαρσίας.	

From an examination of the above chart it is observed that although *Dial.* 17:4 and *Dial.* 112:4 do not reproduce all of the same material, in that instance where they are parallel (*Dial.* 17:4β and *Dial.* 112:4α) they agree almost exactly against their gospel parallel in Mt. 23:27, the presence of καὶ in *Dial.* 112:4 and δὲ in *Dial.* 17:4 hardly being more than stylistic changes. The sequence of the two passages in Justin is inconsistent and is also inconsistent with the order of the gospel parallels; therefore, it will be best to examine each of Justin's passages separately before drawing final conclusions about the source or sources underlying *Dial.* 17:4 and *Dial.* 112:4.

If we follow the order of *Dial.* 17:4, we gain the following picture from the above chart. *Dial.* 17:4α is apparently a harmony of Mt. 23:23 and Lk. 11:42 with abbreviation and slight modification. The beginning οὐαὶ ὑμῖν, γραμματεῖς καὶ Φαρισαῖοι ὑποκριταί apparently comes from Mt. 23:23 (οὐαὶ ὑμῖν, γραμματεῖς καὶ Φαρισαῖοι) and not from the Lukan parallel from which γραμματεῖς and ὑποκριταί are both missing. The next phrase ὅτι ἀποδεκατοῦτε τὸ ἡδύοσμον could have come from either Mt. 23:23 or from Lk. 11:42, both of which have the same reading as Justin; however, Justin's phrase καὶ τὸ πήγανον is paralleled only in Luke. Further, Justin's τὴν δὲ ἀγάπην τοῦ Θεοῦ καὶ τὴν κρίσιν οὐ κατανοεῖτε finds its only parallel in Lk. 11:42 (καὶ παρέρχεσθε τὴν κρίσιν καὶ τὴν ἀγάπην τοῦ Θεοῦ), although the phrases are reversed, the verb is different, and Justin's text is shorter. Therefore, there can be little doubt that either Justin or his source harmonized and abbreviated Mt. 23:23 and Lk. 11:42.

Dial. 17:4β reproduces quite closely the text of Mt. 23:27 for which Luke has no parallel, although either Justin or his source apparently modified this text of Matthew and shortened it.

An examination of *Dial.* 17:4γ again indicates a harmonization of elements from Matthew and Luke. οὐαὶ ὑμῖν, γραμματεῖς, parallels the text of Mt. 23:13 (οὐαὶ δὲ ὑμῖν, γραμματεῖς), but Justin's ὅτι τὰς κλεῖς ἔχετε is not identical to either Matthew or Luke although similar to both; however, it is perhaps closer to Luke, since Matthew does not have the noun at all. But Justin's words καὶ αὐτοὶ οὐκ εἰσέρχεσθε καὶ τοὺς εἰσερχομένους κωλύετε show influence from both Matthew and Luke. αὐτοὶ is peculiar to Luke and εἰσέρχεσθε to Matthew; and Justin and Luke both use a form of the verb κωλύειν, whereas Matthew has οὐδὲ τοὺς εἰσερχομένους ἀφίετε εἰσελθεῖν. Further, Justin's ὁδηγοὶ τυφλοί is paralleled in Mt. 23:16. Therefore, our examination would seem to indicate that *Apol.* 17:4γ was either based on a source that harmonized Mt. 23:13, 16 with Lk. 11:52 or that Justin himself harmonized these verses. Our overall picture of *Dial.* 17:4 is that Justin either harmonized these various texts of Matthew and Luke or else used a source that had already harmonized them.[1]

Now let us turn our attention to Justin's second quotation of this passage, *Dial.* 112:4. *Dial.* 112:4a reproduces quite closely the text of Mt. 23:27 (for which Luke has no parallel) with slight modifications and with abbreviation but in almost complete agreement with the quotation in *Dial.* 17:4. *Dial.* 112:4β again comes closest to the text of Matthew: τὸ ἡδύοσμον ἀποδεκατοῦντες is parallel to either Mt. 23:23 or to

---

[1] Massaux (*Influence de l'Evangile*, p. 518) argues that Justin here combines the texts of Matthew and Luke but that he does not seem to depend on any sources other than the gospels, but Massaux does not seem to realize that this combination of Matthew and Luke may have been an element not of Justin himself but of his source.

Lk. 11:42, both of which are identical in their text of this phrase; but τὴν δὲ κάμηλον καταπίνοντες, τυφλοὶ ὁδηγοί is closest to Mt. 23:24 (for which Luke has no parallel), although Justin's text is shorter than Matthew and the order of the address is reversed. Therefore, we see that in *Dial.* 112:4 Justin either himself shortened and adapted the text of Mt. 23:27, 23, 24 or else used a source that already had these features.[1]

A comparison of *Dial.* 17:4 with *Dial.* 112:4 indicates that although the two texts do not parallel each other exactly they do reproduce almost exactly the same variants from the text of Mt. 23:27 in that portion where they do parallel each other (*Dial.* 17:4β and *Dial.* 112:4α). This indicates that there is no need to conclude that Justin was here quoting from two different sources. Rather, Justin may be quoting in each passage different portions of a larger context,[2] and this larger context was apparently a harmony of Matthew and Luke.[3]

11. DIALOGUE 125:4, DIALOGUE 103:6, APOLOGY 16:6, AND DIALOGUE 93:2

Dial. 125:4

Γέγραπται· Κύριον τὸν θεόν σου προσκυνήσεις καὶ αὐτῷ μόνῳ λατρεύσεις.

Dial. 103:6

῞Υπαγε ὀπίσω μου, σατανᾶ· κύριον τὸν θεόν σου προσκυνήσεις καὶ αὐτῷ μόνῳ λατρεύσεις.

Apol. 16:6

Μεγίστη ἐντολή ἐστι· Κύριον τὸν θεόν σου προσκυνήσεις καὶ αὐτῷ μόνῳ λατρεύσεις ἐξ ὅλης τῆς καρδίας σου καὶ ἐξ ὅλης τῆς ἰσχύος σου, κύριον τὸν θεὸν τὸν ποιήσαντά σε.

Dial. 93:2

᾿Αγαπήσεις κύριον τὸν θεόν σου ἐξ ὅλης τῆς καρδίας σου καὶ ἐξ ὅλης τῆς ἰσχύος σου, καὶ τὸν πλησίον σου ὡς σεαυτόν.

---

[1] With respect to *Dial.* 112:4 Wright maintains (pp. 26 f.) that "it seems quite probable that we have to do with but a summary framework embracing instances of typical pharisaic misplacement of ethical emphasis, according to Justin's context, and not with a purposefully conceived aggregation of harmonistic texts." However, my present analysis refutes this position.

[2] I have reached the same conclusion in my analysis of *Apol.* 16:11 and *Dial.* 76:5 (see above, pp. 22-25).

[3] Baldus argues (p. 43) that these two texts are (1) two different gospel citations and (2) memory citations, but this position cannot stand in view of my present study.

This saying, which appears four times in Justin, is found twice in the synoptic gospels: (1) Mk. 12:30, 31 (paralleled in Mt. 22:37-39 and Lk. 10:27), the so-called great commandment; and (2) Mt. 4:10 and Lk. 4:8 (from Q) in the temptation story. In *Dial.* 125:4 and *Dial.* 103:6 Justin follows more closely the version in Mt. 4:10 and Lk. 4:8, and in *Apol.* 16:6 and *Dial.* 93:2 the text parallels more closely the version of Mk. 12:30, 31, Mt. 22:37-39, and Lk. 10:27. Therefore, I shall examine separately each of these two versions of the saying.

Dial. 125:4	*Dial.* 103:6	Mt. 4:10	Lk. 4:8
	καὶ	τότε	καὶ
ἀποκρίνεται	ἀπεκρίνασθαι	λέγει	ἀποκριθεὶς
γὰρ			
αὐτῷ·	αὐτῷ	αὐτῷ	ὁ Ἰησοῦς
	τὸν Χριστόν·	ὁ Ἰησοῦς·	εἶπεν αὐτῷ·
	Ὕπαγε	ὕπαγε,	
	ὀπίσω μου,		
	σατανᾶ·	σατανᾶ·	
Γέγραπται·		γέγραπται γάρ·	γέγραπται·
Κύριον τὸν	κύριον τὸν	κύριον τὸν	προσκυνήσεις
θεόν σου	θεόν σου	θεόν σου	κύριον τὸν
προσκυνήσεις	προσκυνήσεις	προσκυνήσεις	θεόν σου
καὶ αὐτῷ μόνῳ	καὶ αὐτῷ μόνῳ	καὶ αὐτῷ μόνῳ	καὶ αὐτῷ μόνῳ
λατρεύσεις.	λατρεύσεις.	λατρεύσεις.	λατρεύσεις.

The introduction to this saying in *Dial.* 125:4 (ἀποκρίνεται γὰρ αὐτῷ) and *Dial.* 103:6 (καὶ ἀπεκρίνασθαι αὐτῷ τὸν Χριστόν) perhaps reflects influence from Lk. 4:8 (καὶ ἀποκριθεὶς ὁ Ἰησοῦς εἶπεν αὐτῷ), although it must be realized that the similarity of these three texts may be coincidental (1) because it is quite natural to introduce a saying of Jesus with a form of the verb ἀποκρίνομαι and (2) because *Dial.* 125:4, *Dial.* 103:6, and Lk. 4:8 all use different forms of this verb.

The rebuke ὕπαγε ὀπίσω μου, σατανᾶ of *Dial.* 103:6 is missing from the best manuscripts of Luke [1] but has an approximate parallel in Mt. 4:10

---

[1] Certain manuscripts and versions of Lk. 4:8 add ὕπαγε ὀπίσω μου, σατανᾶ (AW[b]ΓΔΛΠ unc.[9] b l q Cop. [wi. et dz. recent.] Syr. [pesh.] Aeth. [cod.] a); however, these witnesses do not indicate that this reading was old enough to have been derived by Justin from Lk. 4:8. Rather, it appears that the text of Lk. 4:8 has here been harmonized to read like the text of certain manuscripts of its Matthaean parallel. See below.

(ὕπαγε, σατανᾶ). Justin's version (ὕπαγε ὀπίσω μου, σατανᾶ) is apparently the result of harmonization of Mt. 4:10 with Mt. 16:23, where in rebuking Peter Jesus says ὕπαγε ὀπίσω μου, σατανᾶ.[1] The word γέγραπται from *Dial.* 125:4 has a parallel in both Matthew and Luke, and the remaining section of *Dial.* 125:4 and *Dial.* 103:6 (κύριον τὸν θεόν σου προσκυνήσεις καὶ αὐτῷ μόνῳ λατρεύσεις) is identical to Mt. 4:10, whereas the Lukan parallel has the inverted word order προσκυνήσεις κύριον τὸν θεόν σου καὶ αὐτῷ μόνῳ λατρεύσεις.[2]

It is, therefore, apparent that as his source for *Dial.* 125:4 and *Dial.* 103:6 Justin either harmonized Mt. 4:10 and Mt. 16:23 or else used a source that had already harmonized these elements. It is also possible that the introduction to these passages in Justin shows influence from Lk. 4:8; however, this influence is by no means certain.[3] The second version of this saying, the great commandment, appears in *Apol.* 16:6 and *Dial.* 93:2; and I shall now turn to an examination of this material with its gospel parallels.

Apol. 16:6	*Dial.* 93:2	Mt. 22:37-39	Mk. 12:30, 31	Lk. 10:27
Μεγίστη ἐντολή ἐστι·		[37]ὁ δὲ ἔφη αὐτῷ·	[30]καὶ	ὁ δὲ ἀποκριθεὶς εἶπεν·
Κύριον τὸν θεόν σου προσκυνή- σεις καὶ αὐτῷ μόνῳ λατρεύσεις	Ἀγαπήσεις κύριον τὸν θεόν σου	ἀγαπήσεις κύριον τὸν θεόν σου	ἀγαπήσεις κύριον τὸν θεόν σου	ἀγαπήσεις κύριον τὸν θεόν σου
ἐξ ὅλης τῆς καρδίας	ἐξ ὅλης τῆς καρδίας	ἐν ὅλη τῆ καρδία	ἐξ ὅλης τῆς καρδίας	ἐξ ὅλης τῆς καρδίας

---

[1] This harmonization of Mt. 4:10 and Mt. 16:23 appears in many manuscripts of Mt. 4:10 (C²DELMUZΓΩ li355. 209. 346. 543². 28. 33. 71. 157. 248. 349. 482. 517. 692. 892². al. pler., item. retro me b l, post me d h, *similiter* Syr. cur.sa. hl. txt. Cop sa. bo. (2 MSS) Aeth.).

[2] Many manuscripts of Lk. 4:8 have the order κύριον τὸν θεόν σου προσκυνήσεις καὶ αὐτῷ μόνῳ λατρεύσεις (Sinaiticus BDFLWᵇΛΞ 1. 33. 69. 118. 124. 130. 131. 157. al.³⁰ *fere* b c e f ff² g¹·². l q Vg. Goth. Cop. Syr. utr. Aeth.); however, this reading is certainly not original but is rather the result of harmonization to Mt. 4:10.

[3] The fact that the saying in *Dial.* 103:6 is immediately preceded by the words of the voice at Jesus' baptism as recorded in D it. codd. of Lk. 3:22 (Υἱός μου εἶ σύ, ἐγὼ σήμερον γεγέννηκά σε) perhaps supports the position that there is Lukan influence in these texts of Justin.

σου	σου	σου	σου	σου
		και ἐν	και ἐξ	και ἐν
		ὅλῃ τῇ	ὅλης τῆς	ὅλῃ τῇ
		ψυχῇ σου	ψυχῆς σου	ψυχῇ σου
		και ἐν	και ἐξ	και ἐν
		ὅλῃ τῇ	ὅλης τῆς	ὅλῃ τῇ
		διανοίᾳ	διανοίας	ἰσχύϊ
		σου.	σου	σου
και ἐξ	και ἐξ		και ἐξ	και ἐν
ὅλης τῆς	ὅλης τῆς		ὅλης τῆς	ὅλῃ τῇ
ἰσχύος	ἰσχύος		ἰσχύος	διανοίᾳ
σου,	σου,		σου.	σου,
		[38]αὕτη ἐστιν		
		ἡ μεγάλη		
		και πρώτη		
		ἐντολή.		
		[39]δευτέρα	[31]δευτέρα	
		ὁμοία αὐτῇ·	αὕτη·	
	και	ἀγαπήσεις	ἀγαπήσεις	και
	τὸν πλησίον	τὸν πλησίον	τὸν πλησίον	τὸν πλησίον
	σου ὡς	σου ὡς	σου ὡς	σου ὡς
	σεαυτόν.	σεαυτόν.	σεαυτόν.	σεαυτόν.
κύριον τὸν				
θεὸν τὸν				
ποιήσαντά				
σε.				

The opening words of *Apol.* 16:6 (μεγίστη ἐντολή ἐστι) have their closest parallel in Mt. 22:38 (αὕτη ἐστιν ἡ μεγάλη και πρώτη ἐντολή). Then *Apol.* 16:6 ignores the evidence of both the synoptic parallels to the great commandment and the Old Testament text of Deut. 6:5 [1] by reading κύριον τὸν θεόν σου προσκυνήσεις και αὐτῷ μόνῳ λατρεύσεις instead of ἀγαπήσεις κύριον τὸν θεόν σου of the synoptic parallels and *Dial.* 93:2 or ἀγαπήσεις Κύριον τὸν θεόν σου of Deut. 6:5. Rather this section of *Dial.* 16:6 parallels exactly Mt. 4:10, *Dial.* 125:4, and *Dial.* 103:6 already discussed above; but in this same instance *Dial.* 93:2 parallels exactly Mt. 22:37 Mk. 12:30, and Lk. 10:27.

---

[1] Deut. 6:5 και Κύριον τὸν θεόν σου ἐξ ὅλης τῆς διανοίας σου και ἐξ ὅλης τῆς ψυχῆς σου και ἐξ ὅλης τῆς δυνάμεώς σου (Henry Barclay Swete, *The Old Testament in Greek* [Cambridge, 1887], p. 355).

Apol. 16:6 and *Dial.* 93:2 agree with each other against the evidence of the gospels and Deut. 6:5 in reading ἐξ ὅλης τῆς καρδίας σου καὶ ἐξ ὅλης τῆς ἰσχύος σου, omitting the references to both ψυχή and διανοία found in both the synoptic parallels and in Deuteronomy. ἐξ ὅλης τῆς καρδίας σου of Justin's texts finds a parallel in Mk. 12:30 and Lk. 10:27, but Justin's καὶ ἐξ ὅλης τῆς ἰσχύος σου finds its only parallel in Mk. 12:30, this phrase being completely absent from the Matthaean parallel and in the dative case in Lk. 10:27 (ἐν ὅλῃ τῇ ἰσχύϊ σου). An examination of the patristic evidence indicates that this middle section was known in many different combinations and versions in the early church:

Clem. Alex., *Paed.* III, 12 (Stählin, I, *GCS*, p. 284)

Θεόν σου ἐν ὅλῃ καρδίᾳ σου καὶ ἐν ὅλῃ τῇ ψυχῇ σου καὶ ἐν ὅλῃ τῇ ἰσχύι σου, καὶ τὸν πλησίον σου ὡς σεαυτόν.

Clem. Alex., *Liber Quis Dives Salvetur* 27 (Stählin, III, *GCS*, p. 178)

ἀγαπήσεις κύριον τὸν θεόν σου ἐξ ὅλης τῆς ψυχῆς σου καὶ ἐξ ὅλης τῆς δυνάμεώς σου.

Basil, *Regulae Brevius Tractatae*, Interrogatio CLXIII (Migne, *PG*, XXIII, 1188-1189)

Πρώτη δὲ καὶ μεγάλη ἐντολή· Ἀγαπήσεις Κύριον τὸν Θεόν σου ἐξ ὅλης τῆς καρδίας σου, καὶ ἐξ ὅλης τῆς διανοίας σου, καὶ ἐξ ὅλης τῆς ἰσχύος σου· καὶ δευτέρα ὁμοία ταύτῃ· Ἀγαπήσεις τὸν πλησίον σου ὡς σεαυτόν·

Basil, *Homilia in Psalmum XLIX* (Migne, *PG*, XXIX, 392)

Ἀγαπήσεις Κύριον τὸν Θεόν σου ἐξ ὅλης τῆς καρδίας σου, καὶ ἐξ ὅλης τῆς ψυχῆς σου, καὶ ἐξ ὅλης τῆς διανοίας σου.

Orosius, *Apology* 31, 4 (Zangemeister, p. 658)

diliges Dominum Deum tuum ex toto corde tuo et ex tota anima tua et ex totis viribus tuis; et secundum simile huic: diliges proximum tuum tamquam te ipsum.

Hilarius, *De Trinitate* IX, 24 (Migne, *PL*, X, 300)

ita diligendus ex toto corde et ex totis viribus et ex tota anima: et diligere proximum tamquam se ipsum.

Cyprian, *De Catholicae Ecclesiae Unitate* 15 (Hartel, p. 224)

diliges Dominum Deum tuum de toto corde tuo et de tota anima tua et de tota virtute tua. hoc primum et secundum simile huic: diliges proximum tuum tamquam te.

Cyprian, *Epistola ad Fortunatum* 2 (Hartel, p. 323)

diliges Dominum Deum tuum de toto corde tuo et de tota anima tua et de tota virtute tua. hoc primum et secundum simile huic; diliges proximum tuum tamquam te.

Although none of these fathers agrees exactly with the text of Justin, these texts do demonstrate the wide variety of combinations in which this material circulated. However, the agreement of Justin in including only ἐξ ὅλης τῆς καρδίας σου and καὶ ἐξ ὅλης τῆς ἰσχύος σου in exactly the same form in both *Apol.* 16:6 and *Dial.* 93:2 probably indicates dependence upon a written tradition.

It is also significant that the two passages in Justin end differently: *Dial.* 93:2, apparently following the form of Luke, with the phrase καὶ τὸν πλησίον σου ὡς σεαυτόν and *Apol.* 16:6 with the phrase κύριον τὸν θεὸν τὸν ποιήσαντά σε not found in any of the gospel parallels. Köster has argued convincingly that there is underlying *Barnabas* 19:2 and *Didache* 1:2 a Jewish tradition of the two ways, and in this material we find a parallel to the reading of *Apol.* 16:6 (κύριον τὸν θεὸν τὸν ποιήσαντά σε): [1]

Barn. 19:2 (Lake, I, p. 400)

ἀγαπήσεις τὸν ποιήσαντά σε

Did. 1:2 (Lake, I, p. 308)

πρῶτον ἀγαπήσεις τὸν θεὸν τὸν ποιήσαντά σε, δεύτερον τὸν πλησίον σου ὡς σεαυτόν.

---

[1] *Synoptische Überlieferung*, pp. 133 f., 170 ff. Richard Glover ("The Didache's Quotations and the Synoptic Gospels," *New Testament Studies* V [1958-1959], pp. 12-39) agrees that *Did.* 1:2 supports Justin in his addition of the phrase κύριον τὸν θεὸν τὸν ποιήσαντά σε. Leon E. Wright (pp. 60 f.), on the other hand, maintains that this phrase of Justin should be attributed to oral tradition of Jewish origin. In comparing the phrase of *Apol.* 16:6 and *Did.* 1:2, Wright argues that "Justin's free quotation involving the identical phrase is due probably to the same or to a similar source. His repetition of this idea in a different connection, nevertheless, suggests a rather fluid application more compatible with an oral rather than with a stereotyped documentary version. This, of course, cannot be urged. In neither of Justin's contexts, however, is the idea demanded in a manner suggestive of its being an independent creation. Thus the essential Jewishness of the sentiment here indicated leads one to suspect that Justin, along with the *Didache*, is reproducing from an uncanonical source a sentiment of prior urgency in the sphere of Jewish dogmatics." Köster's study reduces the probability that this phrase is a free quotation by Justin. In the same connection it should be noted that the phrase ὁ ποιήσας τὰ πάντα occurs in the following verse, *Apol.* 16:7; and it is quite possible that Justin actually found the phrase κύριον τὸν θεὸν τὸν ποιήσαντά σε in his source for *Apol.* 16:6 and himself added ὁ ποιήσας τὰ πάντα the second time in *Apol.* 16:7 (see above, pp. 17-20).

The results of the above discussion of *Apol.* 16:6 and *Dial* 93:2 can be summarized in the following table:

Apol. 16:6	Source
Μεγίστη ἐντολή ἐστι·	Mt. 22:38
κύριον τὸν θεόν . . . λατρεύσεις	Mt 4:10
ἐξ ὅλης τῆς καρδίας σου	Mk. 12:30 or Lk. 10:27
καὶ ἐξ ὅλης τῆς ἰσχύος σου	Mk. 12:30
κύριον τὸν θεὸν τὸν ποιήσαντά σε	non-synoptic *Didache*-like material

Dial. 93:2	Source
Ἀγαπήσεις . . . θεόν σου	Mt. 22:37, Mk. 12:30, Lk. 10:27
ἐξ ὅλης τῆς καρδίας σου	Mk. 12:30 or Lk. 10:27
καὶ ἐξ ὅλης τῆς ἰσχύος σου	Mk. 12:30[1]
καὶ τὸν πλησίον σου ὡς σεαυτόν.	Lk. 10:27

Although *Apol.* 16:6 and *Dial.* 93:2 are not parallel in each phrase, there is only a single section that indicates that Justin could not have used the same source for both passages; and that section is the opening clause where *Dial.* 93:2 follows the synoptic parallels (Mt. 22:37, Mk. 12:30, or Lk. 10:27) and *Apol.* 16:6 harmonizes the material from the temptation story (Mt. 4:10). Indeed, it appears that *Apol.* 16:6 is based on a harmony of Mt. 22:38, Mt. 4:10, Mk. 12:30, and non-synoptic *Didache*-like material, and *Dial.* 93:2 is based on a harmony of Mk. 12:30 and Lk. 10:27.[2]

---

[1] Massaux argues (*Influence de l'Evangile*, p. 531) that Justin has in *Dial.* 93:2 freely combined texts of Luke and Matthew and that we can safely exclude the use of Mark, because the passage shows no literary influence from the second gospel. But it has been shown that Justin's text of *Dial.* 93:2 demonstrates no peculiar evidences of Matthew's text but does show dependence upon material found only in Mark. Indeed, Justin's ἐξ ὅλης τῆς καρδίας σου appears as ἐν ὅλῃ τῇ καρδίᾳ σου in Mt. 22:37, and Justin's καὶ ἐξ ὅλης τῆς ἰσχύος is entirely lacking in Matthew's text.

[2] Bousset argues (p. 86) that by comparing Justin's text with *Did.* 1:2 there is evidence of the use of an extra-canonical, pre-canonical source; but it is difficult to understand how a pre-canonical source would have contained what are apparently harmonistic elements. Credner (p. 243) and Semisch (pp. 276-279) maintain that Justin is quoting freely from memory, but this hypothesis overlooks what is apparently a carefully devised harmonistic pattern that can hardly have arisen accidentally through a failure of memory.

12. Apology 16:13 and Dialogue 35:3a

Apol. 16:13	Dial. 35:3a	Mt. 24:5; 7: 15, 16, 19	Mk. 13:6	Lk. 21:8
				ὁ δὲ εἶπεν· βλέπετε μὴ πλανηθῆτε·
		24:5		
πολλοὶ γὰρ	Πολλοὶ	πολλοὶ γὰρ	πολλοὶ	πολλοὶ γὰρ
ἥξουσιν	ἐλεύσονται	ἐλεύσονται	ἐλεύσονται	ἐλεύσονται
ἐπὶ τῷ	ἐπὶ τῷ	ἐπὶ τῷ	ἐπὶ τῷ	ἐπὶ τῷ
ὀνόματί	ὀνόματί	ὀνόματί	ὀνόματί	ὀνόματί
μου,	μου,	μου	μου	μου
		λέγοντες·	λέγοντες	λέγοντες·
		ἐγώ	ὅτι ἐγώ	ἐγώ
		εἰμι	εἰμι,	εἰμι,
		ὁ χριστός,		καὶ· ὁ καιρὸς
		καὶ πολλοὺς	καὶ πολλοὺς	ἤγγικεν· μὴ
		πλανή-	πλανή-	πορευθῆτε
		σουσιν.	σουσιν.	ὀπίσω αὐτῶν.
		7:15		
		Προσέχετε		
		ἀπὸ τῶν		
		ψευδο-		
		προφητῶν,		
		οἵτινες		
		ἔρχονται		
ἔξωθεν μὲν	ἔξωθεν	πρὸς ὑμᾶς		
ἐνδεδυμένοι	ἐνδεδυμένοι	ἐν ἐνδύμασιν		
δέρματα	δέρματα			
προβάτων,	προβάτων,	προβάτων,		
ἔσωθεν δὲ	ἔσωθεν δέ	ἔσωθεν δέ		
ὄντες λύκοι	εἰσι λύκοι	εἰσιν λύκοι		
ἅρπαγες·	ἅρπαγες.	ἅρπαγες.		
ἐκ τῶν		7:16 ἀπὸ τῶν		
ἔργων		καρπῶν		
αὐτῶν		αὐτῶν		
ἐπιγνώσεσθε		ἐπιγνώσεσθε		
αὐτούς.		αὐτούς.	Mt. 3:10	Lk. 3:9
πᾶν δὲ		7:19 πᾶν	πᾶν οὖν	πᾶν οὖν

δένδρον,	δένδρον	δένδρον	δένδρον
μὴ ποιοῦν	μὴ ποιοῦν	μὴ ποιοῦν	μὴ ποιοῦν
καρπὸν	καρπὸν	καρπὸν	καρπὸν
καλόν,	καλὸν	καλὸν	καλὸν
ἐκκόπτεται	ἐκκόπτεται	ἐκκόπτεται	ἐκκόπτεται
καὶ	καὶ	καὶ	καὶ
εἰς πῦρ	εἰς πῦρ	εἰς πῦρ	εἰς πῦρ
βάλλεται.	βάλλεται.	βάλλεται.	βάλλεται.

The opening words of *Apol.* 16:13 (πολλοὶ γὰρ ἥξουσιν ἐπὶ τῷ ὀνόματί μου) and *Dial.* 35:3a (πολλοὶ ἐλεύσονται ἐπὶ τῷ ὀνόματί μου) have their gospel parallels in Mt. 24:5, Mk. 13:6, and Lk. 21:8 with only two minor differences. (1) *Dial.* 35:3a follows exactly the text of Mk. 13:6 omitting γὰρ after πολλοί; however, this omission does not indicate that Justin here used Mark as his source, because such an omission could easily be attributed to stylistic alteration.[1] (2) *Apol.* 16:13, on the other hand, has ἥξουσιν where *Dial.* 35:3a and the gospel parallels all have ἐλεύσονται; but inasmuch as the two passages in Justin agree basically except for this single difference, it is safe to conclude that Justin probably used for both passages a single source that read ἐλεύσονται in agreement with the synoptics and that he retained this reading in *Dial.* 35:3a but altered it in *Apol.* 16:13 to ἥξουσιν.

In the material that follows Justin departs radically from the order of the synoptic gospels. Instead of continuing the saying with the text of Mt. 24:5b and its parallels, Justin's text now parallels the material of Mt. 7:15.[2] Since both passages of Justin agree almost exactly in this combination of material from Mt. 24:5a and Mt. 7:15, we may safely assume that this feature of combining the two texts was an element of Justin's source. The words πολλοὶ γὰρ ἐλεύσονται of Mt. 24:5 apparently suggested the similar phrase οἵτινες ἔρχονται in Mt. 7:15, and we may safely assume that because of their similarity of context the two verses were combined in Justin's source. The ἔξωθεν in *Apol.* 16:13 and *Dial.* 35:3a is apparently an element of Justin's source, in this case a literary improvement to balance the ἔσωθεν that appears later in *Apol.* 16:13

---

[1] The γὰρ in Mt. 24:5 and Lk. 21:8 connects these clauses with the material that immediately precedes them in their respective gospels; in *Dial.* 35:3a there is no reason to connect this material so closely with the preceding section.

[2] Baldus argues (pp. 38 f.) that this material in Justin is not based on Mt. 7:15 but that it should rather be attributed to a memory failure. He believes that the saying πολλοί . . . ἅρπαγες is an unknown and separate saying of Jesus and that it stood in Justin's edition of Matthew between 7:15 and 7:16.

and *Dial.* 35:3a, and that is derived from Mt. 7:15. This attempt at literary balance is pursued even further in *Apol.* 16:13, probably by Justin himself,[1] in emphasizing the balance by using ἔξωθεν μὲν with ἔσωθεν δὲ. Such a minor difference indicates that Justin probably edited the material from his source in incorporating it into the context of his own writings.

Justin twice has ἐνδεδυμένοι δέρματα προβάτων, which we can, therefore, assume was probably an element of his source, because this reading differs from Matthew's ἐν ἐνδύμασιν προβάτων; and Justin's use of the participle ὄντες in *Apol.* 16:13 instead of εἰσι(ν) is apparently stylistic.[2]

In *Apol.* 16:13 Justin continues with material parallel to Mt. 7:16, although Justin's text has ἐκ τῶν ἔργων for Matthew's ἀπὸ τῶν καρπῶν αὐτῶν.[3] The last section of *Apol.* 16:13 is apparently based on Mt. 7:19[4] with the small change of the appearance of δὲ in Justin's text, a particle used here to connect the sentences with the preceding material.

An examination of some of the witnesses of the early fathers indicates that the source that was used by Justin and that combines Mt. 24:5 with Mt. 7:15, 16, (19) was apparently a written document known to other fathers in the early church: [5]

Apostolic Constitutions VI, 13 (Migne, *PG*, I, 944, 945)

"'Ελεύσονται," λέγων, "πρὸς ὑμᾶς ἄνθρωποι ἐν ἐνδύμασι προβάτων· ἔσωθεν δέ εἰσι λύκοι ἅρπαγες· ἀπὸ τῶν καρπῶν αὐτῶν ἐπιγνώσεσθε αὐτούς.

Pseudoclementine *Homilies* XI, 35 (Rehm, p. 172)

Πολλοὶ ἐλεύσονται πρός με ἐν ἐνδύματι προβάτων, ἔσωθεν δέ εἰσι λύκοι ἅρπαγες· ἀπὸ τῶν καρπῶν αὐτῶν ἐπιγνώσεσθε αὐτούς.

Although neither of these passages agrees exactly with the text of

---

[1] The reason this is to be attributed to Justin himself and not to his source is that *Dial.* 35:3a does not contain this extended balance, and it appears that the more elaborate and more stylistic form would naturally be the later version.

[2] So too Massaux, "Le Texte du Sermon," p. 427.

[3] Massaux ("Le Texte du Sermon," p. 428) believes that this change arose because the word καρπός is improper to apply to men, whereas ἐκ τῶν ἔργων αὐτῶν would be a sounder test of a man's morality.

[4] This passage is also paralleled in Mt. 3:10 and Lk. 3:9 (see chart above); however, inasmuch as Justin's source has already followed the text of Mt. 7:15, 16, it is more likely that Mt. 7:19 is the source of this section of the quotation rather than the similar material in either Mt. 3:10 or Lk. 3:9.

[5] The material parallel to Mt. 24:5 is indicated by a single underlining, and the material parallel to Mt. 7:15, 16 by a double underlining.

Justin, they both point to the existence of texts that combined Mt. 24:5 with Mt. 7:15, 16.

We can, therefore, safely conclude that Justin had before him a written source that combined Mt. 24:5 with Mt. 7:15, 16, 19. In *Apol.* 16:13 he apparently quoted this source in full, whereas in *Dial.* 35:3a he quoted only the section containing the material of Mt. 24:5 and Mt. 7:15.[1]

Conclusion

From the above analysis of the *logia* that occur more than once in the writings of Justin Martyr, it is possible to draw certain tentative conclusions about the source or sources from which Justin derived these sayings.

(1) It is certain from the above discussion that Justin did not quote from memory, as Semisch and others have maintained, but that he quoted from one or more written sources.

(2) Although most of the sayings discussed in this chapter could have come from a single source, there are two sayings that indicate that Justin at least occasionally quoted a single saying of Jesus from two different sources (*Apol.* 16:7 and *Dial.* 101:2; *Apol.* 16:6 and *Dial.* 93:2).[2]

(3) There is definite evidence that Justin's sources were written documents known, at least in part, to other fathers in the church (*Apol.* 15:13 and *Dial.* 96:3a; *Dial.* 101:2; *Apol.* 16:10 and *Apol.* 63:5; *Apol.* 16:11 and *Dial.* 76:5; *Apol.* 63:3, *Apol.* 63:13, and *Dial.* 100:1; *Apol.* 16:13 and *Dial.* 35:3a), and the parallel in 2 *Clement* (*Apol.* 16:11 and *Dial.* 76:5) probably indicates that at least some peculiarities of Justin's sources existed prior to the composition of the *Dialogue* and the *Apology*.

(4) Certain passages show elements of careful harmonization of parallel texts of Matthew and Luke (*Apol.* 15:13 and *Dial.* 96:3a; *Apol.* 15:14; *Apol.* 16:11 and *Dial.* 76:5; *Dial.* 76:4, *Dial.* 120:6, and *Dial.* 140:4; *Dial.* 17:4 and *Dial.* 112:4).

(5) That elements from Mark were also harmonized into Justin's sources is also certain (*Apol.* 99:2; *Dial.* 93:2 and *Apol.* 16:6 and perhaps also *Apol.* 16:7 and *Dial.* 101:2).

(6) There is evidence that Justin's source or sources combined similar

---

[1] This result will be reexamined below in the section that discusses the four sayings of *Dial.* 35:3 (pp. 100-106).

[2] The fact that the entire section *Apol.* 15-17 might have been based on a special catechetical source will be discussed in the following chapter. With this in mind it is perhaps not surprising that the only two sayings that indicate that Justin used more than a single source are sayings that have one of their versions in *Apol.* 15-17.

sayings from different parts of the same gospel (*Dial.* 76:7, *Dial.* 100:3, and *Dial.* 51:2; *Dial.* 125:4 and *Dial.* 103:6; *Apol.* 16:13 and *Dial.* 35:3a; and perhaps *Apol.* 16:10 and *Apol.* 63:5).

(7) There are sayings in which Justin quotes from a single gospel (*Apol.* 15:15 and *Apol.* 63:3, *Apol.* 63:13, and *Dial.* 100:1); however, there is no reason to believe that a source that harmonized the synoptic gospels and combined material from different places in the same gospel could not on occasion quote a saying from a single gospel.

(8) Several manuscripts of the gospels reproduce peculiar readings of Justin. Most of these variants are from late manuscripts; therefore, not all of the variants have been listed above; but in most cases the variants in question show features of harmonization of several gospels or combinations of texts from two parts of the same gospel similar to what we find in Justin's text of the same saying. Very possibly these manuscript witnesses have been influenced by texts similar to Justin's sources.

It is apparent from the foregoing conclusions that even before Justin there is at least some evidence for the use of gospel harmonies in the church of the second century.[1] However, an examination of the text of Justin's sayings of Jesus indicates that Justin had before him written sources that harmonized texts from Matthew, Mark, and Luke and that combined material of similar context from different places in the same gospel. It is not possible to decide here whether Justin himself composed his own harmony on models that existed prior to his time or whether he used a written harmony that had been composed before him and that he merely adapted to his own context; but it is certain that either Justin's harmony or a harmony very similar to it was known to several other fathers. Clement of Alexandria and the Pseudoclementine *Homilies* have the closest parallels to Justin's peculiar readings, and Justin most often shows peculiar readings in common with Irenaeus and Origen as well as Clement of Alexandria and the Pseudoclementine *Homilies*. The above conclusions are only tentative and must now be reexamined in light of the collections or groups of sayings found in Justin's writings.

---

[1] So too Köster, *Synoptische Überlieferung*, pp. 264 f.

CHAPTER THREE

COLLECTIONS OR GROUPS OF SAYINGS

(*Apology* 15-17 and *Dialogue* 35:3)

There are in the writings of Justin two sections that contain collections
or groups of sayings, *Apol.* 15-17 and *Dial.* 35:3. Here separate sayings
are presented in such a way that it is necessary not only to study the
separate sayings but also to consider the possibility that the grouping
of these sayings may be significant to help reconstruct the history of the
transmission of this material.

A. APOLOGY 15-17

In *Apol.* 14:4, 5 Justin prefaces the material of *Apol.* 15-17 with these
words:

ἵνα δὲ μὴ σοφίζεσθαι ὑμᾶς δόξωμεν, ὀλίγων τινῶν τῶν παρ' αὐτοῦ τοῦ
Χριστοῦ διδαγμάτων ἐπιμνησθῆναι καλῶς ἔχειν πρὸ τῆς ἀποδείξεως
ἡγησάμεθα, καὶ ὑμέτερον ἔστω ὡς δυνατῶν βασιλέων ἐξετάσαι εἰ ἀληθῶς
ταῦτα δεδιδάγμεθα καὶ διδάσκομεν. βραχεῖς δὲ καὶ σύντομοι παρ' αὐτοῦ
λόγοι γεγόνασιν· οὐ γὰρ σοφιστὴς ὑπῆρχεν, ἀλλὰ δύναμις θεοῦ ὁ λόγος
αὐτοῦ ἦν.

Immediately following this introductory material we find sayings of
Jesus in the greatest concentration that appears in either the *Apology* or
the *Dialogue*: we find the text of *Apol.* 15-17.

Apology 15 [1]

1 Περὶ μὲν οὖν σωφροσύνης τοσοῦτον εἶπεν· Ὃς ἂν ἐμβλέψῃ γυναικὶ
πρὸς τὸ ἐπιθυμῆσαι αὐτῆς ἤδη ἐμοίχευσε τῇ καρδίᾳ παρὰ τῷ θεῷ. 2 καί·
Εἰ ὁ ὀφθαλμός σου ὁ δεξιὸς σκανδαλίζει σε, ἔκκοψον αὐτόν· συμφέρει γάρ
σοι μονόφθαλμον εἰσελθεῖν εἰς τὴν βασιλείαν τῶν οὐρανῶν, ἢ μετὰ τῶν δύο
πεμφθῆναι εἰς τὸ αἰώνιον πῦρ. 3 καί· Ὃς γαμεῖ ἀπολελυμένην ἀφ' ἑτέρου
ἀνδρὸς μοιχᾶται. 4 καί· Εἰσί τινες οἵτινες εὐνουχίσθησαν ὑπὸ τῶν ἀνθρώπων, εἰσὶ δὲ οἳ ἐγεννήθησαν εὐνοῦχοι, εἰσὶ δὲ οἳ εὐνούχισαν ἑαυτοὺς διὰ
τὴν βασιλείαν τῶν οὐρανῶν· πλὴν οὐ πάντες τοῦτο χωροῦσιν. 5 ὥσπερ

---

[1] The text quoted here is from the edition of Goodspeed corrected by comparison
with Otto's text.

καὶ οἱ νόμῳ ἀνθρωπίνῳ διγαμίας ποιούμενοι ἁμαρτωλοὶ παρὰ τῷ ἡμετέρῳ
διδασκάλῳ εἰσί, καὶ οἱ προσβλέποντες γυναικὶ πρὸς τὸ ἐπιθυμῆσαι αὐτῆς·
οὐ γὰρ μόνον ὁ μοιχεύων ἔργῳ ἐκβέβληται παρ' αὐτῷ, ἀλλὰ καὶ ὁ μοιχεῦσαι
βουλόμενος, ὡς οὐ τῶν ἔργων φανερῶν μόνον τῷ θεῷ ἀλλὰ καὶ τῶν
ἐνθυμημάτων. 6 καὶ πολλοί τινες καὶ πολλαὶ ἑξηκοντοῦται καὶ ἑβδομη-
κοντοῦται, οἳ ἐκ παίδων ἐμαθητεύθησαν τῷ Χριστῷ, ἄφθοροι διαμένουσι·
καὶ εὔχομαι κατὰ πᾶν γένος ἀνθρώπων τοιούτους δεῖξαι. 2 τί γὰρ καὶ λέγομεν
τὸ ἀναρίθμητον πλῆθος τῶν ἐξ ἀκολασίας μεταβαλόντων καὶ ταῦτα
μαθόντων; οὐ γὰρ τοὺς δικαίους οὐδὲ τοὺς σώφρονας εἰς μετάνοιαν
ἐκάλεσεν ὁ Χριστός, ἀλλὰ τοὺς ἀσεβεῖς καὶ ἀκολάστους καὶ ἀδίκους.
8 εἶπε δὲ οὕτως· οὐκ ἦλθον καλέσαι δικαίους, ἀλλὰ ἁμαρτωλοὺς εἰς
μετάνοιαν. θέλει γὰρ ὁ πατὴρ ὁ οὐράνιος τὴν μετάνοιαν τοῦ ἁμαρτωλοῦ ἢ
τὴν κόλασιν αὐτοῦ. 9 περὶ δὲ τοῦ στέργειν ἅπαντας ταῦτα ἐδίδαξεν· Εἰ
ἀγαπᾶτε τοὺς ἀγαπῶντας ὑμᾶς, τί καινὸν ποιεῖτε; καὶ γὰρ οἱ πόρνοι
τοῦτο ποιοῦσιν. Ἐγὼ δὲ ὑμῖν λέγω· Εὔχεσθε ὑπὲρ τῶν ἐχθρῶν ὑμῶν καὶ
ἀγαπᾶτε τοὺς μισοῦντας ὑμᾶς καὶ εὐλογεῖτε τοὺς καταρωμένους ὑμῖν καὶ
εὔχεσθε ὑπὲρ τῶν ἐπηρεαζόντων ὑμᾶς. 10 εἰς δὲ τὸ κοινωνεῖν τοῖς
δεομένοις καὶ μηδὲν πρὸς δόξαν ποιεῖν ταῦτα ἔφη· Παντὶ τῷ αἰτοῦντι
δίδοτε καὶ τὸν βουλόμενον δανείσασθαι μὴ ἀποστραφῆτε. εἰ γὰρ δανείζετε
παρ' ὧν ἐλπίζετε λαβεῖν, τί καινὸν ποιεῖτε; τοῦτο καὶ οἱ τελῶναι ποιοῦσιν.
11 ὑμεῖς δὲ μὴ θησαυρίζητε ἑαυτοῖς ἐπὶ τῆς γῆς, ὅπου σὴς καὶ βρῶσις
ἀφανίζει καὶ λῃσταὶ διορύσσουσι· Θησαυρίζετε δὲ ἑαυτοῖς ἐν τοῖς οὐρανοῖς,
ὅπου οὔτε σὴς οὔτε βρῶσις ἀφανίζει. 12 τί γὰρ ὠφελεῖται ἄνθρωπος, ἂν
τὸν κόσμον ὅλον κερδήσῃ, τὴν δὲ ψυχὴν αὐτοῦ ἀπολέσῃ; ἢ τί δώσει αὐτῆς
ἀντάλλαγμα; θησαυρίζετε οὖν ἐν τοῖς οὐρανοῖς, ὅπου οὔτε σὴς οὔτε βρῶσις
ἀφανίζει. 13 καί· Γίνεσθε δὲ χρηστοὶ καὶ οἰκτίρμονες, ὡς καὶ ὁ πατὴρ
ὑμῶν χρηστός ἐστι καὶ οἰκτίρμων, καὶ τὸν ἥλιον αὐτοῦ ἀνατέλλει ἐπὶ
ἁμαρτωλοὺς καὶ δικαίους καὶ πονηρούς. 14 μὴ μεριμνᾶτε δὲ τί φάγητε
ἢ τί ἐνδύσησθε. οὐχ ὑμεῖς τῶν πετεινῶν καὶ τῶν θηρίων διαφέρετε; καὶ ὁ
θεὸς τρέφει αὐτά. 15 μὴ οὖν μεριμνήσητε τί φάγητε ἢ τί ἐνδύσησθε·
οἶδε γὰρ ὁ πατὴρ ὑμῶν ὁ οὐράνιος ὅτι τούτων χρείαν ἔχετε. 16 ζητεῖτε
δὲ τὴν βασιλείαν τῶν οὐρανῶν, καὶ ταῦτα πάντα προστεθήσεται ὑμῖν.
ὅπου γὰρ ὁ θησαυρός ἐστιν, ἐκεῖ καὶ ὁ νοῦς τοῦ ἀνθρώπου. 17 καί·
Μὴ ποιῆτε ταῦτα πρὸς τὸ θεαθῆναι ὑπὸ τῶν ἀνθρώπων· εἰ δὲ μή γε,
μισθὸν οὐκ ἔχετε παρὰ τοῦ πατρὸς ὑμῶν τοῦ ἐν τοῖς οὐρανοῖς.

Apology 16

1 Περὶ δὲ τοῦ ἀνεξικάκους εἶναι καὶ ὑπηρετικοὺς πᾶσι καὶ ἀοργήτους ἃ ἔφη ταῦτά ἐστί· Τῷ τύπτοντί σου τὴν σιαγόνα πάρεχε καὶ τὴν ἄλλην, καὶ τὸν αἴροντά σου τὸν χιτῶνα ἢ τὸ ἱμάτιον μὴ κωλύσῃς. 2 ὃς δ᾽ ἂν ὀργισθῇ, ἔνοχός ἐστιν εἰς τὸ πῦρ. παντὶ δὲ ἀγγαρεύοντί σε μίλιον ἀκολούθησον δύο. λαμψάτω δὲ ὑμῶν τὰ καλὰ ἔργα ἔμπροσθεν τῶν ἀνθρώπων, ἵνα βλέποντες θαυμάζωσι τὸν πατέρα ὑμῶν τὸν ἐν τοῖς οὐρανοῖς. 3 οὐ γὰρ ἀνταίρειν δεῖ· οὐδὲ μιμητὰς εἶναι τῶν φαύλων βεβούληται ἡμᾶς, ἀλλὰ διὰ τῆς ὑπομονῆς καὶ πραότητος ἐξ αἰσχύνης καὶ ἐπιθυμίας τῶν κακῶν ἄγειν πάντας προετρέψατο. 4 ὃ γὰρ καὶ ἐπὶ πολλῶν τῶν παρ᾽ ὑμῖν γεγενημένων ἀποδεῖ-ξαι ἔχομεν· ἐκ βιαίων καὶ τυράννων μετέβαλον, ἡττηθέντες ἢ γειτόνων καρτερίαν βίου παρακολουθήσαντες ἢ συνοδοιπόρων πλεονεκτουμένων ὑπομονὴν ξένην κατανοήσαντες ἢ συμπραγματευομένων πειραθέντες. 5 περὶ δὲ τοῦ μὴ ὀμνύναι ὅλως, τἀληθῆ δὲ λέγειν ἀεί, οὕτως παρεκελεύσατο· Μὴ ὀμόσητε ὅλως· ἔστω δὲ ὑμῶν τὸ ναὶ ναί, καὶ τὸ οὒ οὔ· τὸ δὲ περισσὸν τούτων ἐκ τοῦ πονηροῦ. 6 ὡς δὲ καὶ τὸν θεὸν μόνον δεῖ προσκυνεῖν, οὕτως ἔπεισεν εἰπών· Μεγίστη ἐντολή ἐστι· Κύριον τὸν θεόν σου προσκυνήσεις καὶ αὐτῷ μόνῳ λατρεύσεις ἐξ ὅλης τῆς καρδίας σου καὶ ἐξ ὅλης τῆς ἰσχύος σου, κύριον τὸν θεὸν τὸν ποιήσαντά σε. 7 καὶ προσελθόντος αὐτῷ τινος καὶ εἰπόντος· Διδάσκαλε ἀγαθέ, ἀπεκρίνατο λέγων· Οὐδεὶς ἀγαθὸς εἰ μὴ μόνος ὁ θεός, ὁ ποιήσας τὰ πάντα. 8 οἳ δ᾽ ἂν μὴ εὑρίσκωνται βιοῦντες, ὡς ἐδίδαξε, γνωριζέσθωσαν μὴ ὄντες Χριστιανοί, κἂν λέγωσιν διὰ γλώττης τὰ τοῦ Χριστοῦ διδάγματα· οὐ γὰρ τοὺς μόνον λέγοντας, ἀλλὰ τοὺς καὶ τὰ ἔργα πράττοντας σωθήσεσθαι ἔφη. 9 εἶπε γὰρ οὕτως· Οὐχὶ πᾶς ὁ λέγων μοι Κύριε κύριε εἰσελεύσεται εἰς τὴν βασιλείαν τῶν οὐρανῶν, ἀλλ᾽ ὁ ποιῶν τὸ θέλημα τοῦ πατρός μου τοῦ ἐν τοῖς οὐρανοῖς. 10 ὃς γὰρ ἀκούει μου καὶ ποιεῖ ἃ λέγω ἀκούει τοῦ ἀποστείλαντός με. 11 πολλοὶ δὲ ἐροῦσί μοι· Κύριε κύριε, οὐ τῷ σῷ ὀνόματι ἐφάγομεν καὶ ἐπίομεν καὶ δυνάμεις ἐποιήσαμεν; καὶ τότε ἐρῶ αὐτοῖς· Ἀποχωρεῖτε ἀπ᾽ ἐμοῦ, ἐργάται τῆς ἀνομίας. 12 τότε κλαυθμὸς ἔσται καὶ βρυγμὸς τῶν ὀδόντων, ὅταν οἱ μὲν δίκαιοι λάμψωσιν ὡς ὁ ἥλιος, οἱ δὲ ἄδικοι πέμπωνται εἰς τὸ αἰώνιον πῦρ. 13 πολλοὶ γὰρ ἥξουσιν ἐπὶ τῷ ὀνόματί μου, ἔξωθεν μὲν ἐνδεδυμένοι δέρματα προβάτων, ἔσωθεν δὲ ὄντες λύκοι ἅρπαγες· ἐκ τῶν ἔργων αὐτῶν ἐπιγνώσεσθε αὐτούς. πᾶν δὲ δένδρον, μὴ ποιοῦν καρπὸν καλόν, ἐκκόπτεται

καὶ εἰς πῦρ βάλλεται. 14 κολάζεσθαι δὲ τοὺς οὐκ ἀκολούθως τοῖς διδάγ-
μασιν αὐτοῦ βιοῦντας, λεγομένους δὲ μόνον Χριστιανούς, καὶ ὑφ' ὑμῶν
ἀξιοῦμεν.

Apology 17

1 Φόρους δὲ καὶ εἰσφορὰς τοῖς ὑφ' ὑμῶν τεταγμένοις πανταχοῦ πρὸ πάντων
πειρώμεθα φέρειν, ὡς ἐδιδάχθημεν παρ' αὐτοῦ. 2 κατ' ἐκεῖνο γὰρ τοῦ
καιροῦ προσελθόντες τινὲς ἠρώτων αὐτόν, εἰ δεῖ Καίσαρι φόρους τελεῖν.
καὶ ἀπεκρίνατο· Εἴπατέ μοι, τίνος εἰκόνα τὸ νόμισμα ἔχει; οἱ δὲ ἔφασαν·
Καίσαρος. καὶ πάλιν ἀνταπεκρίνατο αὐτοῖς· Ἀπόδοτε οὖν τὰ Καίσαρος
τῷ Καίσαρι καὶ τὰ τοῦ θεοῦ τῷ θεῷ. 3 ὅθεν θεὸν μὲν μόνον προσκυνοῦμεν,
ὑμῖν δὲ πρὸς τὰ ἄλλα χαίροντες ὑπηρετοῦμεν, βασιλεῖς καὶ ἄρχοντας
ἀνθρώπων ὁμολογοῦντες καὶ εὐχόμενοι μετὰ τῆς βασιλικῆς δυνάμεως
καὶ σώφρονα τὸν λογισμὸν ἔχοντας ὑμᾶς εὑρεθῆναι. 4 εἰ δὲ καὶ ἡμῶν
εὐχομένων καὶ πάντα εἰς φανερὸν τιθέντων ἀφροντιστήσετε, οὐδὲν ἡμεῖς
βλαβησόμεθα, πιστεύοντες, μᾶλλον δὲ καὶ πεπεισμένοι, κατ' ἀξίαν τῶν
πράξεων ἕκαστον τίσειν διὰ πυρὸς αἰωνίου δίκας, καὶ πρὸς ἀναλογίαν ὧν
ἔλαβε δυνάμεων παρὰ θεοῦ τὸν λόγον ἀπαιτηθήσεσθαι, ὡς ὁ Χριστὸς
ἐμήνυσεν εἰπών. Ὧι πλέον ἔδωκεν ὁ θεός, πλέον καὶ ἀπαιτηθήσεται παρ'
αὐτοῦ.

The sayings in *Apol.* 15-17 are introduced by ten citation formulas,
most of which conform to a fixed pattern of (1) describing the subject
matter of the saying or sayings that follow and (2) introducing the sayings
material itself with an aorist form of εἶπον, διδάσκω, φημί, or παρακελεύω: [1]

Apol. 15:1 περὶ μὲν οὖν σωφροσύνης τοσοῦτον εἶπεν (this is followed by
four sayings, *Apol.* 15:1-4).

---

[1] According to Blass-Debrunner-Funk (p. 329), "the aorist serves for a simple
reference to an utterance previously made (especially for a specific pronouncement
of an individual)," but regarding the early Christian fathers this remark is not
sufficient. It must be pointed out that the present and perfect tenses so typical
for the quotation of "scripture" (λέγει, γέγραπται, etc.) are totally lacking in this
section, although they do occur elsewhere in Justin when he is quoting the Old
Testament (see e.g. *Apol.* 38:1, 4, 6; 39:1; *Dial.* 22:1; 26:2; 34:6; 13:1; etc.).
See also Köster (*Synoptische Überlieferung*, pp. 4-6, 25, 63-66, 112-113), who
argues correctly that when the Apostolic Fathers introduce sayings of Jesus with
εἶπεν one can safely conclude that these sayings are not being quoted as γραφή.
The same position can certainly be maintained with regard to Justin, who in using
the aorist apparently does not quote the sayings of Jesus as γραφή.

Apol. 15:7, 8 οὐ γὰρ τοὺς δικαίους οὐδὲ τοὺς σώφρονας εἰς μετάνοιαν ἐκάλεσεν ὁ Χριστός, ἀλλὰ τοὺς ἀσεβεῖς καὶ ἀκολάστους καὶ ἀδίκους. εἶπε δὲ οὕτως (then follows a single saying, *Apol.* 15:8).

Apol. 15:9 περὶ δὲ τοῦ στέργειν ἅπαντας ταῦτα ἐδίδαξεν (here follows a single saying, *Apol.* 15:9).

Apol. 15:10 εἰς δὲ τὸ κοινωνεῖν τοῖς δεομένοις καὶ μηδὲν πρὸς δόξαν ποιεῖν ταῦτα ἔφη (this is followed by eight sayings, *Apol.* 15:10-17).

Apol. 16:1 περὶ δὲ τοῦ ἀνεξικάκους εἶναι καὶ ὑπηρετικοὺς πᾶσι καὶ ἀοργήτους ἃ ἔφη ταῦτά ἐστι (then follow two sayings, *Apol.* 16:1, 2).

Apol. 16:5 περὶ δὲ τοῦ μὴ ὀμνύναι ὅλως, τἀληθῆ δὲ λέγειν ἀεί, οὕτως παρεκελεύσατο (here follows a single saying, *Apol.* 16:5).

Apol. 16:6 ὡς δὲ καὶ τὸν θεὸν μόνον δεῖ προσκυνεῖν, οὕτως ἔπεισεν εἰπών (here follow two sayings, *Apol.* 16:6, 7).

Apol. 16:8, 9 οὐ γὰρ τοὺς μόνον λέγοντας, ἀλλὰ τοὺς καὶ τὰ ἔργα πράττοντας σωθήσεσθαι ἔφη. εἶπε γὰρ οὕτως (here follow five sayings, *Apol.* 16:9-13).

Apol. 17:1 φόρους δὲ καὶ εἰσφορὰς τοῖς ὑφ' ὑμῶν τεταγμένοις πανταχοῦ πρὸ πάντων πειρώμεθα φέρειν, ὡς ἐδιδάχθημεν παρ' αὐτοῦ (here follows a pronouncement story culminating in a saying of Jesus, *Apol.* 17:2).

Apol. 17:4 εἰ δὲ καὶ ἡμῶν εὐχομένων καὶ πάντα εἰς φανερὸν τιθέντων ἀφροντιστήσετε, οὐδὲν ἡμεῖς βλαβησόμεθα, πιστεύοντες, μᾶλλον δὲ καὶ πεπεισμένοι, κατ' ἀξίαν τῶν πράξεων ἕκαστον τίσειν διὰ πυρὸς αἰωνίου δίκας, καὶ πρὸς ἀναλογίαν ὧν ἔλαβε δυνάμεων παρὰ θεοῦ τὸν λόγον ἀπαιτηθήσεσθαι, ὡς ὁ Χριστὸς ἐμήνυσεν εἰπών (here follows a single saying, *Apol.* 17:4).

Verse	Subject Matter	Aorist Verb
15:1	σωφροσύνη	εἶπεν
15:7, 8	καλεῖν εἰς μετάνοιαν	εἶπε
15:9	στέργειν	ἐδίδαξεν
15:10	κοινωνεῖν and ποιεῖν	ἔφη
16:1	ἀνεξικάκους εἶναι	(ἃ) ἔφη (ταῦτά ἐστι)
16:5	ὀμνύναι	παρεκελεύσατο
16:6	προσκυνεῖν	εἰπών
16:8, 9	οὐ λέγοντας ἀλλὰ πράττοντας σωθήσεσθαι	εἶπε
17:1	φόρους φέρειν	(ὡς) ἐδιδάχθημεν (παρ' αὐτοῦ)
17:4	δίκας τίνειν (κατ' ἀξίαν τῶν πράξεων)	εἰπών

Among these introductory formulas four of them (*Apol.* 15:7, 8; *Apol.* 16:8, 9; *Apol.* 17:1; and *Apol.* 17:4) do not conform strictly to the fixed pattern of introducing the subject matter that is commented upon in the sayings as described above; however, each of these sections is concerned with a single subject, and the method of introduction is only slightly different from the normal pattern; the introduction comments on a state of affairs and then introduces one or more *logia* that reflect Jesus' teaching on the subject in question.

The sayings in *Apol.* 15-17 often find their closest gospel parallels in the Sermon on the Mount; however, this is not surprising for a section that intended to be didactic (*Apol.* 14:4 ὀλίγων τινῶν τῶν παρ' αὐτοῦ τοῦ Χριστοῦ διδαγμάτων ἐπιμνησθῆναι). It is, therefore, valuable at this point to determine whether this section has certain formal similarities to early Christian catechisms.

From an examination of certain New Testament texts (especially in Colossians, Ephesians, 1 Peter, 2 Peter, James, and Hebrews), Selwyn[1] and Carrington [2] have described certain features that were common to primitive Christian catechisms. By comparing certain points of agreement between their descriptions of such catechisms with the material from *Apol.* 15-17, we are able to classify Justin's material under certain topics common to most primitive catechisms: [3]

1. Entry into the new life at baptism
   Apol. 15:4 (?); 15:8 (?)
2. Section dealing with the renunciation of heathen idolatry and vice (deals with catechumen behavior)
   Apol. 15:1; 15:2; 15:3; 16:5
3. Worship of God
   Apol. 16:6; 16:7

---

[1] Edward G. Selwyn, *The First Epistle of Peter* (London, 1946), pp. 386-389.

[2] Philip Carrington, *The Primitive Christian Catechism* (Cambridge, 1940), p. 58.

[3] I am not convinced that each of the sayings is properly classified, because at times the subject matter of one saying overlaps into more than a single category. Nor is there any reason to believe that Justin would have been limited by the form of earlier catechisms in composing one for use in his own community. For this reason I regard my classification of these sayings merely as a guide that indicates the probability that the form of *Apol.* 15-17 is in agreement with the form of primitive Christian catechisms. In this regard W. D. Davies has correctly suggested that Carrington and Selwyn have both "probably too much systematized what was often fluid and amorphous, but their data do at least reveal clearly what the main body of that teaching was which was transmitted through the medium of catechesis" (p. 370).

4. The catechumen is instructed to be submissive to God and to the elders (description of social virtues)

Apol. 15:4 (?); 15:9; 15:10; 15:13; 15:14; 15:15; 15:16; 15:17; 16:1; 16:2; 16:10; 17:2; 17:4

4. Duty of watchfulness and prayer with suggestion of temptation and afflictions to come (eschatological section) [1]

Apol. 15:11 (?); 15:12 (?); 16:11; 16:12; 16:13; 17:4

In the early church, catechisms served as the basis of the instruction given to catechumens before baptism. Such material was probably preserved orally in the primitive church but was eventually preserved in written form by the second or third century. Baptism into the church was generally accompanied by an exhortation to live according to the commands of God and/or Jesus, and in the course of the development of Christian tradition the words of Jesus necessarily became an essential part of such exhortation and, therefore, of the catechisms themselves.

Hippolytus records the following at the close of the baptismal ceremony: "And when these things are completed, let each one hasten to do good works, and to please God and to live aright, devoting himself to the Church, practising the things he has learned, advancing in the services of God" (*Treatise on the Apostolic Tradition*, XXXII, 12). We might, therefore, expect to find a certain emphasis on baptism in *Apol.* 15-17 if, in fact, this section is based on a catechism used in Justin's school in Rome; yet the references to baptism are questionable, if not entirely lacking. It must, however, be recalled that this section in Justin's *Apology* is addressed specifically to the Roman rulers (δυνατῶν βασιλέων *Apol.* 14:4), and Justin's concern is to cite for them a few precepts of Christ (ὀλίγων τινῶν τῶν παρ' αὐτοῦ τοῦ Χριστοῦ διδαγμάτων ἐπιμνησθῆναι *Apol.* 14:4). Although Justin might naturally make use of a Christian catechism as the basis of this section in citing certain precepts of Christ, a discussion of the teaching of Jesus *specifically within the context of the baptism of catechumens* would be unsuitable for Justin's audience; and the absence of such baptismal material is, therefore, not only understandable but desirable.

The material in *Apol.* 15-17 shows certain similarities to 1 *Clement* 13:1, 2, *Didache* 1-6, and *Barnabas* 18-20, all of which were probably used for

---

[1] It is possible that *Dial.* 35:3 is also related to this catechetical material but that it was not included in full in *Apol.* 15-17; however, *Apol.* 16:13 has a parallel in *Dial.* 35:3 a (see above, pp. 44-47), and the presence of this saying in this section of *Apol.* 15-17 may indicate that the four sayings in *Dial.* 35:3 are from the same corpus of sayings included by Justin in *Apol.* 15-17.

catechetical purposes.[1] Both 1 *Clem.* 13:1, 2 and *Did.* 1-6 resemble *Apol.* 15-17 in deriving much of their material from the Sermon on the Mount (or the Sermon on the Plain) or from the pre-synoptic tradition incorporated by Matthew in the Sermon on the Mount (or by Luke in the Sermon on the Plain). In his analysis of 1 *Clement* Köster lists the closest parallels to the seven sayings found in 1 *Clem.* 13:2 as follows:

Saying 1 Mt. 5:7
Saying 2 Mk. 11:25
Saying 3 Mt. 7:12
Saying 4 Lk. 6:38a
Saying 5 Mt. 7:2a (cf. also Lk. 6:37)
Saying 6
Saying 7 Mt. 7:2b (cf. also Lk. 6:38b)

Köster demonstrates convincingly that the sayings are derived not from the synoptic gospels but from the free tradition of the church and suggests that although no definite conclusions can be reached concerning the source of the entire section 1 *Clem.* 13:2, we may perhaps be dealing with a rendering of an oral but firmly fixed catechism.[2]

Did. 1-6 is also largely catechetical, containing directions for imparting instruction to catechumens followed in 7:1-3 by directions for administering baptism. As was the case with 1 *Clem.* 13, so too with *Did.* 1-6 the closest gospel parallels are found principally in Mt. 5-7, Lk. 6, or in material similar in subject matter to sayings found in Mt. 5-7 or Lk. 6. Köster concludes that the source of the sayings in *Did.* 1-6 is to be found in both the written gospels and in the oral tradition of the church.[3]

The sayings material found in *Apol.* 15-17 is very similar to the catechetical material found in 1 *Clem.* 13 and *Did.* 1-6. It will be seen in what follows that there is not so much detailed agreement in words, but the similarity is rather in the character of material used. In all cases the material is based on either Mt. 5-7, Lk. 6, on the free tradition contained in Mt. 5-7 or Lk. 6, or on gospel material similar in nature to the sayings found in Matthew's Sermon on the Mount.

---

[1] Hans Windisch, *Der Barnabasbrief* (Tübingen, 1920), pp. 405 f.; Rudolf Knopf, *Die Lehre der zwölf Apostel* (Tübingen, 1920), p. 2; Martin Dibelius, *Geschichte der urchristlichen Literatur* (Berlin, 1926), pp. 68 ff.; Berthold Altaner, *Patrologie*, 3rd Edition (Frieburg, 1951), p. 38; Johannes Quasten, *Patrology* (Westminster, Maryland, 1950), Vol. I, pp. 30 f.; see also Köster, *Synoptische Überlieferung*, pp. 132, 160 f.

[2] *Synoptische Überlieferung*, pp. 12-16.

[3] *Ibid.*, pp. 167-172, 217-241.

It is significant that the patristic material found in *Did.* 1-6, 1 *Clem.* 13, and *Barn.* 18-20 has often been regarded by scholars as catechetical. The similarity of the material found in *Apol.* 15-17 with regard to both the character of the material used and the structure of the section makes it highly probable that this material is also catechetical in form. It is, however, impossible at this point to determine whether Justin was making use of a traditional catechism or whether we are dealing with a catechetical composition of Justin himself written according to the formal pattern of traditional catechisms but based on written gospel material. This question can be answered only by examining in detail each of the sayings embodied in *Apol.* 15-17, and to this task I shall now turn.

1. *Sayings based on a single gospel*

There are in *Apol.* 15-17 twelve sayings that are apparently based on material from a single synoptic gospel, eight of which are based on Matthew and four of which are based on Luke.

a. *Sayings that reflect dependence on Matthew only*

1) *Apology* 15:1

Apol. 15:1	Mt. 5:28
	ἐγὼ δὲ λέγω ὑμῖν ὅτι
Ὃς ἂν ἐμβλέψῃ γυναικὶ	πᾶς ὁ βλέπων γυναῖκα
πρὸς τὸ ἐπιθυμῆσαι αὐτῆς	πρὸς τὸ ἐπιθυμῆσαι αὐτὴν
ἤδη ἐμοίχευσε	ἤδη ἐμοίχευσεν αὐτὴν
τῇ καρδίᾳ	ἐν τῇ καρδίᾳ αὐτοῦ.
παρὰ τῷ θεῷ.	

That *Apol.* 15:1 is in some way related to Mt. 5:28 is certain, but it is important for our purposes to determine whether Justin actually used the text of Matthew or some other text as his source; and the witness of the early fathers is most helpful in this investigation:

Origen, *De Principiis* III, 1, 6 (Koetschau, V, *GCS*, p. 202)
ὃς ἐὰν ἐμβλέψῃ γυναῖκα πρὸς τὸ ἐπιθυμῆσαι, ἤδη ἐμοίχευσεν ἐν τῇ καρδίᾳ αὐτοῦ.

Origen, *Contra Celsum* III, 44 (Koetschau, I, *GCS*, p. 240)
ὃς ἐὰν ἐμβλέψῃ γυναικὶ πρὸς τὸ ἐπιθυμῆσαι, ἤδη ἐμοίχευσεν αὐτὴν ἐν τῇ καρδίᾳ αὐτοῦ.

Origen, *Commentary on John* XX, 23 (Preuschen, IV, *GCS*, p. 356)
Ὃς ἂν ἐμβλέψῃ γυναῖκα πρὸς τὸ ἐπιθυμῆσαι αὐτὴν, ἤδη ἐμοίχευσεν αὐτὴν ἐν τῇ καρδίᾳ αὐτοῦ.

Origen, *Selecta in Ezechiel* 6 (Lommatzsch, Vol. 14, pp. 195f.)

ὃς ἂν ἐμβλέψῃ γυναῖκα πρὸς τὸ ἐπιθυμῆσαι αὐτῆς, ἤδη ἐμοίχευσεν αὐτὴν ἐν τῇ καρδίᾳ αὐτοῦ.

Cyril of Jerusalem, *Catechesis* XIII, 5 (Migne, *PG*, XXXIII, 777)

ᵒΟς ἐὰν ἐμβλέψῃ γυναικὶ πρὸς τὸ ἐπιθυμῆσαι, ἤδη ἐμοίχευσεν αὐτήν.

Clem. Alex., *Paed.* III, 5, 33 (Stählin, I, *GCS*, p. 255)

"ὁ γὰρ ἐμβλέψας," φησί, "περιεργότερον ἤδη ἥμαρτεν"

Clem. Alex., *Strom.* II, 14, 61 (Stählin, II, *GCS*, p. 146)

καὶ ὁ ἐμβλέψας πρὸς ἐπιθυμίαν κρίνεται;

Clem. Alex., *Strom.* III, 14, 94 (Stählin, II, *GCS*, p. 239)

πᾶς ὁ βλέπων γυναῖκα πρὸς τὸ ἐπιθυμῆσαι ἤδη ἐμοίχευσεν αὐτήν.

Clem. Alex., *Strom.* IV, 18, 114 (Stählin, II, *GCS*, p. 298)

ʽΟ ἐμβλέψας τῇ γυναικὶ πρὸς ἐπιθυμίαν ἤδη μεμοίχευκεν.

Apost. Const. I, 1 (Migne, *PG*, I, 560)

Πᾶς ὅστις ἐμβλέψει εἰς τὴν γυναῖκα τοῦ πλησίου πρὸς τὸ ἐπιθυμῆσαι αὐτήν, ἤδη ἐμοίχευσεν αὐτὴν ἐν τῇ καρδίᾳ αὐτοῦ.

From the above quotations we see that many of the fathers agree with Justin's reading ὃς (ἐ)ὰν ἐμβλέψῃ instead of with Matthew's πᾶς ὁ βλέπων: Origen, *De Principiis* III, 1, 6; *Contra Celsum* III, 44; *Commentary on John* XX, 23; *Selecta in Ezekiel* 6; Cyril of Jerusalem, *Catechesis* XXX, 5. And several other texts at least agree with Justin in using the compound verb ἐμβλέπειν instead of the simple Matthaean verb βλέπειν, although they do not use the same form of the verb as in Justin's text: Clem. Alex., *Paed.* III, 5, 33; *Strom*' II, 14, 61; *Strom.* IV, 18, 114; *Apost. Const.* I, 1.[1]

Justin's use of the dative γυναικὶ for Matthew's accusative γυναῖκα is also known to other fathers;[2] however, this variant is certainly a grammatical change demanded by the use of the dative case with the verb ἐμβλέπειν and may have been made independently by several of the

---

[1] It should be noted that in each of the above quotations, with the exception of *Apost. Const.* I, 1, the Matthaean form πᾶς does not appear in the text. This observation seems to point to the conclusion that among the early fathers this Matthaean saying circulated in written form in texts beginning ὃς (ἐ)ὰν ἐμβλέψῃ and ὁ ἐμβλέψας; the large number of collected variants from different fathers reduces the possibility that this variant can be attributed to memory failure. Rather written texts with these variants must have been known to the fathers.

[2] Origen, *Contra Celsum* III, 44; Cyril of Jerusalem, *Catechesis* XIII, 5; Clem. Alex., *Strom.* IV, 18, 114.

fathers.[1] It appears, however, from the collected evidence that the accusative form γυναῖκα had survived from Mt. 5:28 in the sources used by some of the fathers even though the verb βλέπειν had been altered to ἐμβλέπειν.

In the Matthaean phrase πρὸς τὸ ἐπιθυμῆσαι αὐτὴν ἤδη ἐμοίχευσεν αὐτήν, the early fathers apparently noticed the grammatical error involved in the use of the accusative αὐτὴν with the verb ἐπιθυμεῖν.[2] This error was generally corrected either by omitting αὐτὴν completely [3] or by changing αὐτὴν to the genitive αὐτῆς as in Justin's case.[4] Justin's reading ἐπιθυμῆσαι αὐτῆς ἤδη ἐμοίχευσε is in agreement with those fathers and manuscript witnesses that corrected Matthew's text by using the genitive αὐτῆς, and the omission of the second αὐτὴν in *Apol.* 15:1 is possibly a stylistic change made either by Justin or his source in improving upon the faulty Greek of the text of Mt. 5:28, although Origen, *De Principiis* III, 1, 6 also omits this second αὐτὴν in agreement with *Apol.* 15:1.

Whereas Mt. 5:28 concludes ἐν τῇ καρδίᾳ αὐτοῦ, Justin's text ends with the words τῇ καρδίᾳ παρὰ τῷ θεῷ, a reading found only in Justin and supported by none of the patristic parallels or manuscript witnesses. The reason for this peculiar variant in *Apol.* 15:1 is probably to be sought in the fact that the reading τῇ καρδίᾳ παρὰ τῷ θεῷ would have more meaning to Justin's pagan catechumens than the Matthaean phrase ἐν τῇ καρδίᾳ αὐτοῦ.[5]

---

[1] See Blass-Debrunner-Funk, 202; Walter Bauer, *Griechisch-Deutsches Wörterbuch zu den Schriften des Neuen Testaments und der übrigen urchristlichen Literatur*, 5th edition (Berlin, 1958), p. 504. So too Baldus (p. 82) and Massaux ("Le Texte du Sermon," p. 419). The example of Clement of Alexandria might be cited in support of this view: whereas *Strom.* III, 14, 94 has πᾶς ὁ βλέπων γυναῖκα, *Strom.* IV, 18, 114 has ὁ ἐμβλέψας τῇ γυναικὶ using the dative with the verb ἐμβλέπειν. However, Origen does not seem to follow this example: whereas *De Principiis* III, 1, 6 has ὃς ἐὰν ἐμβλέψῃ γυναῖκα and *Commentary on John* XX, 23 has ὃς ἂν ἐμβλέψῃ γυναῖκα, *Contra Celsum* III, 44 has ὃς ἐὰν ἐμβλέψῃ γυναικί.

[2] Blass-Debrunner-Funk, 171 (1); Bauer, pp. 579 f.; Henry George Liddell and Robert Scott. *A Greek-English Lexicon* (Oxford, 1953), pp. 634 f.

[3] Origen, *De Principiis*, III, 1, 6; *Contra Celsum*, III, 44; Cyril of Jerusalem *Catechesis* XIII, 5; Clem. Alex., *Strom.* III, 14, 94; so too the later manuscripts ΔΠ suppl. mg. Sinaiticus*.

[4] Origen, *Selecta in Ezekiel* 6; so too the manuscripts Sinaiticus[b] ΜΣ 1. 209. 22. 346. 21. 262. 265. 472. 485. 697.

[5] Baldus has argued (p. 82) that this παρὰ τῷ θεῷ is added with reference to the heathen audience, and Wright suggested (p. 37) that "the added παρὰ τῷ θεῷ (with God) leaves no doubt of the difficulty which Justin felt as to the practical value of this verse for ethical purposes. Certainly a pagan audience would have been unconvinced by the teaching as it stood. Hence the necessity of buttressing the already explanatory ἐν τῇ καρδίᾳ (in his heart) with the complementary παρὰ τῷ θεῷ, suggesting a dimension of ethical sanction and judgment beyond challenge."

The cumulative evidence of this analysis leads us to the conclusion that either Justin used the text of Mt. 5:28, improving upon its incorrect Greek and making necessary didactic changes (τῇ καρδίᾳ παρὰ τῷ θεῷ) to suit the context of *Apol.* 15-17; or else he used a written source that had already made these alterations. Only later in the larger context of my discussion of *Apol.* 15:1-4 will it be possible to draw final conclusions about the source for this verse. But it is, nevertheless, certain that the improved text of *Apol.* 15:1 is later than the parallel in Mt. 5:28 and is in some way related to the Matthaean text.

2) *Apology* 15:4

Apol. 15:4	Mt. 19:12, 11
	¹²εἰσὶν γὰρ εὐνοῦχοι
	οἵτινες ἐκ κοιλίας
	μητρὸς ἐγεννήθησαν
Εἰσί	οὕτως, καὶ εἰσὶν
τινες οἵτινες	εὐνοῦχοι οἵτινες
εὐνουχίσθησαν ὑπὸ	εὐνουχίσθησαν ὑπὸ
τῶν ἀνθρώπων,	τῶν ἀνθρώπων,
εἰσὶ δὲ οἳ	
ἐγεννήθησαν εὐνοῦχοι,	
εἰσὶ δὲ	καὶ εἰσὶν εὐνοῦχοι
οἳ εὐνούχισαν	οἵτινες εὐνούχισαν
ἑαυτοὺς διὰ τὴν	ἑαυτοὺς διὰ τὴν
βασιλείαν τῶν οὐρανῶν·	βασιλείαν τῶν οὐρανῶν.
	ὁ δυνάμενος
	χωρεῖν χωρείτω.
	¹¹ὁ δὲ εἶπεν αὐτοῖς·
πλὴν οὐ πάντες	οὐ πάντες
τοῦτο χωροῦσιν.	χωροῦσιν τὸν λόγον τοῦτον,
	ἀλλ' οἷς δέδοται.

The text of *Apol.* 15:4 has parallels to most of the phrases in Mt. 19:12, 11; however, the order of the phrases is quite different in the two passages. A comparison of the two passages does not reveal which of the two versions is the older, but a comparison of the contexts of both *Apol.* 15:4 and Mt. 19:11, 12 reveals that Justin is probably dependent on Matthew's

---

Massaux (p. 419) likewise maintains that "Justin ajoute au texte matthéen παρὰ τῷ θεῷ; cette addition parait intentionelle; Justin écrit pour les païens; il doit dès lors faire comprendre comment on peut commettre l'adultère dans son coeur; c'est devant Dieu, explique Justin."

text rather than on a source older than Matthew. The context of both Mt. 19:11, 12 and *Apol.* 15:4 is concerned with the subject of divorce (Mt. 19:9 and *Apol.* 15:3), but it is probable that Mt. 19:10-12 originally stood in a context that was concerned with self-denial.[1] It is, therefore, the author of the gospel of Matthew who has first placed this saying into the context of divorce; and inasmuch as this context of divorce is preserved in Justin's text, we can be relatively certain that Justin is here dependent either on Mt. 19:12, 11 or on a postsynoptic source that was itself based on this text of Matthew.

3) *Apology* 15:11

Apol. 15:11	Mt. 6:19, 20
ὑμεῖς δὲ μὴ θησαυρίζητε ἑαυτοῖς ἐπὶ τῆς γῆς, ὅπου σὴς καὶ βρῶσις ἀφανίζει καὶ λῃσταὶ διορύσσουσι· Θησαυρίζετε δὲ ἑαυτοῖς ἐν τοῖς οὐρανοῖς, ὅπου οὔτε σὴς οὔτε βρῶσις ἀφανίζει.	[19]Μὴ θησαυρίζετε ὑμῖν θησαυροὺς ἐπὶ τῆς γῆς, ὅπου σὴς καὶ βρῶσις ἀφανίζει, καὶ ὅπου κλέπται διορύσσουσιν καὶ κλέπτουσιν· [20]Θησαυρίζετε δὲ ὑμῖν θησαυροὺς ἐν οὐρανῷ, ὅπου οὔτε σὴς οὔτε βρῶσις ἀφανίζει, καὶ ὅπου κλέπται οὐ διορύσσουσιν οὐδὲ κλέπτουσιν·

The text of *Apol.* 15:11 is very close to the gospel parallel in Mt. 6:19, 20 with the exception of certain minor variants, all of which are apparently stylistic variants that were made either by Justin or by his source to improve upon the Greek of the Matthaean version. The use of the verb θησαυρίζητε in Justin for θησαυρίζετε θησαυροὺς in Matthew is an improvement in the Greek probably for the purpose of suppressing a Semitism.[2] The change from ὑμῖν in Mt. 6:19 and 6:20 to ἑαυτοῖς twice in *Apol.* 15:11 is an improvement in the Greek,[3] especially when the object θησαυροὺς is omitted.

---

[1] Alan Hugh M'Neile argues (*The Gospel According to St. Matthew* [London, 1955], p. 275) that "it is probable that vv. 10-12 originally stood in another context, following some utterance on self-denial for the sake of the Kingdom of Heaven, which might include the renunciation of marriage (cf. Lk. xiv. 26, xviii. 29)."

[2] So too Massaux, "Le Texte du Sermon," p. 422. That the form of Mt. 16:19, 20 is Hebraic is especially evident from the parallelism and tautology of the verse (M'Neile, p. 83).

[3] Blass-Debrunner-Funk, 282 (1).

The difference between ληϲταὶ διορύϲϲουϲι in *Apol.* 15:11 and κλέπται διορύϲϲουϲιν καὶ κλέπτουϲιν in Mt. 6:19 is apparently the result of economy and emphasis. Matthew's phrase κλέπται . . . κλέπτουϲιν is awkward, and further there is a difference in meaning between κλέπτηϲ and ληϲτήϲ, the latter having more of a connotation of violence.[1] Apparently either Justin or his source felt that κλέπται was inadequate for the intended meaning and substituted the stronger word ληϲταί.[2]

The use of ἐν τοῖϲ οὐρανοῖϲ in Justin in place of Matthew's ἐν οὐρανῷ is significant. Although Justin does occasionally have the singular οὐρανῷ (*Dial.* 36:6; 56:23; 78:1; 85:6; 94:1; 106:4; 112:1; 128:3; 132:1), he has the plural ἐν τοῖϲ οὐρανοῖϲ in all sayings of Jesus in which the phrase occurs (*Apol.* 15:11, 12, 17; 16:2, 9); and it will be noticed that all of these sayings are in the section *Apol.* 15-17. On three occasions (*Apol.* 15:17; 16:2; 16:9) the plural form in Justin (ἐν τοῖϲ οὐρανοῖϲ) is in agreement with the gospel parallels (Mt. 6:1; 5:6; 7:21); however, on two occasions (*Apol.* 15:11, 12) either Justin or his source has substituted the plural (ἐν τοῖϲ οὐρανοῖϲ) for the singular (ἐν οὐρανῷ) of their gospel parallels (Mt. 6:20 in both cases). This preference for the plural ἐν τοῖϲ οὐρανοῖϲ is apparently a consistent element of Justin's source, although there is no apparent difference in the meaning of the two phrases. It is, therefore, apparent that *Apol.* 15:11 is later than the text of Mt. 6:19, 20 and that it is based on this Matthaean *logion*, the style of which has been improved either by Justin or by his source.

4) *Apology* 15:15

This passage has already been discussed in the previous chapter (pp. 14-17) where it was concluded that Justin here "used either Mt. 6:31, 32 with modifications and assimilation to *Apol.* 15:14 or a source that contained these same elements" (p. 17).

---

[1] See Bauer, pp. 859, 935. With reference to John 10:1 in which the words κλέπτηϲ and ληϲτήϲ occur together, C. K. Barrett argues (*The Gospel According to St. John* [New York, 1956], p. 305) that "the words are not synonymous (though John may not have intended any clear distinction between them here). Judas, who pilfered money from the money-box, was a κλέπτηϲ (12:6), Barabbas, who was implicated in murder and perhaps armed revolt (Mk. 15:7), was a ληϲτήϲ (18:40)."

[2] Massaux believes (Le Texte du Sermon," p. 422) that Justin substituted ληϲταί for κλέπται because the former is more suitable with the verb διορύϲϲω.

5) *Apology* 15:17

Apol. 15:17	Mt. 6:1
	Προσέχετε δὲ τὴν
	δικαιοσύνην ὑμῶν
Μὴ ποιῆτε ταῦτα πρὸς	μὴ ποιεῖν ἔμπροσθεν
τὸ θεαθῆναι	τῶν ἀνθρώπων πρὸς
ὑπὸ τῶν ἀνθρώπων·	τὸ θεαθῆναι αὐτοῖς·
εἰ δὲ μή γε,	εἰ δὲ μή γε,
μισθὸν οὐκ ἔχετε	μισθὸν οὐκ ἔχετε
παρὰ τοῦ πατρὸς ὑμῶν	παρὰ τῷ πατρὶ ὑμῶν
τοῦ ἐν τοῖς οὐρανοῖς.	τῷ ἐν τοῖς οὐρανοῖς·

The differences between *Apol.* 15:17 and its gospel parallel Mt. 6:1 are minor but sufficient to indicate Justin's relationship to the Matthaean *logion*. Either Justin's text is based on a pre-synoptic source that did not have the reference to δικαιοσύνη found in Mt. 6:1, or else Justin or his source was deliberately avoiding the Matthaean reference to δικαιοσύνη. Although the noun δικαιοσύνη occurs in Justin's writings forty-four times, the term occurs only twice in the *Apology* (2:2; 6:1), perhaps because its Biblical significance would not have been properly understood by the readers of the writing addressed formally to a pagan audience.[1] It is, therefore, possible that Justin or his source altered Mt. 6:1 to avoid the reference to δικαιοσύνη. This omission of προσέχετε δὲ τὴν δικαιοσύνην ὑμῶν by Justin required that the infinitive ποιεῖν be changed to the imperative ποιῆτε to insure parallelism with the other parts of *Apol.* 15:10-16,[2] and this change also demanded the transfer of τῶν ἀνθρώπων with the preposition ὑπὸ instead of Matthew's ἔμπροσθεν to the position of αὐτοῖς in Mt. 6:1.[3]

Although it has not been possible to prove conclusively that *Apol.* 15:17 is actually based on Mt. 6:1 rather than on Matthew's source, the difference between παρὰ with the dative in Mt. 6:1 and παρὰ with the genitive in *Apol.* 15:17 is indicative that Justin's text is later than Matthew's. παρὰ with the genitive means *from*, but with the dative παρά

---

[1] Another instance in which Justin does not have δικαιοσύνη where it occurs in his gospel parallel is in *Apol.* 15:16, which will be discussed below (p. 91).

[2] δίδοτε (15:10), ἀποστραφῆτε (15:10), μὴ θησαυρίζητε (15:11), θησαυρίζετε (15:11), θησαυρίζετε (15:12), γίνεσθε (15:13), μὴ μεριμνᾶτε (15:14), μεριμνήσατε (15:15), ζητεῖτε (15:16).

[3] Massaux ("Le Texte du Sermon," p. 438) argues that this change preserved the essence of the teaching of Jesus but at the same time gives to the phrase an aspect more Greek and less Biblical.

means *at* or *by*, *beside, near, with*.[1] Certainly the use of the genitive is to be preferred in this *logion*, and the difference here apparently indicates that Justin improved upon Matthew's version of the saying.

That *Apol.* 15:17 is based on Mt. 6:1 rather than on Matthew's presynoptic source is probable; however, it is not possible to exclude completely the possibility that Justin's text actually preserved an older reading than that found in Mt. 6:1.

6) *Apology* 16:5

Apol. 16:5	Mt. 5:34, 37
	³⁴ἐγὼ δὲ λέγω ὑμῖν
Μὴ ὀμόσητε ὅλως·	μὴ ὀμόσαι ὅλως·
	μήτε ἐν τῷ οὐρανῷ,
	ὅτι θρόνος ἐστὶν τοῦ θεοῦ·
ἔστω δὲ ὑμῶν	³⁷ἔστω δὲ ὁ λόγος ὑμῶν
τὸ ναὶ ναί, καὶ τὸ οὒ οὔ·	ναὶ ναί, οὒ οὔ·
τὸ δὲ περισσὸν τούτων	τὸ δὲ περισσὸν τούτων
ἐκ τοῦ πονηροῦ.	ἐκ τοῦ πονηροῦ ἐστιν.

It is apparent from the above chart that *Apol.* 16:5 is related in some way to Mt. 5:34, 37; however, there is another important parallel to this verse in James 5:12, and it will be useful for our purpose to compare the entire version of this saying in Matthew with that in the Epistle of James before trying to determine the relationship of either of these passages to *Apol.* 16:5.[2]

Mt. 5:34-37	Jas. 5:12
³⁴ἐγὼ δὲ λέγω ὑμῖν	Πρὸ πάντων δέ, ἀφελφοί
μὴ ὀμόσαι ὅλως·	μου, μὴ ὀμνύετε,
μήτε ἐν τῷ οὐρανῷ	μήτε τὸν οὐρανὸν
ὅτι θρόνος ἐστὶν τοῦ θεοῦ·	
³⁵μήτε ἐν τῇ γῇ,	μήτε τὴν γῆν
ὅτι ὑποπόδιόν ἐστιν τῶν	

---

[1] See Blass-Debrunner-Funk, 237 and 238 (especially 238, where it is stated that παρά is least used with the dative); cf. also Liddell and Scott, p. 1302 and Bauer, pp. 1208 ff.

[2] The text of 2 Cor. 1:19 is hardly significant here, and the manuscript variants are probably the result of later assimilation to Mt. 5:37 or Jas. 5:12. (2 Cor. 1:19 ὁ τοῦ θεοῦ γὰρ υἱὸς Χριστὸς Ἰησοῦς ὁ ἐν ὑμῖν δι' ἡμῶν κηρυχθείς, δι' ἐμοῦ καὶ Σιλουανοῦ καὶ Τιμοθέου, οὐκ ἐγένετο ναὶ καὶ οὔ, ἀλλὰ ναὶ ἐν αὐτῷ γέγονεν [p⁴⁶ 424² vg. read τὸ ναὶ καὶ τὸ οὔ]).

ποδῶν αὐτοῦ· μήτε εἰς
Ἱεροσόλυμα, ὅτι πόλις ἐστὶν
τοῦ μεγάλου βασιλέως·
³⁶μήτε ἐν τῇ κεφαλῇ σου   μήτε ἄλλον τινὰ ὅρκον·
ὀμόσῃς, ὅτι οὐ δύνασαι μίαν
τρίχα λευκὴν ποιῆσαι ἢ
μέλαιναν.
³⁷ἔστω δὲ ὁ λόγος ὑμῶν   ἤτω δὲ ὑμῶν
ναὶ ναί, οὒ οὔ·   τὸ ναὶ ναί, καὶ τὸ οὒ οὔ,
τὸ δὲ περισσὸν τούτων   ἵνα μὴ ὑπὸ
ἐκ τοῦ πονηροῦ ἐστιν.   κρίσιν πέσητε.

A comparison of these two texts reveals, first of all, that although Matthew regards this material as a saying of Jesus, there is no citation formula to introduce the material in the Epistle of James as a saying of Jesus.[1] Secondly, the form of the saying in James is a more simple parenetic form than the text of Matthew, where each example is elaborated and where the command is not what one should do but what one should say.[2] It, therefore, appears that the form of the saying in Jas. 5:12 is older than Matthew's version,[3] although it is not certain that it was Matthew who first regarded this text as a saying of Jesus.

When we compare the text of *Apol.* 16:5 with Mt. 5:34-37 and Jas. 5:12, we find that Justin's ἔστω δὲ ὑμῶν τὸ ναὶ ναί, καὶ τὸ οὒ οὔ is closer to James' ἤτω δὲ ὑμῶν τὸ ναὶ ναί, καὶ τὸ οὒ οὔ than to Matthew's ἔστω δὲ ὁ λόγος ὑμῶν ναὶ ναί, οὒ οὔ; however, it would be unsound to conclude that Justin is here dependent on the Epistle of James because (1) Justin's ἔστω is paralleled in Mt. 5:37 and not in James (ἤτω); (2) μὴ ὀμόσητε ὅλως in *Apol.* 16:5 is closer to Mt. 5:34 (μὴ ὀμόσαι ὅλως) than to Jas. 5:12 (μὴ ὀμνύετε); and (3) Justin's τὸ δὲ περισσὸν τούτων ἐκ τοῦ πονηροῦ appears in Matthew as τὸ δὲ περισσὸν τούτων ἐκ τοῦ πονηροῦ ἐστιν, but the text of Jas. 5:12 reads ἵνα μὴ ὑπὸ κρίσιν πέσητε. This evidence would seem to

---

[1] Martin Dibelius points out (*Der Brief des Jakobus* [Göttingen, 1957], p. 231) that the fact that James does not introduce this material with a citation formula does not mean that the author did not regard it as a saying of Jesus. The verse is obviously parenetic in form, and such material would generally be regarded as originating with a saying of Jesus, although it would not necessarily be introduced as such.

[2] *Ibid.*, p. 231.

[3] So too Dibelius, *Der Brief des Jakobus*, pp. 230 f.; Dibelius, *Die Formgeschichte des Evangeliums*, p. 241; Ernst Lohmeyer, *Das Evangelium des Matthäus* (Göttingen, 1958), p. 134. M'Neile (pp. 67 f.), on the other hand, implies that the text of James is based on Mt. 5:34-37. Cf. Davies, pp. 401 ff.

indicate that *Apol.* 16:5 was here based on a text of Mt. 5:34, 37 that had either been harmonized in part with Jas. 5:12 or with the parenetic tradition that underlies Jas. 5:12. The evidence of several of the fathers indicates a widespread knowledge of a text similar to *Apol.* 16:5.

Eusebius, *Demonstratio Evangelica* III, 3, 103 (Heikel, VI, *GCS*, p. 109)
ἔστω γὰρ ὑμῶν τὸ ναὶ ναί, τὸ οὒ οὔ.

Clem. Alex., *Strom.* V, 14, 99 (Stählin, II, *GCS*, p. 391)
ἔστω ὑμῶν τὸ ναὶ καὶ τὸ οὒ οὔ.

Clem. Alex., *Strom.* VII, 11, 67 (Stählin, III, *GCS*, p. 48)
ἔσται ὑμῶν τὸ ναὶ ναὶ καὶ οὒ οὔ.

Eusebius, *Commentary in Psalm* 14, 4 (Migne, *PG*, XXIII, 152)
ἐφ' ᾧ βεβαιοῦνται τὸ, Ναὶ ναὶ, καὶ τὸ, Οὒ οὔ.

Pseudoclementine *Homilies* 19, 2 (Rehm, *GCS*, p. 253)
Ἔστω ὑμῶν τὸ ναὶ ναὶ καὶ τὸ οὒ οὔ, τὸ δὲ περισσὸν τούτων ἐκ τοῦ πονηροῦ ἐστιν.

Pseudoclementine *Homilies* 3, 55 (Rehm, *GCS*, p. 77)
Ἔστω ὑμῶν τὸ ναὶ ναί, τὸ οὒ οὔ · τὸ γὰρ περισσὸν τούτων ἐκ τοῦ πονηροῦ ἐστιν.

Cyril of Alexandria, *De Adoratione et Veritate* VI (Migne, *PG*, LXVIII 472)
Ἔστω ὑμῶν, τὸ Ναὶ, ναὶ, καὶ τὸ Οὒ, οὔ · τὸ δὲ περισσὸν τούτων, ἐκ τοῦ διαβόλου ἐστίν.

Gregory of Nyssa, *In Canticle of Canticles*, Homily XIII (Migne, *PG*, XLIV, 1040)
Ἔστω δὲ ὑμῶν ὁ λόγος τὸ, Ναὶ, ναί · καὶ τὸ, Οὒ, οὔ · τὸ δὲ περισσότερον τούτων, ἐκ τοῦ διαβόλου ἐστίν.

A comparison of these texts points to the possibility of a common text or tradition that may have read:

ἔστω ὑμῶν τὸ ναὶ ναί, καὶ τὸ οὒ οὔ · τὸ δὲ περισσὸν τούτων ἐκ τοῦ πονηροῦ ἐστιν,

a reading identical to Pseudoclementine *Homilies* 19, 2. The addition of καὶ and the omission of γὰρ in Pseudo-clementine *Homilies* 3, 55 is probably a stylistic change, and the appearance in Cyril and Gregory of διαβόλου for πονηροῦ is apparently an interpretative personalization of what in the original reading could be either a masculine or a neuter noun. Justin's departure from this form of the saying is minor and can be easily explained. The δὲ is obviously a stylistic connective, and the omission of the final ἐστιν is not significant.

It is, therefore, apparent that there existed a parenetic saying about swearing that was based on Mt. 5:34-37 harmonized either with Jas. 5:12 or with the parenetic teaching that lies behind Jas. 5:12 and that this saying was known to several patristic writers after Justin.[1]

7) *Apology* 16:9

Apol. 16:9

    Οὐχὶ πᾶς ὁ λέγων μοι
    Κύριε κύριε εἰσελεύσεται
    εἰς τὴν βασιλείαν τῶν οὐρανῶν
    ἀλλ' ὁ ποιῶν τὸ θέλημα
    τοῦ πατρός μου τοῦ ἐν
    τοῖς οὐρανοῖς.

Mt. 7:21

    Οὐ πᾶς ὁ λέγων μοι
    κύριε κύριε, εἰσελεύσεται
    εἰς τὴν βασιλείαν τῶν οὐρανῶν,
    ἀλλ' ὁ ποιῶν τὸ θέλημα
    τοῦ πατρός μου τοῦ ἐν
    τοῖς οὐρανοῖς.

The only difference between the text of Justin and the text of Matthew is the use of οὐχὶ in *Apol.* 16:9 where Mt. 7:21 has οὐ; however, this variation is minor and casts no doubt on the conclusion that the text of *Apol.* 16:9 is ultimately based on a text substantially identical with Mt. 7:21.[2]

8) *Apology* 16:12

The *logion* in *Apol.* 16:12 is paralleled, at least in part, seven times in the synoptic gospels. The version of Q is found in Mt. 8:12b and Lk. 13:28, and a second version peculiar to Matthew is found in Mt. 13:42, 43. In addition Mt. 13:50 produces the saying in a version identical to Mt. 13:42; and Mt. 22:13, 24:51b, and 25:30 are identical to Mt. 8:12b,

---

[1] The text of Epiphanius, *Adversus Haereses* XIX, 6, 21 may perhaps be the final proof that this kind of reading arose from an attempt to harmonize Mt. 5:34 with Jas. 5:12: καὶ πάλιν ἐν τῷ εὐαγγελίῳ λέγοντος· μὴ ὀμνύναι μήτε τὸν οὐρανὸν μήτε τὴν γῆν μήτε ἕτερόν τινα ὅρκον, ἀλλ' ἤτω ὑμῶν τὸ ναὶ ναὶ καὶ τὸ οὒ οὒ. τὸ περισσότερον γὰρ τούτων ἐκ τοῦ πονηροῦ ὑπάρχει (Holl, I, *GCS*, p. 223). Here the first part is almost identical to Jas. 5:12 and the final sentence to Mt. 5:37. And although the text of Epiphanius is actually closer to the form of James, the saying is introduced as one coming from the gospel (ἐν τῷ εὐαγγελίῳ), which by the time of Epiphanius must have meant, in this instance, our canonical Matthew. The variant reading of Mt. 5:37 τὸ ναὶ ναί, καὶ τὸ οὒ οὔ (Θ 213. 1360. 1 184) is certainly not original and is probably the result of assimilation to Jas. 5:12 or to the parenetic tradition that underlies *Apol.* 16:5 and the other patristic sources quoted above.

[2] So too Massaux, "Le Texte du Sermon," p. 415 and *L'Influence de l'Evangile,* p. 487.

perhaps indicating that the phrase ἐκεῖ ἔσται ὁ κλαυθμὸς καὶ ὁ βρυγμὸς τῶν ὀδόντων had almost become proverbial.[1]

Apol. 16:12	Mt. 13:42, 43 (and 13:50)	Mt. 8:12b (and 22:13; 24:51b; 25:30)	Lk. 13:28
	42 (and 13:50)		
	καὶ βαλοῦσιν αὐτοὺς εἰς τὴν κάμινον τοῦ πυρός·		
τότε κλαυθμὸς ἔσται	ἐκεῖ ἔσται ὁ κλαυθμὸς	ἐκεῖ ἔσται ὁ κλαυθμὸς	ἐκεῖ ἔσται ὁ κλαυθμὸς
καὶ βρυγμὸς τῶν ὀδόντων,	καὶ ὁ βρυγμὸς τῶν ὀδόντων.	καὶ ὁ βρυγμὸς τῶν ὀδόντων.	καὶ ὁ βρυγμὸς τῶν ὀδόντων,
ὅταν οἱ μὲν δίκαιοι λάμψωσιν ὡς ὁ ἥλιος,	43τότε οἱ δίκαιοι ἐκλάμψουσιν ὡς ὁ ἥλιος ἐν τῇ βασιλείᾳ τοῦ πατρὸς αὐτῶν. ὁ ἔχων ὦτα ἀκουέτω.		ὅταν ὄψησθε Ἀβραὰμ καὶ Ἰσαὰκ καὶ Ἰακὼβ ...
οἱ δὲ ἄδικοι πέμψωνται εἰς τὸ αἰώνιον πῦρ.			

The fact that Mt. 8:12b and Lk. 13:28 agree completely in their wording ἐκεῖ ἔσται ὁ κλαυθμὸς καὶ ὁ βρυγμὸς τῶν ὀδόντων indicates that this reading was original in Q, and the text of Mt. 13:42, 13:50, 22:13, 24:51b, and 25:30 supports the fact that this reading is pre-Matthaean. It is, therefore, certain that Justin's wording (τότε κλαυθμὸς ἔσται καὶ βρυγμὸς τῶν ὀδόντων) is based either on our gospels or on a text later than our gospels. Although there are seven gospel texts that parallel at least part of *Apol.* 16:12, only Mt. 13:42, 43 has parallels to all of Justin's

---

[1] M'Neile maintains (p. 106) that this phrase might have been "a stereotyped formula in Christian teaching."

phrases. The syntax of *Apol.* 16:12 (τότε ... ὅταν ...) is more stylistic and more fluent Greek than the awkward version of Mt. 5:42f. (ἐκεῖ ἔσται ... τότε ...).[1] Further, either Justin or his source has twice omitted ὁ from Matthew's version (before κλαυθμὸς and before βρυγμὸς). The difference between the aorist subjunctive λάμψωσιν in *Apol.* 16:12 and the future indicative ἐκλάμψουσιν in Mt. 13:43 can be explained by Justin's use of ὅταν, which requires this revision;[2] and the μὲν in *Apol.* 16:12 (balanced by the δὲ in the following clause) is only a stylistic device introduced either by Justin or his source.

The final phrase of *Apol.* 16:12 (οἱ δὲ ἄδικοι πέμψωνται εἰς τὸ αἰώνιον πῦρ) is related to Mt. 13:42a as follows:

Mt. 13:42a	*Apol.* 16:12
αὐτούς	has become οἱ δὲ ἄδικοι
βαλοῦσιν	has become πέμψωνται
εἰς τὴν κάμινον τοῦ πυρός	has become εἰς τὸ αἰώνιον πῦρ

The pronoun αὐτούς of Mt. 13:42a, having no antecedent in *Apol.* 16:12, had to be substituted by a noun (οἱ ἄδικοι); the active verb βαλοῦσιν in Mt. 13:42a, which has its subject (angels) in the previous verse (Mt. 13:41), had to be altered to the passive verb πέμψωνται to preserve the meaning; and in attempting to avoid Matthew's allusion to Gehenna (εἰς τὴν κάμινον τοῦ πυρός),[3] either Justin or his source substituted the phrase εἰς τὸ αἰώνιον πῦρ.

From this analysis it is certain that either Justin made certain changes in Mt. 13:42, 43 in adapting this saying of Jesus to his own context or else used a source based on Mt. 13:42, 43 and in which these changes had already been made.

With regard to the above eight sayings that reflect dependence on Matthew only, it should be noted that sayings 1, 2, 3, 5, 6, and 7 have parallels only in Matthew and in none of the other synoptic gospels, whereas sayings 4 and 8 follow the reading of Matthew although there is a parallel in Mark and/or Luke.

---

[1] Although ὅταν is found in Lk. 13:28, the fact that it introduces material completely different from that found in *Apol.* 16:12 probably indicates that Luke has not influenced Justin here.

[2] The change from the use of the verb ἐκλάμπω in Mt. 13:43 to λάμπω in *Apol.* 16:12 is perhaps only a matter of preference; however, it is interesting that the word occurs nowhere else in the New Testament.

[3] M'Neile (p. 202) regards this phrase as a reference to Gehenna, an allusion that would have had little significance to Justin's pagan audience.

b. Sayings that reflect dependence on Luke only

1) *Apology* 15:3

Apol. 15:3	Mt. 5:32b	Mt. 19:9	Mk. 10:12	Lk. 16:18b
		λέγω δὲ ὑμῖν ὅτι		
Ὅς γαμεῖ	καὶ ὃς ἐάν	ὃς ἂν	καὶ ἐὰν αὐτὴ	καὶ ὁ
ἀπο-	ἀπο-	ἀπο-	ἀπο-	ἀπο-
λελυμένην	λελυμένην	λύσῃ	λύσασα	λελυμένην
ἀφ' ἑτέρου		τὴν γυναῖκα	τὸν ἄνδρα	ἀπὸ ἀνδρὸς
ἀνδρὸς		αὐτοῦ μὴ ἐπὶ πορνείᾳ	αὐτῆς	
	γαμήσῃ,	καὶ γαμήσῃ ἄλλην,	γαμήσῃ ἄλλον,	γαμῶν
μοιχᾶται.	μοιχᾶται.	μοιχᾶται.	μοιχᾶται.	μοιχεύει.

The above gospel tradition about divorce has been derived from two traditions (1) the version of Q found in Mt. 5:32b and Lk. 16:18b and (2) the Markan version (10:12) paralleled in Mt. 19:9.[1] The text of *Apol.* 15:3 parallels the Q form of this saying recorded in Mt. 5:32b and Lk. 16:18b, and two features of Justin's text indicate that Justin used not the pre-synoptic Q version of this saying but a post-synoptic tradition. (1) The fact that both Mt. 5:32b and Lk. 16:18b have the verb for marry (γαμήσῃ in Mt. 5:32 and γαμῶν in Lk. 16:18) near the end of the saying immediately before μοιχᾶται (Matthew) and μοιχεύει (Luke) indicates that it probably occurred here in Q; however, in Justin's version γαμεῖ occurs at the beginning of the saying. (2) The phrase ἀπὸ ἀνδρὸς in Lk. 16:18b was apparently added by Luke for clarity and was, therefore, not in Q; however, it is paralleled in *Apol.* 15:3 (ἀφ' ἑτέρου ἀνδρὸς).

The phrase ὃς γαμεῖ ἀπολελυμένην of *Apol.* 15:3 does not have an exact parallel in either Mt. 5:32b (καὶ ὃς ἐὰν ἀπολελυμένην γαμήσῃ) or Lk. 16:18b (καὶ ὁ ἀπολελυμένην ... γαμῶν); however, a second century patristic text written a few decades after the death of Justin indicates a link here between *Apol.* 15:3 and Lk. 16:18b:

Theophilus of Antioch III, 12 (Migne, *PG*, VI, 1140)

καὶ ὁ γαμῶν, φησὶν, ἀπολελυμένην ἀπὸ ἀνδρὸς μοιχεύει.

[1] Bultmann, p. 140. Bultmann further maintains that the Q form is original and explains the Markan form, which answered the need of providing divorce laws not only for men but also for women.

The relationship of this text of Theophilus to Lk. 16:18b is certain, the only difference between the two being the transfer of the participle γαμῶν to the beginning of the saying; and this word order found in Theophilus is parallel to Justin's order (ὃς γαμεῖ ἀπολελυμένην).

The middle section of *Apol.* 15:3 (ἀφ' ἑτέρου ἀνδρὸς) finds its only parallel in Lk. 16:18b (ἀπὸ ἀνδρὸς). The verb μοιχᾶται of *Apol.* 15:3 is identical to Mt. 5:32b (also Mt. 19:9 and Mk. 10:12), whereas Lk. 16:18b has μοιχεύει; however, there was apparently some difference in meaning between μοιχάω and μοιχεύω. μοιχεύω was used in Attic Greek principally of men, and in the New Testament the verb is usually employed with reference to the sixth commandment (Mt. 5:27; 19:18; Mk. 10:19; Lk. 18:20; Rom. 13:9; Jas. 2:11); the Doric verb μοιχάω, on the other hand, was used of both men and women and apparently carried no special connotation of the Mosaic commandment in the New Testament.[1] Although it might be argued that Justin derived μοιχᾶται from Mt. 5:32b, it is possible that he knew the Old Testament connotations of the verb μοιχεύω and substituted the neutral verb μοιχάω to avoid a connotation perhaps undesirable in a writing addressed to pagans.[2]

That *Apol.* 15:3 is dependent on Lk. 16:18b or on a text based on Lk. 16:18b is certain, but it should also be admitted that Justin's text perhaps shows features of harmonization with Mt. 5:32b.[3]

2) *Apology* 16:1

Apol. 16:1	Mt. 5:39, 40	Lk. 6:29
	39ἐγὼ δὲ λέγω	
	ὑμῖν μὴ	
	ἀντιστῆναι	
	τῷ πονηρῷ·	
	ἀλλ' ὅστις	

---

[1] Blass-Debrunner-Funk, 101; Friedrich Hauck, "μοιχεύω, μοιχάω, κ.τ.λ.," *Theologisches Wörterbuch zum Neuen Testament*, ed. Gerhard Kittel, Vol. IV (Stuttgart, 1957), pp. 737-743. Liddell-Scott, however, makes no distinction between the two verbs and regards them rather as synonyms (p. 1141).

[2] The appearance of μοιχᾶται in several manuscripts of Lk. 16:18 b (KMXII al.²⁰) is also probably the result either of harmonization with Mt. 5:32 b or influence from the tradition found in Justin's text.

[3] Baldus (p. 64) maintains that Justin is dependent on Mt. 5:32 to which he has himself added the phrase ἀφ' ἑτέρου ἀνδρός. Likewise, Massaux ("Le Texte du Sermon," p. 421) argues that Justin added ἀφ' ἑτέρου ἀνδρός to Mt. 5:32 and did not use Luke; however, for the reasons mentioned above I find it more reasonable to conclude that Justin is here either directly or indirectly dependent on Lk. 16:18 b.

Τῷ τύπτοντί σου	σε ῥαπίζει	τῷ τύπτοντί σε
τὴν	εἰς τὴν δεξιὰν	ἐπὶ τὴν
σιαγόνα	σιαγόνα σου,	σιαγόνα
πάρεχε	στρέψον αὐτῷ	πάρεχε
καὶ τὴν ἄλλην,	καὶ τὴν ἄλλην·	καὶ τὴν ἄλλην,
καὶ τὸν	⁴⁰καὶ τῷ	καὶ ἀπὸ τοῦ
αἴροντά σου	θέλοντί σοι	αἴροντός σου
τὸν χιτῶνα ἢ	κριθῆναι καὶ	τὸ ἱμάτιον καὶ
	τὸν χιτῶνά	
	σου λαβεῖν,	
	ἄφες αὐτῷ καὶ	
τὸ ἱμάτιον	τὸ ἱμάτιον.	τὸν χιτῶνα
μὴ κωλύσῃς.		μὴ κωλύσῃς.

That *Apol.* 16:1 is based on Lk. 6:29 or on a post-synoptic text based on Lk. 6:29 is certain, because in two instances in which Justin differs from Luke the text of *Apol.* 16:1 is obviously an improvement of the Lukan reading. (1) Luke's τῷ τύπτοντί σε ἐπὶ τὴν σιαγόνα πάρεχε καὶ τὴν ἄλλην is the only known instance of τύπτειν ἐπί with the accusative;[1] Justin's τῷ τύπτοντί σου τὴν σιαγόνα πάρεχε καὶ τὴν ἄλλην, on the other hand, is better Greek. (2) Luke's construction κωλύειν ἀπό is uncommon, whereas Justin's use of κωλύειν with the accusative is more common both in the New Testament and in classical Greek.[2] It might be argued that if Luke faithfully preserved the reading of his source Q, Justin's improvements might as well be based on the pre-synoptic text used by Luke. But Justin's use of a synoptic or post-synoptic source elsewhere makes the use of a pre-synoptic text unlikely in this instance.

The difference between τὸ ἱμάτιον καὶ τὸν χιτῶνα in Lk. 6:29 and τὸν χιτῶνα ἢ τὸ ἱμάτιον in *Apol.* 16:1 apparently arose from a misunderstanding either by Justin or his source of the meaning of Luke's text. Whereas ἱμάτιον probably belongs to the verb αἴροντός and χιτῶνα to the verb κωλύσῃς in Luke, Justin or his source apparently thought that both nouns were the objects of the verb αἴροντός. The change from καὶ to ἢ comes naturally from the alteration in meaning, and the inversion of the order of χιτῶνα and ἱμάτιον may be only a stylistic change made in order to mention second the outer and more valuable garment.[3] These results

---

[1] Alfred Plummer, *A Critical and Exegetical Commentary on the Gospel According to S. Luke* (Edinburgh, 1956), p. 185.

[2] *Ibid.*; Blass-Debrunner-Funk, 180 (1).

[3] The fact that Mt. 5:40 lists χιτῶνα before ἱμάτιον does not indicate a Matthaean influence in Justin's text. Rather the absence of any definite influence from Matthew leaves little doubt that this small agreement is coincidental.

leave little doubt that either Justin or his source is here based on the text of Lk. 6:29.[1]

3) *Apology* 16:10

It has already been argued above that *Apol.* 16:10 was probably based on a text of Lk. 10:16 that added a fourth line to the gospel text (see above, pp. 20-22).

4) *Apology* 17:4

Apol. 17:4 ᾧ πλέον ἔδωκεν ὁ θεός, πλέον ἀπαιτηθήσεται παρ' αὐτοῦ. This saying from *Apol.* 17:4 does not have an exact parallel in any of the gospels or in the patristic literature; however, there are rather close parallels in Lk. 12:48 and in many writings of the early church, where we find both a longer and a shorter version of this *logion*:

The Longer Version

Lk. 12:48 (Nestle Text)
παντὶ δὲ ᾧ ἐδόθη πολύ, πολὺ ζητηθήσεται παρ' αὐτοῦ, καὶ ᾧ παρέθεντο πολύ, περισσότερον αἰτήσουσιν αὐτόν.

Lk. 12:48, Codex D (quoted from Bousset, p. 107)
παντὶ δὲ ᾧ ἔδωκαν πολύ, ζητηθήσεται ἀπ' αὐτοῦ περισσότερον καὶ ᾧ παρέθεντο πολύ, πλέον ἀπαιτήσουσιν αὐτόν.

Macarius of Egypt, *Homilies* XXXIX, 6 (Migne, *PG*, XXXIV, 720)
παντὶ δὲ ᾧ ἐδόθη πολύ, πολὺ ζητήσεται παρ' αὐτοῦ καὶ ᾧ πολὺ παρέθεντο, περισσότερον ἀπαιτήσουσιν αὐτόν.

The Shorter Version

Apostolic Constitutions II, 18 (Migne, *PG*, I, 629)
ᾧ γάρ, φησί, παρέθεντο πολύ, περισσότερον ἀπαιτήσουσιν παρ' αὐτοῦ.

Epiphanius, *Ancoratus* 26, 8 (Holl, I, *GCS*, p. 35)
ᾧ δίδοται περισσότερον, περισσότερον ἀπαιτήσουσιν αὐτόν.

Clem. Alex., *Strom.* II, 23 (Stählin, II, *GCS*, p. 194)
ᾧ πλεῖον ἐδόθη, οὗτος καὶ ἀπαιτηθήσεται.[2]

A comparison of these texts with the text of *Apol.* 17:4 reveals two

---

[1] Köster argues (*Synoptische Überlieferung*, pp. 226 ff., 264) that *Did.* 1:4 shows evidence of harmonization of Mt. 5:39, 40 and Lk. 6:29, but there is no evidence of any connection between the passage in *Didache* and Justin's text.

[2] The text of Migne (*PG*, VIII, 1097) reads ᾧ πλαῖον ἐδόθη, οὗτος καὶ πλεῖον ἀπαιτηθήσεται, but a comparison of this reading with the other editions of Clement supports the reading of the edition of Stählin.

significant features: (1) Lk. 12:48 alone uses the verb αἰτέω; all other parallels use the compound verb ἀπαιτέω (ἀπαιτήσουσιν in Codex D, Macarius, *Apostolic Constitutions*, and Epiphanius and the passive form ἀπαιτηθήσεται in Clement of Alexandria and Justin);[1] and (2) there is great disagreement among the texts in their use of πολύ, πλεῖον (πλέον),[2] and περισσότερον in different combinations and order; but inasmuch as the meaning of the saying is altered by changing these words, such alterations may have been made by the individual authors to suit their respective contexts and intentions. These two features account for many of the differences among the several texts under consideration; however, it is now necessary to examine separately each of these parallel texts.

Codex D of Lk. 12:48 has only minor differences from the version of the Nestle text. The change from the passive ἐδόθη in Lk. 12:48 (Nestle) to the active ἔδωκαν in Codex D is probably only stylistic, as are the changes from πολύ and παρ' αὐτοῦ in Lk. 12:48 to περισσότερον and ἀπ' αὐτοῦ in Codex D. Further the difference between περισσότερον in Lk. 12:48 (Nestle) and πλέον in Codex D is perhaps only stylistic, and the change from αἰτήσουσιν to the compound verb ἀπαιτήσουσιν in Codex D may be only an improvement in the Greek of Luke's text.

The differences between Macarius and Lk. 12:48 are also minor. The change from the future ζητηθήσεται in Lk. 12:48 to the present ζητήσεται in Macarius is probably stylistic, as in the change from παρέθεντο πολύ in Lk. 12:48 to πολύ παρέθεντο in Macarius. Further, Macarius also has the compound verb ἀπαιτήσουσιν for Luke's αἰτήσουσιν, a difference I have already discussed above.

The text of *Apostolic Constitutions* and the text of Epiphanius parallel only the second part of Lk. 12:48 making certain minor variations. The additions of γὰρ in *Apostolic Constitutions* is probably to provide a smooth connection with the preceding material, and the change in Epiphanius to δίδοται and περισσότερον is probably only stylistic. Both texts support the reading of the compound verb ἀπαιτήσουσιν, and the author of the *Apostolic Constitutions* has apparently improved upon the Greek of Luke by changing αὐτόν to παρ' αὐτοῦ.[3]

---

[1] The change from the simple to the compound verb is not significant, because the verb ἀπαιτέω is the better Greek for the idea expressed. The change is, therefore, probably one of stylistic improvement. See Bauer, pp. 50 f., 158 and Liddell-Scott, pp. 44, 175.

[2] πλεῖον and πλέον are variant forms of the same word, and there is no difference in meaning between the two forms; see Bauer, pp. 1363 ff. and Liddell-Scott, p. 1415.

[3] ἀπαιτέω τὶ ἀπό τινος is better Greek than the accusative; see Bauer, p. 158 and Lk. 6:30.

But whereas *Apostolic Constitutions* and Epiphanius have apparently based their text on the second part of Lk. 12:48, Clement of Alexandria has apparently either harmonized elements from the first and second parts of Lk. 12:48 or else used a harmony that had already done this before him.[1] The change from πολύ in Lk. 12:48 to πλεῖον is probably only stylistic, but the use of ἐδόθη in Clement is probably from the first part of Lk. 12:48. The final phrase of Clement οὗτος καὶ ἀπαιτηθήσεται has no close parallel in either half of Lk. 12:48; however, it does use the compound verb ἀπαιτέω although in the passive mood.

Apol. 17:4 reveals features in common with this text of Clement of Alexandria; however, Justin departs less radically from the Lukan parallel than does Clement's text. Both Clement and Justin begin ᾧ πλεῖον (πλέον), and both use the passive form ἀπαιτηθήσεται. Justin's use of the active ἔδωκεν ὁ θεός instead of the passive form found in all other parallels can probably be attributed to Justin's desire to change what could be interpreted as a general proverbial statement into a statement about God's requirements from men, and the appearance of παρ᾽ αὐτοῦ is probably an improvement upon the accusative αὐτόν.[2]

The small but significant agreements of Clement and Justin here leads to the suspicion that the two fathers might have used a common source, which could have read ᾧ πλεῖον (πλέον) ἐδόθη, πλεῖον (πλέον) καὶ ἀπαιτηθήσεται αὐτόν.[3] If this were the case, then Clement here reproduced exactly the first part of his source (ᾧ πλεῖον ἐδόθη); but realizing the difficulty of ἀπαιτήσεται αὐτόν, he changed this phrase to οὗτος καὶ ἀπαιτηθήσεται. Justin, on the other hand, changed in the first part from the passive to the active form ἔδωκεν ὁ θεός; and realizing the difficulty of ἀπαιτηθήσεται αὐτόν, he changed this reading to ἀπαιτηθήσεται παρ᾽ αὐτοῦ.

This analysis of *Apol.* 17:4 reveals that Justin is remotely dependent upon the text of Lk. 12:48, although it appears that he did not use the gospel itself but that he used rather a post-synoptic harmony of Lk. 12: 48a and 12:48b known also to Clement of Alexandria.

---

[1] That the apparently harmonistic form of Lk. 12:48 found in Clement (and Justin) is a post-synoptic version and not the original pre-synoptic text used as a source by Luke is supported by the fact that Lk. 12:48 b was probably originally an independent saying, which Luke here joined to the material underlying 12:47, 48a (Bultmann, pp. 84, 119).

[2] See p. 74 n. 2.

[3] I do not intend to press this point too far; however, the possibility of this mutual dependence upon a common source is presented here as a reasonable solution to the problem of the history of transmission of this saying by Justin and Clement of Alexandria.

With regard to the above four sayings that reflect dependence on Luke only, it should be noted that saying 4 has a parallel only in Luke, whereas sayings 2 and 3 follow the reading of Luke although there is a parallel in Matthew, and saying 1 follows Luke although there are parallels in both Matthew and Mark.

2. Sayings showing features of harmonization of Matthew and Luke

a. Apology 15:8a

Apol. 15:8a	Mt. 9:13	Mk. 2:17	Lk. 5:32
οὐκ ἦλθον	οὐ γὰρ ἦλθον	οὐκ ἦλθον	οὐκ ἐλήλυθα
καλέσαι	καλέσαι	καλέσαι	καλέσαι
δικαίους,	δικαίους	δικαίους	δικαίους
ἀλλὰ	ἀλλὰ	ἀλλὰ	ἀλλὰ
ἁμαρτωλοὺς	ἁμαρτωλούς.	ἁμαρτωλούς.	ἁμαρτωλοὺς
εἰς μετάνοιαν.			εἰς μετάνοιαν.

The saying in *Apol.* 15:8a is identical to the text of Mt. 9:13[1] and Mk. 2:17 with the exception of the addition of εἰς μετάνοιαν found only in Lk. 5:32. The text of *Apol.* 15:8a, therefore, shows evidence of harmonization of Matthew and/or Mark with Luke, and such a harmonized text apparently influenced later patristic writers[2] and manuscript traditions[3] that show evidence of the same sort of reading found in *Apol.* 15:8.

There is, however, some uncertainty whether Justin intended to include *Apol.* 15:8b (θέλει γὰρ ὁ πατὴρ ὁ οὐράνιος τὴν μετάνοιαν τοῦ ἁμαρτωλοῦ ἢ τὴν κόλασιν αὐτοῦ) as a part of this saying of Jesus. Wright maintains that this second half of *Apol.* 15:8 is not a saying of Jesus but rather a "complement" that "seems clearly in the nature of an explanation."[4] Resch,[5]

---

[1] Although Matthew's text actually has οὐ γὰρ rather than οὐκ ἦλθον found in *Apol.* 15:8 a and Mk. 2:17, this difference is minor. The γὰρ of Matthew's text is only a connective, which is unimportant to the meaning of the saying and which, when removed, requires that οὐ be changed to οὐκ.

[2] The patristic witnesses that have readings identical to *Apol.* 15:8 are too numerous to list here; but among these are Pseudo-Justin, *De Resurrectione* 7:23; Epiphanius, *Against Heresies* 51, 5, 1; Eusebius, *Demonstratio Evangelica* IV, 10, 11; Basil, *Mort. Reg.* LII, 3; Augustine, *Epist.* 102.

[3] Mt. 9:13 +εἰς μετάνοιαν CEGKLMSUVmg·XYΓmg· ΘΩ 118². fam. 13. 543. 32*. 700. 892. al. pler. c g1·2·vg. (3 MSS.) Syr. s.hl.mg.hier. Cop. sa·bo·(aliq·) Aeth.; Mk. 2:17 + εἰς μετάνοιαν CΓל (exc. K) 118mg·. 131. 22³. fam. 13. 543. 32. 1071, al. pler. a c g1 r1 vg. (1 MS) Syr. hier. Cop. bo·(aliq·) Geo.²; Lk. 5:32 ἦλθον C³D 1. 28. 157. 47 ev· al.pauc.

[4] p. 76.

[5] pp. 98 f.

Bousset,[1] and Ropes,[2] on the other hand, believe that it was Justin's intention to quote this material as a saying of Jesus. That *Apol.* 15:8b was not regarded by Justin as part of the saying of Jesus is supported by the fact that in *Apol.* 15-17 there are besides *Apol.* 15:8 four instances in which Justin comments on a preceding saying of Jesus (*Apol.* 15:5; 16:3; 16:14; 17:3); and in each instance the verse in question is linked to the saying upon which it is commenting by a connective word (ὥσπερ καὶ in 15:5; δὲ in 16:14; γὰρ in 16:3; ὅθεν in 17:3), just as *Apol.* 15:8b is linked by the connective word γὰρ to the preceding saying. This close similarity of form leaves little doubt that *Apol.* 15:8b was not regarded by Justin as part of the *logion* but that it was written as an explanation complementing the preceding saying of Jesus.

b. *Apology* 15:9

Apol. 15:9	Mt. 5:46, 47, 44	Lk. 6:32, 33, 27, 28
Εἰ ἀγαπᾶτε	⁴⁶ἐὰν γὰρ ἀγαπήσητε	³²καὶ εἰ ἀγαπᾶτε
τοὺς ἀγαπῶντας	τοὺς ἀγαπῶντας	τοὺς ἀγαπῶντας
ὑμᾶς,	ὑμᾶς,	ὑμᾶς,
τί καινὸν ποιεῖτε;	τίνα μισθὸν ἔχετε;	ποία ὑμῖν χάρις ἐστίν;
	οὐχὶ καὶ οἱ	καὶ γὰρ οἱ ἁμαρτωλοὶ
	τελῶναι τὸ	τοὺς ἀγαπῶντας
	αὐτὸ ποιοῦσιν;	αὐτοὺς ἀγαπῶσιν.
	⁴⁷καὶ ἐὰν	³³καὶ γὰρ ἐὰν
	ἀσπάσησθε	ἀγαθοποιῆτε
	τοὺς ἀδελφοὺς	τοὺς ἀγαθοποιοῦντας
	ὑμῶν μόνον,	ὑμᾶς,
	τί περισσὸν	ποία ὑμῖν
	ποιεῖτε;	χάρις ἐστίν;
καὶ γὰρ	οὐχὶ καὶ	καὶ
οἱ πόρνοι	οἱ ἐθνικοὶ	οἱ ἁμαρτωλοὶ
τοῦτο	τὸ αὐτὸ	τὸ αὐτὸ
ποιοῦσιν.	ποιοῦσιν;	ποιοῦσιν.
Ἐγὼ δὲ	⁴⁴ἐγὼ δὲ	²⁷Ἀλλὰ
ὑμῖν λέγω·	λέγω ὑμῖν·	ὑμῖν λέγω
		τοῖς ἀκούουσιν·

---

[1] p. 98. Bousset argues that the phrase ὁ πατὴρ ὁ οὐράνιος which he regards as a peculiarity of Justin's source, lends weight to the probability that Justin read these words in his source.

[2] James Hardy Ropes, *Die Sprüche Jesus, Texte und Untersuchungen* XIV, 2 (Leipzig, 1896), pp. 98 f.

Εὔχεσθε ὑπὲρ	ἀγαπᾶτε τοὺς	ἀγαπᾶτε τοὺς
τῶν ἐχθρῶν ὑμῶν	ἐχθροὺς ὑμῶν	ἐχθροὺς ὑμῶν,
καὶ ἀγαπᾶτε τοὺς		καλῶς ποιεῖτε
μισοῦντας ὑμᾶς καὶ		τοῖς μισοῦσιν ὑμᾶς,
εὐλογεῖτε τοὺς		²⁸εὐλογεῖτε τοὺς
καταρωμένους ὑμῖν		καταρωμένους ὑμᾶς,
καὶ εὔχεσθε ὑπὲρ	καὶ προσεύχεσθε	προσεύχεσθε
	ὑπὲρ	περὶ
τῶν ἐπηρεαζόντων	τῶν διωκόντων	τῶν ἐπηρεαζόντων
ὑμᾶς.	ὑμᾶς.	ὑμᾶς.

The opening words of *Apol.* 15:9 εἰ ἀγαπᾶτε τοὺς ἀγαπῶντας ὑμᾶς agree exactly with the reading of Lk. 6:32 as opposed to the reading ἐὰν γὰρ ἀγαπήσητε τοὺς ἀγαπῶντας ὑμᾶς in Mt. 5:46; however, Justin's τί καινὸν ποιεῖτε is quite different from Matthew's τίνα μισθὸν ἔχετε and Luke's ποία ὑμῖν χάρις ἐστιν. Nor does Justin's reading find a parallel in any of the patristic witnesses. Indeed, it appears that either Justin or his source is responsible for this alteration made perhaps for stylistic or, more probably, for dogmatic or catechetical reasons in order to emphasize not the personal benefits of loving one's neighbor but rather the "newness" of the Christian ethic involving a command to love.[1] Further, the verb ποιεῖτε was probably suggested by ποιοῦσιν in the following clause of *Apol.* 15:9 and the gospel parallels. Justin repeats his question τί καινὸν ποιεῖτε again in *Apol.* 15:10b apparently for the same dogmatic or catechetical reason that he uses the phrase in *Apol.* 15:9.

The phrase καὶ γὰρ οἱ πόρνοι τοῦτο ποιοῦσιν also finds no exact parallel in the gospels, although Mt. 5:46 (οὐχὶ καὶ οἱ τελῶναι τὸ αὐτὸ ποιοῦσιν;)[2],

---

[1] That this interpretation is consistent with Justin's use of καινός elsewhere is supported by the fact that Justin almost always uses the word καινός to refer to either the New Covenant (*Dial.* 11:3, 4; 12:2; 34:1; 43:1; 51:3; 67:9; 118:3; 122:5), to the New Lawgiver (*Dial.* 14:3; 18:1), or to the New Law given by him (*Dial.* 12:3; 34:1); and on one occasion (*Dial.* 14:3) Justin records that the New Lawgiver (καινὸς νομοθέτης) demands the performance of other works and not the imitation of the old and evil works (ἄλλων ἔργων πρᾶξιν καὶ μὴ τῶν παλαιῶν καὶ φαύλων τὴν μίμησιν). Wright maintains (p. 61) that Justin's τί καινὸν ποιεῖτε is a significant expression of the emergent self-consciousness of the early Christian community representing in history a peculiar, indeed, a "new" people, and this interpretation is possible. Baldus, on the other hand, attributes this phrase in Justin to a failure of memory in his attempt to quote τί περισσὸν ποιεῖτε of Mt. 5:47 (p. 44); whereas Massaux (pp. 428 f.) argues that this phrase in *Apol.* 15:9 was merely suggested by the τί περισσὸν ποιεῖτε of Mt. 5:47.

[2] That Justin is actually not dependent upon Mt. 5:46 here is probable because of the fact that this phrase from Matthew's gospel is closely paralleled below in *Apol.* 15:10 c (τοῦτο καὶ οἱ τελῶναι ποιοῦσιν).

Mt. 5:47 (οὐχὶ καὶ οἱ ἐθνικοὶ τὸ αὐτὸ ποιοῦσιν;), Lk. 6:32 (καὶ γὰρ οἱ ἁμαρτωλοὶ τοὺς ἀγαπῶντας αὐτοὺς ἀγαπῶσιν), and Lk. 6:33 (καὶ οἱ ἁμαρτωλοὶ τὸ αὐτὸ ποιοῦσιν) are all approximate parallels. It is probable with reference to these two sections of Matthew and Luke that Matthew (τελῶναι and ἐθνικοί) probably preserves the reading of Q, which Luke has generalized to ἁμαρτωλοί in both instances in the interest of his Gentile audience.[1] ἁμαρτωλοί might also be regarded as an exaggeration of Q's τελῶναι and ἐθνικοί, and this exaggeration might have been carried even further by Justin (πόρνοι), for whom the meaning of the other words might have not been strong enough to convey the desired meaning. Such a progression implies that Justin's reading is a later form than that of Q or of our gospels, although it is not certain whether Justin was here dependent on our synoptic gospels or on a post-synoptic source.

The words ἐγὼ δὲ ὑμῖν λέγω of *Apol.* 15:9 have an almost exact parallel in Mt. 5:47 (ἐγὼ δὲ λέγω ὑμῖν), but the Lukan order ὑμῖν λέγω is evident. Justin's reading εὔχεσθε ὑπὲρ τῶν ἐχθρῶν ὑμῶν does not appear in Matthew or Luke; however, this reading is confirmed again in several allusions in Justin [2] and in other early fathers:

Apol. 14:3
καὶ ὑπὲρ τῶν ἐχθρῶν εὐχόμενοι, καὶ τοὺς ἀδίκως μισοῦντας πείθειν πειρώμενοι.

Dial. 35:8
διὸ καὶ ὑπὲρ ὑμῶν καὶ ὑπὲρ τῶν ἄλλων ἁπάντων ἀνθρώπων τῶν ἐχθραινόντων ἡμῖν εὐχόμεθα.

Dial. 96:3
ὑπὲρ τῶν ἐχθρῶν εὔχεσθαι

Dial. 133:6
εὔχεσθαι καὶ ὑπὲρ τῶν ἐχθρῶν καὶ ἀγαπᾶν τοὺς μισοῦντας καὶ εὐλογεῖν τοὺς καταρωμένους.[3]

Oxyrhynchus Papyrus 1224 (Klostermann, *Apocrypha* II, p. 26)
κ)αὶ π(ρ)οσεύχεσθε ὑπὲρ (τῶν ἐχθ)ρῶν ὑμῶν.

---

[1] So too John Martin Creed, *The Gospel According to St. Luke* (London, 1953), p. 94.

[2] *Dial.* 85:7, on the other hand, confirms the reading of the gospel texts: Ἰησοῦς ἐκέλευσεν ἀγαπᾶν καὶ τοὺς ἐχθρούς; however, this reference is not inconsistent with my thesis that a written source is probably behind this reading of *Apol.* 15:9. Certainly in making a mere allusion Justin could have recalled more readily the text of the gospels, whereas elsewhere he might be employing his special source.

[3] This text also confirms Justin's καὶ ἀγαπᾶτε τοὺς μισοῦντας ὑμᾶς καὶ εὐλογεῖτε τοὺς καταρωμένους ὑμῖν, a reading found in this form in none of our gospels (see below).

Didache 1:3 (Lake, I, p. 308)

Τούτων δὲ τῶν λόγων ἡ διδαχή ἐστιν αὕτη· εὐλογεῖτε τοὺς καταρωμένους ὑμῖν καὶ προσεύχεσθε ὑπὲρ τῶν ἐχθρῶν ὑμῶν, νηστεύετε δὲ ὑπὲρ τῶν διωκόντων ὑμᾶς· ποία γὰρ χάρις, ἐὰν ἀγαπᾶτε τοὺς ἀγαπῶντας ὑμᾶς; οὐχὶ καὶ τὰ ἔθνη τὸ αὐτὸ ποιοῦσιν; ὑμεῖς δὲ ἀγαπᾶτε τοὺς μισοῦντας ὑμᾶς, καὶ οὐκ ἔξετε ἐχθρόν.

Pseudoclementine *Homilies* XII, 32 (Rehm, *GCS*, p. 190)

δίκαιος πειρᾶται καὶ ἐχθροὺς ἀγαπᾶν καὶ λοιδοροῦντας εὐλογεῖν, ἔτι μὴν καὶ ὑπὲρ ἐχθρῶν εὔχεσθαι.

It is difficult to believe that these sources all accidentally agreed in misquoting the gospel text; rather it appears that they preserved another reading coming from a catechetical tradition which in turn is dependent on liturgical praxis of the post-apostolic church.[1]

The phrase καὶ ἀγαπᾶτε τοὺς μισοῦντας ὑμᾶς in *Apol.* 15:9 seems to have combined ἀγαπᾶτε of Mt. 5:44 or Lk. 6:27 with τοῖς μισοῦσιν ὑμᾶς of Lk. 6:27 here corrected for reasons of syntax to the accusative case. And Justin's εὐλογεῖτε τοὺς καταρωμένους ὑμῖν is based on Lk. 6:28 (εὐλογεῖτε τοὺς καταρωμένους) with the single improvement of altering ὑμᾶς to the dative ὑμῖν.[2] Both of these readings are in turn supported by *Dial.* 133:6 (see above). The final phrase καὶ εὔχεσθε ὑπὲρ τῶν ἐπηρεαζόντων ὑμᾶς is closest to Lk. 6:28 except for the use of the preposition ὑπὲρ from Matthew's text, a change made perhaps to conform with Justin's conscious desire to produce better Greek than that of the gospels.[3]

My investigation has led to the conclusion that either Justin or his source used elements from both Matthew and Luke, harmonizing and rearranging this material; and there is even evidence to indicate that Justin used a written source which came from a catechetical tradition which in turn was dependent on liturgical praxis of the post-apostolic church and which itself harmonized elements from both Matthew and Luke.

c. *Apology* 15:10

Apol. 15:10	Mt. 5:42, 47, 46	Lk. 6:30, 34, 32
a) Παντὶ τῷ	42 τῷ	30 παντὶ

---

[1] So too Massaux, "Le Texte du Sermon," p. 431. Further, the verb νηστεύετε in *Did.* 1:3 shows the influence of the early church in its concern for fasting, an indication perhaps of the use of this verse for catechetical reasons (see also Köster, *Synoptische Überlieferung*, p. 224 and Dibelius, *Formgeschichte*, p. 249).

[2] Blass-Debrunner-Funk, 152 (1).

[3] εὔχομαι ὑπέρ τινος (Bauer, p. 651).

αἰτοῦντι	αἰτοῦντί σε	αἰτοῦντί σε
δίδοτε καὶ	δός, καὶ	δίδου, καὶ
τὸν βουλόμενον	τὸν θέλοντα	ἀπὸ τοῦ
	ἀπὸ σοῦ	αἴροντος
δανείσασθαι	δανείσασθαι	τὰ σὰ
μὴ ἀποστραφῆτε.	μὴ ἀποστραφῆς.	μὴ ἀπαίτει.
b) εἰ γὰρ	⁴⁷καὶ ἐὰν	³⁴καὶ ἐὰν
δανείζετε	ἀσπάσησθε τοὺς	δανείσητε
παρ' ὧν	ἀδελφοὺς	παρ' ὧν
ἐλπίζετε	ὑμῶν	ἐλπίζετε
λαβεῖν,	μόνον,	λαβεῖν
τί καινὸν	τί περισσὸν	ποία ὑμῖν
ποιεῖτε;	ποιεῖτε;	χάρις ἐστίν;
	οὐχὶ καὶ	καὶ ἁμαρτωλοὶ
	οἱ ἐθνικοὶ	ἁμαρτωλοῖς
	τὸ αὐτὸ	δανείζουσιν ἵνα
	ποιοῦσιν;	ἀπολάβωσιν τὰ ἴσα.
	⁴⁶ἐὰν γὰρ ἀγαπήσητε	³²καὶ εἰ ἀγαπᾶτε
	τοὺς ἀγαπῶντας	τοὺς ἀγαπῶντας
	ὑμᾶς,	ὑμᾶς,
	τίνα μισθὸν ἔχετε;	ποία ὑμῖν χάρις ἐστιν;
c) τοῦτο καὶ	οὐχὶ καὶ	καὶ γὰρ
οἱ τελῶναι	οἱ τελῶναι	οἱ ἁμαρτωλοὶ
	τὸ αὐτὸ	τοὺς ἀγαπῶντας
ποιοῦσιν.	ποιοῦσιν;	αὐτοὺς ἀγαπῶσιν.

The opening phrase of *Apol.* 15:10a παντὶ τῷ αἰτοῦντι combines elements from both Mt. 5:42 (τῷ αἰτοῦντί) and Lk. 6:30 (παντὶ αἰτοῦντί),[1] but Justin's omission of σε found in both Matthew and Luke (and consequently in Q) can probably best be attributed to Justin's conciseness,[2] plus the fact that *Apol.* 15:10a here uses the plural δίδοτε where both Matthew (δός) and Luke (δίδου) use the singular. But Justin's use of the present imperative is closer to Luke's δίδου (also a present imperative) than to Matthew's δός (second aorist imperative).

---

[1] Q probably read the same as Matthew here and was strengthened by Luke to παντὶ αἰτοῦντί. That such a harmonization of Mt. 5:42 and Lk. 6:30 existed before Justin's time is supported by the reading of *Did.* 1:5, which has παντὶ τῷ αἰτοῦντί σε. See also Köster, *Synoptische Überlieferung*, pp. 226 ff. Further evidence of such harmonization is indicated by many manuscript witnesses of Lk. 6:30 that read παντὶ τῷ αἰτοῦντί σε (ADEHMPSUVXΓΔΛΞ al. pler. a c e f g²).

[2] So too Massaux, "Le Texte du Sermon," p. 431.

Justin's τὸν βουλόμενον has its closest parallel in Mt. 5:42 (τὸν θέλοντα); however, the change of verbs is here probably only for stylistic reasons.[1] Further, δανείσασθαι μὴ ἀποστραφῆτε in Apol. 15:10a has its parallel in Mt. 5:42 (δανείσασθαι μὴ ἀποστραφῇς) except for the change to the plural as with δίδοτε above. It is, therefore, apparent that Apol. 15:10a either harmonized Matthew and Luke or used a post-synoptic harmony.

Apol. 15:10b is apparently more closely related to Lk. 6:34 than to the parallel in Mt. 5:47. The γάρ of Apol. 15:10b is obviously added for the purpose of connecting this saying more closely with Apol. 15:10a. The change from ἐὰν δανείσητε in Lk. 6:30 to the indicative εἰ δανείζετε in Apol. 15:10 is probably a deliberate change to the indicative of reality to make more definite the significance of the saying.[2] Further, the form of Apol. 15:9 (εἰ ἀγαπᾶτε . . .) may have influenced this change. Only the phrase τί καινὸν ποιεῖτε of Apol. 15:10 differs from Luke; however, it has probably come into this text under the same influence that underlies its use in Apol. 15:9.[3]

For the parallel to Apol. 15:10c we must turn again to Matthew. Although Mt. 5:47 reads οὐχὶ καὶ οἱ ἐθνικοὶ τὸ αὐτὸ ποιοῦσιν; an even closer parallel is found in Mt. 5:46 (οὐχὶ καὶ οἱ τελῶναι τὸ αὐτὸ ποιοῦσιν;). The effect of changing what in Matthew's text is a question to an exclamation in Justin's version has the effect of strengthening the meaning, especially inasmuch as this verse already follows upon a question (τί καινὸν ποιεῖτε;).

The overall picture of Apol. 15:10 is significant. The first part is clearly a harmony of Mt. 5:42 and Lk. 6:30; the second part is based on Lk. 6:34, and the third part on Mt. 5:46. Indeed, Justin's source for Apol. 15:10 was a carefully constructed harmony of elements from Matthew and Luke.[4]

---

[1] Blass-Debrunner-Funk, 101 argues that βούλομαι is "more the considered will" and that θέλω is used more in Asia Minor and in Koine Greek. Perhaps Justin or his source here made the change in verbs to express more accurately the desired meaning.

[2] Blass-Debrunner-Funk, 372. This variant is further found in Lk. 6:34 (ADEFʷHKLPX al.pler.) perhaps under the influence of the textual tradition that underlies Apol. 15:10.

[3] Credner suggests (Beiträge, p. 223) that in both instances the variant τί καινὸν ποιεῖτε comes from an early Aramaic text mh ḥsd' ḏkwn = ποία χάρις ὑμῖν or τίνα μισθὸν ἔχετε that was misread as mh ḥdt' ḏkwn = τί καινὸν ποιεῖτε; but since none of our other evidence points to an Aramaic source but rather to a post-synoptic source, we must reject this hypothesis as fanciful.

[4] Bousset (p. 79) also believes that Justin's source for this saying in Apol. 15:10 must have been a source in which all of these elements stood; however, he concludes that this text was a pre-canonical source rather than a post-synoptic

d) *Apology* 15:14

This verse has been discussed above (pp. 14-17), where it was established that either Justin himself combined and edited Mt. 6:25f. and Lk. 12:22ff. or that he used a source that had already harmonized these elements.

e. *Apology* 16:7

In the previous chapter I have already analyzed this saying (pp. 17-20) and concluded that Justin has here harmonized elements from Matthew with material from either Mark or Luke.

f. *Apology* 16:11

This verse has already been discussed (pp. 22-25), and I have shown that Justin here used a harmony of Mt. 7:22f. and Lk. 13:26f. and that this harmony was known to other fathers in substantially the same form as that used by Justin.

g. *Apology* 17:2

Apol. 17:2	Mt. 22:15-21	Mk. 12:13-17	Lk. 20:20-25
			²⁰Καὶ παρατηρήσαντες ἀπέστειλαν
	¹⁵Τότε	¹³Καὶ	ἐγκαθέτους
	πορευθέντες	ἀποστέλλουσιν	ὑποκρινομένους
	οἱ Φαρισαῖοι	πρὸς αὐτὸν	ἑαυτοὺς
	συμβούλιον	τινας τῶν	δικαίους εἶναι,
	ἔλαβον	Φαρισαίων καὶ	ἵνα ἐπιλάβωνται
	ὅπως αὐτὸν	τῶν Ἡρῳδιανῶν	αὐτοῦ λόγου,
κατ᾽ ἐκεῖνο	παγιδεύσωσιν	ἵνα αὐτὸν	ὥστε παραδοῦναι
γὰρ τοῦ	ἐν λόγῳ.	ἀγρεύσωσιν	αὐτὸν τῇ ἀρχῇ
καιροῦ	¹⁶καὶ	λόγῳ.	καὶ τῇ ἐξουσίᾳ
	ἀποστέλλουσιν	¹⁴καὶ	τοῦ ἡγεμόνος.
προσελθόντες	αὐτῷ τοὺς	ἐλθόντες	²¹καὶ
τινὲς	μαθητὰς αὐτῶν	λέγουσιν	ἐπηρώτησαν
ἠρώτων	μετὰ τῶν	αὐτῷ·	αὐτὸν
αὐτόν,	Ἡρῳδιανῶν		λέγοντες·
	λέγοντας·		
	διδάσκαλε,	διδάσκαλε,	διδάσκαλε,

harmony as I have maintained. But the fact that Justin here has elements not found in Q but peculiar to either Matthew or Luke and that Justin's text shows certain improvements upon the readings of Matthew and Luke refutes Bousset's argument.

	οἴδαμεν ὅτι ἀληθὴς εἶ καὶ τὴν ὁδὸν τοῦ θεοῦ ἐν ἀληθείᾳ διδάσκεις, καὶ οὐ μέλει σοι περὶ οὐδενός, οὐ γὰρ βλέπεις εἰς πρόσωπον ἀνθρώπων·	οἴδαμεν ὅτι ἀληθὴς εἶ καὶ οὐ μέλει σοι περὶ οὐδενός· οὐ γὰρ βλέπεις εἰς πρόσωπον ἀνθρώπων, ἀλλ᾽ ἐπ᾽ ἀληθείας τὴν ὁδὸν τοῦ θεοῦ διδάσκεις.	οἴδαμεν ὅτι ὀρθῶς λέγεις καὶ διδάσκεις καὶ οὐ λαμβάνεις πρόσωπον, ἀλλ᾽ ἐπ᾽ ἀληθείας τὴν ὁδὸν τοῦ θεοῦ διδάσκεις·
	[17]εἰπὸν οὖν ἡμῖν, τί σοι δοκεῖ;		
εἰ δεῖ Καίσαρι φόρους τελεῖν.	ἔξεστιν δοῦναι κῆνσον Καίσαρι ἢ οὔ;	ἔξεστιν δοῦναι κῆνσον Καίσαρι ἢ οὔ; δῶμεν ἢ μὴ δῶμεν;	[22]ἔξεστιν ἡμᾶς Καίσαρι φόρον δοῦναι ἢ οὔ;
	[18]γνοὺς δὲ ὁ Ἰησοῦς τὴν πονηρίαν αὐτῶν εἶπεν·	[15]ὁ δὲ εἰδὼς αὐτῶν τὴν ὑπόκρισιν εἶπεν αὐτοῖς·	[23]κατανοήσας δὲ αὐτῶν τὴν πανουργίαν εἶπεν πρὸς αὐτούς·
	τί με πειράζετε ὑποκριταί;	τί με πειράζετε;	
	[19]ἐπιδείξατέ μοι τὸ νόμισμα τοῦ κήνσου οἱ δὲ προσήνεγκεν αὐτῷ δηνάριον.	φέρετέ μοι δηνάριον ἵνα ἴδω. [16]οἱ δὲ ἤνεγκαν.	[24]δείξατέ μοι δηνάριον·
καὶ ἀπεκρίνατο· Εἴπατέ μοι	[20]καὶ λέγει αὐτοῖς·	καὶ λέγει αὐτοῖς·	

τίνος εἰκόνα	τίνος ἡ εἰκὼν	τίνος ἡ εἰκὼν	τίνος ἔχει εἰκόνα
τὸ νόμισμα	αὕτη καὶ ἡ	αὕτη καὶ ἡ	καὶ
ἔχει;	ἐπιγραφή;	ἐπιγραφή;	ἐπιγραφήν;
οἱ δὲ ἔφασαν·	²¹λέγουσιν·	οἱ δὲ εἶπαν	οἱ δὲ εἶπαν·
		αὐτῷ·	
Καίσαρος.	Καίσαρος.	Καίσαρος·	Καίσαρος.
καὶ πάλιν	τότε	¹⁷ὁ δὲ Ἰησοῦς	²⁵ὁ δὲ
ἀνταπεκρίνατο	λέγει	εἶπεν	εἶπεν
αὐτοῖς·	αὐτοῖς·	αὐτοῖς·	πρὸς αὐτούς·
Ἀπόδοτε οὖν	ἀπόδοτε οὖν	τὰ Καίσαρος	τοίνυν ἀπόδοτε
τὰ Καίσαρος	τὰ Καίσαρος	ἀπόδοτε	τὰ Καίσαρος
τῷ Καίσαρι καὶ	Καίσαρι καὶ	Καίσαρι καὶ	Καίσαρι καὶ
τὰ τοῦ θεοῦ	τὰ τοῦ θεοῦ	τὰ τοῦ θεοῦ	τὰ τοῦ θεοῦ
τῷ θεῷ.	τῷ θεῷ.	τῷ θεῷ.	τῷ θεῷ.

This passage from Justin is not merely a saying of Jesus but rather a short version of the entire pericope of the question concerning the payment of tribute to Caesar. The opening words of *Apol.* 17:2 (κατ᾽ ἐκεῖνο γὰρ τοῦ καιροῦ προσελθόντες τινὲς) are not exactly parallel to any of the synoptic gospels, although προσελθόντες of *Apol.* 17:2 is perhaps reminiscent of Mk. 12:14 (ἐλθόντες). The phrase ἠρώτων αὐτόν, εἰ δεῖ Καίσαρι φόρους τελεῖν of *Apol.* 17:2 has parallels, however, in Luke. ἠρώτων αὐτόν of *Apol.* 17:2 is close to ἐπηρώτησαν αὐτὸν of Lk. 20:21, and Justin's φόρους τελεῖν is closer to φόρον δοῦναι of Lk. 20:22 than to δοῦναι κῆνσον of Mt. 22:17 or Mk. 12:14;[1] however, the relationship between this introduction and the synoptic parallels is so small that it is probable that this introductory material is a free composition of Justin based only loosely on the gospel sources.

The next phrase of *Apol.* 17:2 καὶ ἀπεκρίνατο· Εἴπατέ μοι, τίνος εἰκόνα τὸ νόμισμα ἔχει does not have an exact parallel in any of the gospels, although its closest parallel is found in Lk. 20:24, where τίνος ἔχει εἰκόνα is the closest parallel to τίνος εἰκόνα . . . ἔχει of *Apol.* 17:2. And the following οἱ δὲ ἔφασαν· Καίσαρος of *Apol.* 17:2 again finds no exact parallel in the synoptic gospels, nor indeed does it contain any elements that reveal

---

[1] The use of φόρους in the context of tribute to Caesar occurs again in Lk. 23:2 (τοῦτο εὕραμεν διαστρέφοντα τὸ ἔθνος ἡμῶν καὶ κωλύοντα φόρους Καίσαρι διδόναι, καὶ λέγοντα ἑαυτὸν χριστὸν βασιλέα εἶναι). The only occurrence of φόρους τελεῖν in the New Testament is in Rom. 13:6 (διὰ τοῦτο γὰρ καὶ φόρους τελεῖτε· λειτουργοὶ γὰρ θεοῦ εἰσιν εἰς αὐτὸ τοῦτο προσκαρτεροῦντες); however, there is nothing about the context of Rom. 13:6 to indicate that *Apol.* 17:2 is dependent upon Paul. I should rather incline to the position that *Apol.* 17:2 is here dependent upon Lk. 20:22, if indeed there is any written source behind this entire introductory section.

dependence upon any single gospel.[1] Καίσαρος, of course, occurs in all three of the synoptic gospels.

Justin then proceeds to introduce the saying of Jesus with the phrase καὶ πάλιν ἀνταπεκρίνατο αὐτοῖς, a formula unlike its parallel form in the synoptic gospels.[2] As in the case of all pronouncement stories, the point of the pericope is contained in a saying of Jesus, which generally comes at the end of the story. All of the preceding material is subordinate to this saying of Jesus, and it is perhaps for this reason that the text of *Apol.* 17:2 does not agree closely with any of the gospel parallels in the introductory material, although I have pointed above to certain features in *Apol.* 17:2 peculiar to the text of Lk. 20:22ff.

The actual saying of Jesus as contained in *Apol.* 17:2 (ἀπόδοτε οὖν τὰ Καίσαρος τῷ Καίσαρι καὶ τὰ τοῦ θεοῦ τῷ θεῷ) is identical to the text of Mt. 22:21 except that Matthew does not have τῷ before Καίσαρι in the best manuscripts.[3] From this investigation it appears that either Justin or his source abbreviated the introductory section of this material, although using many terms peculiar to the Lukan parallel; and for the saying of Jesus itself, Justin or his source is apparently based on Mt. 22:21 in a version similar to that underlying certain later manuscript witnesses.

---

[1] Whereas *Apol.* 17:2 has οἱ δὲ ἔφασαν· Καίσαρος, Mt. 22:21 has λέγουσιν· Καίσαρος, Mk. 12:16 has οἱ δὲ εἶπαν αὐτῷ· Καίσαρος, and Lk. 20:24 has οἱ δέ εἶπαν· Καίσαρος.

[2] The verb ἀνταπεκρίνατο of *Apol.* 17:2 is similar to some variant manuscripts of Mark and Luke at this point:

Mk. 12:17 καὶ (om. 433 Syr.s. Arm.) ἀποκριθεὶς ὁ Ἰησοῦς (om. ὁ Ἰησοῦς W 238. 517. Geo.A) AS(W)ΧΓΠΣΦ⸖ p 45vid. fam. 1. fam. 13. 22 543. 28. 157. (517.) al.pler. Syr. (s.)hl. Geo.) Aeth. (Arm.); ἀποκριθεὶς δὲ ὁ Ἰησοῦς (om. ὁ Ἰησοῦς Θ 565) D(Θ) (565). 700. it.pler. vg.pler.

Lk. 20:25 ἀποκριθέντες δὲ ACΔΛΠ unc.7 al.pler. f Goth. Syr. pesh.; ἀποκριθέντες ΔΓ 1. 118. 131. 209. 239. it.pler. vg.

However, this manuscript evidence by no means indicates that Justin's ἀνταπεκρίνατο is related to such a textual variant, because in each case the gospel texts have a participial form of the verb ἀποκρίνομαι coupled with the finite verb whereas *Apol.* 17:2 uses the aorist indicative of the derived verb ἀνταποκρίνομαι. Indeed, Justin or his source may have chosen to use this word, independent of the similar form in the manuscript variants of Mt. 12:17 and Lk. 20:25, especially when we realize that the use of such a verb is quite natural in a dialogue such as exists between Jesus and his interrogators in the text of *Apol.* 17:2.

[3] The order of the Markan parallel is different, and is lacking in Mk. 12:17. The text of Lk. 20:25, in turn, has τοίνυν ἀπόδοτε where *Apol.* 17:2 reads ἀπόδοτε οὖν. It is significant that several manuscripts of Mt. 22:21 add τῷ before Καίσαρι (ΔΚΟΔΘΠ 27. 265. 291. 474. 489. 565. 700. 892. 1219. 1346) and are perhaps dependent on the same tradition that underlies Justin here. The addition of τῷ here is an indication that what was in Matthew a proper name is now used as a title or office (Blass-Debrunner-Funk), 254 (1); Bauer, pp. 781 f.).

3. Sayings that show features of harmonization of Matthew with Mark

a. Apology 15:2

Apol. 15:2	Mt. 5:29	Mt. 18:9	Mk. 9:47
Εἰ ὁ	εἰ δὲ ὁ	καὶ εἰ ὁ	καὶ ἐὰν ὁ
ὀφθαλμός σου	ὀφθαλμός σου	ὀφθαλμός σου	ὀφθαλμός σου
ὁ δεξιὸς	ὁ δεξιὸς		
σκανδαλίζει	σκανδαλίζει	σκανδαλίζει	σκανδαλίζῃ
σε,	σε,	σε,	σε,
ἔκκοψον	ἔξελε .	ἔξελε	ἔκβαλε
αὐτὸν·	αὐτὸν	αὐτὸν	αὐτόν·
	καὶ βάλε	καὶ βάλε	
	ἀπὸ σοῦ·	ἀπὸ σοῦ·	
συμφέρει γάρ	συμφέρει γάρ	καλόν σοί	καλόν σέ
σοι	σοι	ἐστιν	ἐστιν
μονόφθαλμον	ἵνα ἀπόληται	μονόφθαλμον	μονόφθαλμον
εἰσελθεῖν εἰς	ἓν τῶν	εἰς τὴν	εἰσελθεῖν εἰς
τὴν βασιλείαν	μελῶν σου	ζωὴν	τὴν βασιλείαν
τῶν οὐρανῶν,	καὶ μὴ	εἰσελθεῖν,	τοῦ θεοῦ,
ἢ μετὰ τῶν	ὅλον τὸ	ἢ δύο ὀφθαλ-	ἢ δύο ὀφθαλ-
δύο	σῶμά	μοὺς ἔχοντα	μοὺς ἔχοντα
πεμφθῆναι	σου βληθῇ	βληθῆναι	βληθῆναι
εἰς τὸ	εἰς	εἰς τὴν	εἰς τὴν
αἰώνιον πῦρ.	γέενναν.	γέενναν	γέενναν,
		τοῦ πυρός.	

The opening phrase of *Apol.* 15:2 (εἰ ὁ ὀφθαλμός σου ὁ δεξιὸς σκανδαλίζει σε finds its gospel parallel in Mt. 5:29, the only difference being Justin's omission of the connective particle δὲ of Matthew's text. Justin's ἔκκοψον αὐτόν has no gospel parallel in this verse, but it obviously has its origin in Mt. 5:30 (ἔκκοψον αὐτήν) and/or Mt. 18:8 (ἔκκοψον αὐτὸν), where the reference is to cutting off the right hand (in Mt. 18:9 the hand or the foot). This reading finds further patristic support a few years later in Clement of Alexandria and in the fifth century in Theodoret:

Clem. Alex., *Paed.* III, 11, 70 (Stählin, I, *GCS*, p. 274)
εἰ σκανδαλίζει σε ὁ ὀφθαλμός σου, ἔκκοψον αὐτόν.

Clem. Alex., *Liber Quis Dives Salvetur* 24 (Stählin, III, *GCS*, p. 175)
κἂν ὁ δέξιός σου ὀφθαλμὸς σκανδαλίζῃ σε, ταχέως ἔκκοψον αὐτόν.

Theodoret, *Eccles. Hist.* II, 31, 12-13 (Schneidweiler, *GCS*, p. 173)
"εἰ ὁ ὀφθαλμός σου ὁ δεξιὸς σκανδαλίζει σε, ἔκκοψον αὐτόν, καὶ βάλε

ἀπὸ σοῦ." ταῦτα δὲ καὶ περὶ χειρὸς καὶ ποδὸς ὁ δεσπότης ἐνομοθέτησε καὶ προστέθεικε· "συμφέρει γάρ σοι ἵνα ἀπόληται ἓν τῶν μελῶν σου, καὶ μὴ ὅλον τὸ σῶμά σου βληθῇ εἰς γέενναν.

The rest of *Apol.* 15:2 shows evidence of harmonization of Matthew and Mark. Justin's phrase συμφέρει γάρ σοι is apparently derived from Mt. 5:29, whereas Mt. 18:9 and Mk. 9:47 have καλόν σοί (σέ) ἐστιν. μονόφθαλμον of *Apol.* 15:2 has a parallel in both Mt. 18:9 and Mk. 9:47; however, Justin's following phrase εἰσελθεῖν εἰς τὴν βασιλείαν τῶν οὐρανῶν is certainly based on Mk. 9:47 (εἰσελθεῖν εἰς τὴν βασιλείαν τοῦ θεοῦ), of which Justin or his source has changed βασιλείαν τοῦ θεοῦ to βασιλείαν τῶν οὐρανῶν.[1]

Justin's phrase ἢ μετὰ τῶν δύο πεμφθῆναι εἰς τὸ αἰώνιον πῦρ has no exact parallel in Matthew or Mark; however, Justin's text is certainly based on Mt. 18:9 and/or Mk. 9:47, which read ἢ δύο ὀφθαλμοὺς ἔχοντα βληθῆναι εἰς τὴν γέενναν (τοῦ πυρός). The verb πέμπω never occurs in the gospels or in the rest of the New Testament in this context; however, Justin five times uses πέμπω in similar contexts (*Apol.* 16:12 πέμπωνται εἰς τὸ αἰώνιον πῦρ;[2] *Apol.* 28:1 εἰς τὸ πῦρ πεμφθήσεσθαι; *Apol.* 52:3 εἰς τὸ αἰώνιον πῦρ πέμψει; *Dial.* 45:4 εἰς κρίσιν καὶ καταδίκην τοῦ πυρὸς ... πεμφθῶσιν; *Dial.* 120:5 ἐπὶ τὴν καταδίκην τοῦ ἀσβέστου πυρὸς ... πέμπειν).

From this analysis it is certain that either Justin or his source has harmonized Mt. 5:29 and Mk. 9:47 (and perhaps Mt. 18:9).[3]

b. *Apology* 16:6

This passage has already been analyzed along with its parallels in Justin (see above, pp. 37-43), where it was concluded that *Apol.* 16:6 reflects harmonization of Mt. 22:38, Mt. 4:10, Mk. 12:30, and non-synoptic *Didache*-like material.

---

[1] This preference of βασιλεία τῶν οὐρανῶν over βασιλεία τοῦ θεοῦ is a long recognized feature of Matthew's gospel. That Justin shared a similar preference for βασιλεία τῶν οὐρανῶν over βασιλεία τοῦ θεοῦ is demonstrated by the fact that although he has βασιλεία τῶν οὐρανῶν eleven times (*Apol.* 15:2; 15:4; 15:16; 16:9; 61:4; *Dial.* 51:2; 51:3; 76:4; 105:6; 120:6; 140:4), Justin never uses the phrase βασιλεία τοῦ θεοῦ.

[2] In both *Apol.* 15:2 and 16:12 (see above, p. 69) Justin is apparently avoiding a reference to Gehenna, and in both instances he uses the same construction: the verb πέμπω with εἰς τὸ αἰώνιον πῦρ; and although this construction is absent from the New Testament, it has been shown above that it is consistent with Justin's style.

[3] Baldus (p. 62) and Massaux (*Influence de l'Evangile*, 468) both argue that Justin is dependent on Mt. 5:29 and Mt. 18:9; however, they fail to account for the Markan phrase εἰσελθεῖν εἰς τὴν βασιλείαν (τῶν οὐρανῶν) in Justin's text.

4. *Sayings that combine different parts of the same gospel*

a. *Apology* 15:12

Apol. 15:12	Mt. 16:26; 6:20	Mk. 8:36, 37	Lk. 9:25
τί γὰρ	16:26 τί γὰρ	36 τί γὰρ	τί γὰρ
ὠφελεῖται	ὠφεληθήσεται	ὠφελεῖ	ὠφελεῖται
ἄνθρωπος,	ἄνθρωπος	ἄνθρωπον	ἄνθρωπος
ἂν τὸν κόσμον	ἐὰν τὸν κόσμον	κερδῆσαι τὸν	κερδήσας τὸν
ὅλον κερδήσῃ,	ὅλον κερδήσῃ,	κόσμον ὅλον	κόσμον ὅλον
τὴν δὲ ψυχὴν	τὴν δὲ ψυχὴν	καὶ ζημιωθῆναι	ἑαυτὸν δὲ
αὐτοῦ	αὐτοῦ	τὴν ψυχὴν	ἀπολέσας ἢ
ἀπολέσῃ;	ζημιωθῇ;	αὐτοῦ;	ζημιωθείς;
ἢ τί	ἢ τί	37τί γὰρ	
δώσει αὐτῆς	δώσει ἄνθρωπος	δοῖ ἄνθρωπος	
ἀντάλλαγμα;	ἀντάλλαγμα τῆς	ἀντάλλαγμα τῆς	
	ψυχῆς αὐτοῦ;	ψυχῆς αὐτοῦ;	
θησαυρίζετε	6:20 θησαυρίζετε		
οὖν	δὲ ὑμῖν		
	θησαυροὺς		
ἐν τοῖς	ἐν		
οὐρανοῖς,	οὐρανῷ,		
ὅπου οὔτε	ὅπου οὔτε		
σὴς οὔτε	σὴς οὔτε		
βρῶσις	βρῶσις		
ἀφανίζει.	ἀφανίζει,		
	καὶ ὅπου		
	κλέπται οὐ		
	διορύσσουσιν		
	οὐδὲ κλέπτουσιν·		

The phrase τί γὰρ ὠφελεῖται ἄνθρωπος of *Apol.* 15:12 has its parallel in Lk. 9:25, which is here identical to Justin's text.[1] Justin's ἂν τὸν κόσμον ὅλον κερδήσῃ, however, has its closest parallel in Mt. 16:26 (ἐὰν τὸν κόσμον ὅλον κερδήσῃ). The phrase τὴν δὲ ψυχὴν αὐτοῦ ἀπολέσῃ of *Apol.* 15:12 is apparently based on τὴν δὲ ψυχὴν αὐτοῦ from Mt. 16:26 and ἀπολέσας from Lk. 9:25, here altered to ἀπολέσῃ to parallel the previous

---

[1] Several manuscript witnesses of Mt. 16:26 (CDEFGHKMSUVWX ΓΔΠΣ‫ 118. 209. 28. 565. 892. al.pler. it.pler. vg. Arm.) read τί γὰρ ὠφελεῖται ἄνθρωπος; however, this reading is probably not original but is the result of the same harmonization apparent in *Apol.* 15:12.

κερδήση of *Apol.* 15:12.[1] Further evidence of this harmonization of ἀπολέσας from Luke into the otherwise Matthaean material is evident in Clement of Alexandria:

Strom. VI, 14, 112 (Stählin, II, *GCS*, p. 488)

"τί γὰρ ὄφελος, ἐὰν τὸν κόσμον κερδήσης," φησί, "τὴν δὲ ψυχὴν ἀπολέσης;"

The wording of the second question in *Apol.* 15:12 (ἢ τί δώσει αὐτῆς ἀντάλλαγμα;) is obviously based on the Matthaean parallel, but either Justin or his source has omitted from Mt. 16:26 the subject ἄνθρωπος, obvious from the first part of Justin's text. Further, Matthew's τῆς ψυχῆς αὐτοῦ, also known from the previous question, has been replaced in *Apol.* 15:12 by the pronoun αὐτῆς.

The second part of *Apol.* 15:12 is obviously based on Mt. 6:20 with assimilation to *Apol.* 15:11b (see above, p. 61f.). The addition of οὖν in *Apol.* 15:12 serves the obvious function of relating the saying to the preceding material. The problems related to Matthew's use of ὑμῖν θησαυροὺς have already been discussed above (p. 61f.), and Justin has apparently chosen in *Apol.* 15:12 to use the imperative θησαυρίζετε alone. Further, Justin's preference for ἐν τοῖς οὐρανοῖς over ἐν οὐρανῷ has already been analyzed (p. 62f.), and it was argued that ἐν τοῖς οὐρανοῖς was apparently a consistent element of Justin's source.

This analysis points to the conclusion that *Apol.* 15:12 reflects combination of Mt. 16:26 and Mt. 6:20 with some evidence of harmonization of material from Lk. 9:25.

b. *Apology* 15:16

Apol. 15:16	Mt. 6:33; 6:21	Lk. 12:31, 34
ζητεῖτε	6:33 ζητεῖτε	31πλὴν ζητεῖτε
δὲ	δὲ πρῶτον	
τὴν βασιλείαν	τὴν βασιλείαν	τὴν βασιλείαν
τῶν οὐρανῶν,		
	καὶ τὴν	
	δικαιοσύνην αὐτοῦ,	αὐτοῦ,
καὶ ταῦτα πάντα	καὶ ταῦτα πάντα	καὶ ταῦτα
προστεθήσεται ὑμῖν.	προστεθήσεται ὑμῖν.	προστεθήσεται ὑμῖν.

---

[1] It is also possible that ἀπολέση of *Apol.* 15:12 is derived from Mt. 16:25 (ὃς γὰρ ἐὰν θέλη τὴν ψυχὴν αὐτοῦ σῶσαι, ἀπολέσαι αὐτήν· ὃς ἀπολέση τὴν ψυχὴν αὐτοῦ ἕνεκεν ἐμοῦ, εὑρήσει αὐτήν); but it is not unlikely that Justin or his source had both Mt. 16:25 and Lk. 9:25 in mind in inserting ἀπολέση into a phrase that is otherwise based on Mt. 16:26.

ὅπου γὰρ	6:21 ὅπου γὰρ	34 ὅπου γὰρ
ὁ θησαυρός ἐστιν	ἐστιν ὁ θησαυρός σου,	ἐστιν ὁ θησαυρὸς ὑμῶν,
ἐκεῖ	ἐκεῖ ἔσται	ἐκεῖ
καὶ ὁ νοῦς	καὶ ἡ καρδία	καὶ ἡ καρδία
τοῦ ἀνθρώπου.	σου.	ὑμῶν ἔσται.

The first part of *Apol.* 15:16 (ζητεῖτε δὲ τὴν βασιλείαν τῶν οὐρανῶν, καὶ ταῦτα πάντα προστεθήσεται ὑμῖν) is more closely related to Mt. 6:33 than to the Lukan parallel, but it is not possible to determine definitely whether Justin's source here was Matthew's pre-synoptic source Q, the Gospel of Matthew itself, or a post-synoptic text based on Mt. 6:33.

The absence of πρῶτον in Justin's text gives to the passage a slightly less forceful meaning than the Matthaean parallel. The words τῶν οὐρανῶν in *Apol.* 15:16 are certainly an addition made by either Justin or his source; the absence of these words from both Matthew and Luke indicates that they were probably not in Q. Further, we have seen that Justin or his source has a special fondness for the phrase βασιλεία τῶν οὐρανῶν (see above, p. 88). This inclination probably accounts for the addition here, but it is also significant that Justin's audience would probably have misunderstood the word βασιλεία without the addition τῶν οὐρανῶν.

The absence of Matthew's καὶ τὴν δικαιοσύνην αὐτοῦ from Justin's text may be a deliberate suppression made by Justin, who may have regarded the word as too technical for his pagan audience.[1] Justin's καὶ ταῦτα πάντα προστεθήσεται ὑμῖν is identical to Mt. 6:33, whereas the Lukan parallel does not have πάντα. Further evidence supporting Justin's text here is provided by Clement of Alexandria:

Strom. IV, 6, 34 (Stählin, II, *GCS*, p. 263)

   ζητεῖτε δὲ πρῶτον τὴν βασιλείαν τῶν οὐρανῶν καὶ τὴν δικαιοσύνην.

Paed. II, 12, 120 (Stählin, I, *GCS*, p. 229)

   ζητεῖτε πρῶτον τὴν βασιλείαν τῶν οὐρανῶν, καὶ ταῦτα πάντα προστεθήσεται ὑμῖν.

That Clement is in some way dependent upon the Matthaean version of this saying is indicated by the appearance of Matthew's πρῶτον in both of the above quotations. Clement, however, both times agrees with Justin's reading βασιλείαν τῶν οὐρανῶν, and *Paed.* II, 12, 120 is identical to Justin's text except for the inclusion of πρῶτον not found in *Apol.* 15:16 and the absence of δὲ in Clement's text, a difference of no real significance.

---

[1] See above, p. 63. So too Massaux, *Influence de l'Evangile*, p. 486.

This evidence leads to the conclusion that Justin shared with Clement a text related to Mt. 6:33, but it has not been possible to determine whether Justin used a presynoptic or a post-synoptic version of this saying or whether he used the gospel itself as his source.

Apol. 15:16b reproduces a saying apparently related to Mt. 6:21 and/or Lk. 12:34. Although Justin's version of this saying differs considerably from the gospel parallels, there are patristic texts that show features in common with Justin's version:

Clem. Alex., *Strom.* VII, 12, 77 (Stählin, III, *GCS*, p. 55)
"ὅπου γὰρ ὁ νοῦς τινος," φησίν, "ἐκεῖ καὶ ὁ θησαυρὸς αὐτοῦ."

Clem. Alex., *Liber Quis Dives Salvetur* 17, 1 (Stählin, III, *GCS*, p. 170)
ὅπου γὰρ ὁ νοῦς τοῦ ἀνθρώπου, ἐκεῖ καὶ ὁ θησαυρὸς αὐτοῦ.

Macarius of Egypt, *Homily* XLIII, 3 (Migne, *PG*, XXXIV, 773)
Ὅπου ὁ νοῦς σου, ἐκεῖ καὶ ὁ θησαυρός σου.

All three passages have νοῦς in agreement with Justin as opposed to καρδία in Matthew and Luke, and *Quis Dives Salvetur* 17, 1 even has Justin's ὁ νοῦς τοῦ ἀνθρώπου.[1] The dependence of these fathers on a common tradition is certain, but it is impossible to determine whether such a reading existed before Justin or whether he himself was its author. But it is, nevertheless, certain that there is underlying *Apol.* 15:16 a source related either to Mt. 6:33 and Mt. 6:21 (and/or Lk. 12:34) or to the gospel material itself.

c. *Apology* 16:2

Apol. 16:2	Mt. 5:22, 41, 16
a) ὃς δ᾽ ἂν ὀργισθῇ	[22]πᾶς ὁ ὀργιζόμενος
	τῷ ἀδελφῷ αὐτοῦ
ἔνοχος ἐστιν	ἔνοχος ἔσται
εἰς τὸ πῦρ.	τῇ κρίσει.
b) παντὶ δὲ	[41]καὶ ὅστις
ἀγγαρεύοντί σε	σε ἀγγαρεύσει
μίλιον	μίλιον ἕν,
ἀκολούθησον δύο.	ὕπαγε μετ᾽ αὐτοῦ δύο.
c) λαμψάτω δὲ	[16]οὕτως λαμψάτω

---

[1] Massaux argues (p. 437) that this substitution in Justin is due to his philosophical formation and to his tendency to generalize; the word καρδία with all its Jewish connotations was unsuitable for Justin's pagan audience, for whom νοῦς would be more comprehensible. Wright, too, maintains (p. 31) that the substitution of νοῦς for καρδία gives the quotation "the quasi-philosophical turn" appropriate for Justin's audience.

ὑμῶν τὰ καλὰ ἔργα	τὸ φῶς ὑμῶν
ἔμπροσθεν τῶν ἀνθρώπων,	ἔμπροσθεν τῶν ἀνθρώπων,
ἵνα βλέποντες	ὅπως ἴδωσιν
	ὑμῶν τὰ καλὰ ἔργα
θαυμάζωσι	καὶ δοξάσωσιν
τὸν πατέρα ὑμῶν	τὸν πατέρα ὑμῶν
τὸν ἐν τοῖς οὐρανοῖς.	τὸν ἐν τοῖς οὐραοῖς.

Apol. 16:2a has its gospel parallel in Mt. 5:22; however, Justin's ὃς δ' ἂν ὀργισθῇ is closer to the form of Mt. 5:21 (ὃς δ' ἂν φονεύσῃ) than to the form of Mt. 5:22 (πᾶς ὁ ὀργιζόμενος). The use of the present ἐστιν in *Apol.* 16:2, where Matthew has the future ἔσται, is an example of the futuristic use of the present by Justin [1] and is only a stylistic preference. Justin's εἰς τὸ πῦρ is probably a later reading than Matthew's τῇ κρίσει: in Matthew's context the phrase ἔνοχος τῇ κρίσει refers to legal proceedings before the proper authorities; [2] such an interpretation would certainly have had little meaning for Justin's audience, and for this reason either Justin or his source altered the text to the often used εἰς τὸ πῦρ. [3] It is, therefore, quite probable that either *Apol.* 16:2a or Justin's source is here based on Mt. 5:22 influenced perhaps by the form of Mt. 5:21.

Apol. 16:2b has its closest parallel in Mt. 5:41; however, Justin's phrase παντὶ δὲ ἀγγαρεύοντί σε apparently follows the form of Mt. 5:42 (τῷ αἰτοῦντί σε)[4] rather than the form of Mt. 5:41 (ὅστις σε ἀγγαρεύσει). Further, the use of the verb ἀκολούθησον in *Apol.* 16:2b to replace ὕπαγε μετ' αὐτοῦ of Mt. 5:41 may also have influenced the use of the dative in place of Matthew's construction. [5] In the Pseudoclementine literature we find a version of this saying similar to Justin's text:

Pseudoclementine *Homilies* XV, 5 (Rehm, *GCS*, p. 214)
ἀγγαρεύοντι δὲ μίλιον συναπέρχεσθαι δύο

This passage contains two peculiarities of Justin's text. The dative participle ἀγγαρεύοντι is an element found in both Justin and in Pseudo-Clement, and both likewise lack Matthew's ἔν. It is possible that these agreements point to a written tradition; however, there are also two

---

[1] Blass-Debrunner-Funk, 323. C. F. D. Moule, *An Idiom Book of New Testament Greek* (Cambridge, 1953), p. 7.

[2] M'Neile, p. 61; Willoughby C. Allen, *A Critical and Exegetical Commentary on the Gospel According to S. Matthew* (Edinburgh, 1951), p. 49.

[3] See above, p. 80.

[4] See above, pp. 8of.

[5] Blass-Debrunner-Funk, 193.

differences between the two texts. *Apol.* 16:2b has παντί, which does not occur in Pseudo-Clement or in Mt. 5:41; but, even more significant, Justin reads ἀκολούθησον for Pseudo-Clement's συναπέρχεσθαι and Matthew's ὕπαγε μετ' αὐτοῦ. Nevertheless, it seems probable that the agreement of *Apol.* 16:2b and Pseudoclementine *Homilies* XV, 5 points to a common tradition that was based on Mt. 5:41 and that Justin apparently adapted for his own use.

Apol. 16:2c finds its closest parallel in Mt. 5:16, although there are several significant differences between the two texts, the most significant of which is Justin's reading λαμψάτω δὲ ὑμῶν τὰ καλὰ ἔργα for Matthew's λαμψάτω τὸ φῶς ὑμῶν, a variant widely attested among the fathers:

Clem. Alex., *Strom.* III, 4, 36 (Stählin, II, *GCS*, p. 212)
τὰ ἀγαθὰ ὑμῶν ἔργα λαμψάτω.

Clem. Alex., *Strom.* IV, 26, 171 (Stählin, II, *GCS*, p. 324)
λαμψάτω γάρ σου τὰ ἔργα.

Eusebius, *Commentary in Psalm* 28 (*Migne, PG*, XXIII, 253)
Λαμψάτω τὰ ἔργα ὑμῶν ἔμπροσθεν τῶν ἀνθρώπων, ὅπως, βλέποντες τὰ καλὰ ὑμῶν ἔργα, δοξάσωσι τὸν Πατέρα ὑμῶν τὸν ἐν τοῖς οὐρανοῖς.

Tertullian, *De Cultu Feminarum* 13 (Migne, *PL*, I, 1447)
Luceant opera vestra

Tertullian, *De Idolatria* (Migne, *PL*, I, 759)
Sed luceant, inquit, opera vestra.

Origen, *Exhortatio ad Martyrium* 18 (Koetschau, I, *GCS*, p. 17)
λαμψάντων αὐτοῦ τῶν καλῶν ἔργων ἔμπροσθεν τῶν ἀνθρώπων.

Origen, *In Evangelium Joannis* II, 1, 5 (Preuschen, IV, *GCS*, p. 53)
παρὰ μὲν τὸ λάμπειν αὐτοῦ τὰ ἔργα ἔμπροσθεν τῶν ἀνθρώπων φωτός.

This wide agreement of evidence indicates that this tradition must have existed in a fixed text known to many of the church fathers, and the substitution of τὰ καλὰ ἔργα for Matthew's τὸ φῶς points to a post-Matthaean period in which the church discipline was concerned with the good works of its members.[1] Justin's use of the participle βλέποντες for Matthew's ἴδωσιν is supported by Eusebius, *Commentary in Psalm* 28 (see above); however, none of the patristic parallels supports Justin's

---

[1] Bousset maintains (p. 75) that these parallels point to the use of a written fixed text, which is possibly a pre-canonical source; however, there is no indication that this source is pre-canonical. On the contrary, the emphasis on good works probably points to a post-synoptic tradition based on Mt. 5:16.

use of the verb θαυμάζω, which Massaux maintains Justin deliberately substituted in order to avoid the verb δοξάζω, which had too Christian a flavor for a teaching destined for pagans.[1] This analysis indicates that for the saying in *Apol.* 16:2c either Justin or his source is based on Mt. 5:16.

d. *Apology* 16:6

This passage has already been analyzed along with its parallels in Justin (see above, pp. 37-43) where it was concluded that *Apol.* 16:6 reflects harmonization of Mt. 22:38, Mt. 4:10, Mk. 12:30, and non-synoptic *Didache*-like material.

e. *Apology* 16:13

I have already discussed this passage above along with its parallel *Dial.* 35:3a (pp. 44-47) where it was determined that Justin used a source that combined Mt. 24:5 with Mt. 7:15, 16, 19.

5. *Results*

The foregoing analysis of the individual *logia* found in *Apol.* 15-17 confirms the conclusions of the previous chapter. It has been demonstrated in this study of *Apol.* 15-17 (1) that Justin did not quote the sayings of Jesus from memory but that he used one or more written sources often quoted by other fathers in a form almost identical to Justin's version, and this patristic agreement occurs most often and most strikingly in Clement of Alexandria, Pseudoclementine *Homilies,* and Origen; (2) that Justin's text shows features of harmonization of Matthew and Luke; (3) that Justin's text occasionally harmonizes elements from Mark with other synoptic material; (4) that different parts of the same gospel were often combined into a single saying of Jesus; (5) that Justin occasionally quotes from a single gospel (either Matthew or Luke); and (6) that many late manuscripts preserve a textual tradition that reveals the influence of readings similar to those found in Justin. Each of these conclusions confirms the results reached in the last chapter, but it is now possible to go beyond these results and recognize the pattern that underlies the grouping of several sayings in *Apol.* 15-17.

---

[1] p. 442. He feels that the verb θαυμάζω was more suited to a pagan audience, and this observation is probably correct. Only in the Septuagint and in the New Testament does the verb δοξάζω have a meaning similar to its use in Mt. 5:16, and Justin may have realized that his pagan audience would not have fully comprehended this meaning. See Gerhard Kittel, "δοξάζω," *Theologisches Wörterbuch zum Neuen Testament,* Vol. II, pp. 256 f.; see also Liddell-Scott, p. 444.

a. *Apology* 15:1-4

In *Apol.* 15:1-4 we find four separate sayings of Jesus connected in Justin's text by the word καί.[1] This method of joining the four sayings would seem to indicate that these *logia* were known by Justin not to be a literary unit and that they were combined either by Justin or by his source through the use of the connective καί. Had the sayings been regarded as a literary or oral unit, one would not expect such an artificial method of joining them; however, there is underlying this group of sayings a definite pattern that is obvious from the following chart:

Apol.	*Gospel Parallels*			*Remarks*
15:1	*Mt.* 5:28			Justin used a source based on Mt. 5:28 and known to other fathers
15:2	*Mt.* 5:29	*Mt.* 18:9 *Mk.* 9:47		Either Justin or his source harmonized all three passages
15:3	(*Mt.* 5:32*b*)	Mt. 19:9 Mk. 10:12	*Lk.* 16:18*b*	Either Justin or his source used Lk. 16:18b (and perhaps Mt. 5:32b)
15:4	*Mt.* 19:11, 12			Either Justin or his source reworked the text of these verses

The above table seems to indicate not that Justin was accidentally combining in *Apol.* 15:1-4 four separate *logia* but rather that he had before him a written source that harmonized material from Matthew, Mark, and Luke. I have shown that in *Apol.* 15:1 Justin used a written source based on Mt. 5:28 and known to other church fathers. After

---

[1] Justin uses καί to connect sayings of Jesus in two other places, in the group of sayings in *Apol.* 15:10-17 (see below, p. 97) and in *Dial.* 35:3 (see below p. 100).

quoting from Mt. 5:28 this source of Justin proceeded to the material of Mt. 5:29, but this verse suggested the related material of Mt. 18:9 and its gospel parallel in Mk. 9:47, all of which were harmonized in Justin's source. Returning to the context of Matthew 5, Justin's source omitted Mt. 5:30-32a.[1] Instead Justin's source resumed with Mt. 5:32b, not quoting this verse itself but rather the Lukan version of the text suggested by this verse (Lk. 16:18b). But Justin's source then continued neither with Matthew 5 nor with Luke 16 but rather with Mt. 19:11, 12, the verse immediately following the Matthaean parallel of Lk. 16:18b (i.e. Mt. 19:9 [2]).

Our analysis of these four verses in *Apology* 15 would, therefore, lead us to the conclusion that Justin seems to have used as his source for *Apol.* 15:1-4 a carefully composed gospel harmony of elements from Matthew, Mark, and Luke.

b. *Apology* 15:10-17

These eight verses are combined in *Apology* 15 in such a way that we might expect that they have been drawn by Justin from a source in their present form. Instead of being isolated sayings, these several *logia* are joined together in a block except for the insertion of καί after *Apol.* 15:12 and again after *Apol.* 15:16.[3] And on three occasions either Justin or his source has added the connective δέ to these sayings to make this group a closer literary unit (15:11; 15:13; 15:14). The following table presents in synopsis the conclusions reached about these sayings in *Apol.* 15:10-17:

Apol. 15:10 harmony of Mt. 5:42, Lk. 6:30, Lk. 6:34, and Mt. 5:46

Apol. 15:11 based on Mt. 6:19, 20

Apol. 15:12 combines Mt. 16:26 and Mt. 6:20 (+ influence from Lk. 9:25)

Apol. 15:13 harmony of Lk. 6:36 and Mt. 5:45 (+ influence from Lk. 6:35 and Mt. 5:48)

---

[1] Massaux maintains ("Le Texte du Sermon," p. 417) that this omission is justifiable. "Mt 5:30 ferait double emploi; il s'agit là du scandale; or, Justin, loin de multiplier les répétitions, abrège, Mt. 5:31 renvoie a l'Ancien Testament: cette reminiscense de l'A.T. n'avait aucun intérêt pour les païens, lecteurs de l'apologie. Quant a Mt. 5:32 a, il révélait une discipline qui n'aurait pas été comprise des païens ou qui était peut-être abrogée a l'époque de Justin."

[2] Mt. 19:10 was justifiably omitted because it contained not a saying of Jesus but rather a statement of the apostles upon which Jesus comments in Mt. 19:11 f.

[3] Justin uses καί to connect sayings in two other places, *Apol.* 15:1-4 (see above, pp. 96) and *Dial.* 35:3 (see below, p. 100).

Apol. 15:14 harmony of Mt. 6:25, 26 and Lk. 12:22-24

Apol. 15:15 Mt. 6:31, 32 with minor changes and assimilation to
   Apol. 15:14

Apol. 15:16 related to Mt. 6:33 and Mt. 6:21 (and/or Lk. 12:34)

Apol. 15:17 Mt. 6:1 with minor changes and assimilation to the form
   of *Apol.* 15:10-16

Justin or his source seems to have followed the text of the Sermon on
the Mount and harmonized this material with related material from the
Lukan parallel and from other parts of Matthew. Indeed it appears that
this entire section was based on a written source that followed the text
of Matthew 5 and 6, harmonizing related elements from Matthew and
Luke with this material from the Sermon on the Mount.

c. *Apology* 16:1, 2

That *Apol.* 16:1 and 16:2 are grouped together is not surprising,
because both verses are based on material either contained in or suggested
by Matthew 5. Although I have argued that *Apol.* 16:1 is based on the
text of Lk. 6:29, this passage finds its gospel parallel in Mt. 5:39, 40.
Apol. 16:2 is based on Mt. 5:22, 41, 16, material in close proximity to the
Matthaean parallel to *Apol.* 16:1. It is, therefore, not surprising to find
these four sayings combined in the text of *Apol.* 16:1, 2. And as was the
case in *Apol.* 15:11, 13, 14, either Justin or his source has in *Apol.* 16:2
added the particle δέ to connect more closely the two sayings.

d. *Apology* 16:6, 7

The two sayings in *Apol.* 16:6, 7 are derived from two different parts
of the synoptic gospels, and it appears that the only connection between
the two is their unity of theme, the worship of God. Justin has perhaps
attempted to bring these two verses into closer relationship by balancing
the phrase κύριον τὸν θεὸν τὸν ποιήσαντά σε of *Apol.* 16:6 with the phrase
ὁ ποιήσας τὰ πάντα in Apol. 16:7.[1]

e. *Apology* 16:9-13

Inasmuch as *Apol.* 16:9-13 also appears in Justin's text as a single
unit, it seems important, now that I have examined each of these verses
separately, to determine whether any conclusions can be drawn about
this section as a whole. The following table summarizes the results of the
investigation of the individual verses:

---

[1] See above, p. 42 n. 1.

Apol. 16:9 almost identical to Mt. 7:21
Apol. 16:10 based on a variant version of Lk. 10:16
Apol. 16:11 harmony of Mt. 7:22, 23 and Lk. 13:26, 27
Apol. 16:12 based on Mt. 13:42, 43
Apol. 16:13 combines Mt. 24:5

This chart does not seem to reveal any significant pattern, but on closer examination significant results emerge. *Apol.* 16:9 reproduces almost verbatim the text of Mt. 7:21; however, it is important to remember that the Lukan parallel to this verse is Lk. 6:46. The following verse Lk. 6:47 has been incorporated into the text of Lk. 10:16 in *Apol.* 16:10. Thus although Lk. 6:46f. does not appear in either *Apol.* 16:9 or 16:10, the Lukan context has provided the bridge between the material in *Apol.* 16:9 and 16:10.

In *Apol.* 16:11 Justin's source apparently returns to the order of the text of Matthew, resuming with Mt. 7:22, 23 and harmonizing this material with Lk. 13:26, 27. Then following the Lukan order, we find in Lk. 13:28 ἐκεῖ ἔσται ὁ κλαυθμὸς κ.τ.λ., which is parallel to Mt. 13:42 and it is with this material that Justin continues by reworking the text of Mt. 13:42, 43 in *Apol.* 16:12. In *Apol.* 16:13 Justin's source again returns to the order of Matthew 7, harmonizing Mt. 24:5 with Mt. 7:15, 16, 19.

This progression can be diagrammed as follows:

Apol. 16:9 *Mt.* 7:21 ———————→ Lk. 6:46
                   | ↓
Apol. 16:10   ↓   Lk. 6:47 ————————→ *Lk.* 10:16
Apol. 16:11 *Mt.* 7:22f. and *Lk.* 13:26f.
                   | ↓
Apol. 16:12   ↓   Lk. 13:28 ————————→ *Mt.* 13:42f.
Apol. 16:13 *Mt.* 7:15, 16, 19, and *Mt.* 24:5

And to group these sayings into an even more unified section, either Justin or his source has twice added connective particles: γάρ in *Apol.* 16:10 and δέ in *Apol.* 16:11.

Therefore, we can conclude with certainty that these five verses are based on a source that was a carefully composed harmony of material from Matthew and Luke and that was based on the order of Matthew 7.[1] It has already been argued above that the entire section *Apol.* 15-17 may

---

[1] The same conclusion has been reached by Köster (*Synoptische Überlieferung*, pp. 86 ff.), who analyzes this material in detail.

have been based on a single source different from the source underlying the rest of Justin's sayings of Jesus,[1] and I have tried to indicate that this section has many features in common with primitive Christian catechisms.[2] It is, therefore, quite probable from the foregoing discussion that there is underlying *Apol.* 15-17 a primitive Christian catechism in use in Justin's school in Rome, a catechism that was known in similar form to Clement of Alexandria, Origen, and the author of the Pseudo-clementine *Homilies*, a catechism based primarily on the text of the Sermon on the Mount but that harmonized related material from Mark, Luke, and from other parts of Matthew, and a catechism whose tradition was of great influence in later manuscript witnesses of the synoptic gospels.

B. Dialogue 35:3

εἶπε γάρ. 1) Πολλοὶ ἐλεύσονται ἐπὶ τῷ ὀνόματί μου, ἔξωθεν ἐνδεδυμένοι δέρματα προβάτων, ἔσωθεν δέ εἰσι λύκοι ἅρπαγες. καί· 2) Ἔσονται σχίσματα καὶ αἱρέσεις. καί. 3) Προσέχετε ἀπὸ τῶν ψευδοπροφητῶν, οἵτινες ἐλεύσονται πρὸς ὑμᾶς, ἔξωθεν ἐνδεδυμένοι δέρματα προβάτων, ἔσωθεν δέ εἰσι λύκοι ἅρπαγες. καί· 4) Ἀναστήσονται πολλοὶ ψευδόχριστοι καὶ ψευδοαπόστολοι, καὶ πολλοὺς τῶν πιστῶν πλανήσουσιν.

Dial. 35:3 contains four anti-heretical sayings of Jesus here appearing together for the first time in extant patristic literature and joined in Justin's text by the connective καί.[3] Parallels to three of the four sayings appear in the synoptic gospels, and parallels to each of the four sayings appear in the patristic literature. I shall, therefore, proceed to a separate study of each of the four sayings with its gospel and patristic parallels and then try to assess the reason for the appearance of the four sayings together in *Dial.* 35:3.

1. *The First Logion*

This saying has already been discussed in detail with its parallel text *Apol.* 16:13 (see above, pp. 44-47, 95) where it was demonstrated that as his source for this *logion* Justin used a text that harmonized Mt. 24:5 with Mt. 7:15, (16, 19), a source known in similar form to the authors of the *Apostolic Constitutions* (6, 13) and the Pseudoclementine *Homilies* (XI, 35).

---

[1] See above, p. 47 n. 2.

[2] See above, pp. 54-57.

[3] Justin connects sayings of Jesus with the particle καί in two other places, *Apol.* 15:1-4 (see above, p. 96) and *Apol.* 15:10-17 (see above, p. 97).

2. The Second Logion

Ἔσονται σχίσματα καὶ αἱρέσεις.

Dial. 35:3b presents two major difficulties: (1) there are no gospel parallels to this saying and only a single instance in the entire New Testament where the terms σχίσματα and αἱρέσεις occur in the same context, I Cor. 11:18f;[1] and (2) although this saying has no gospel parallels, it has three close parallels in the early patristic literature:

Syriac Didascalia VI, 5 (quoted from Resch, Agrapha, p. 100)[2]

ὡς καὶ ὁ κύριος καὶ σωτὴρ ἡμῶν ἔφη ὅτι ἔσονται αἱρέσεις καὶ σχίσματα.

Didymus, De Trinitate III, 22 (Migne, PG, XXXIX, 920)

ὁ ἀποδεχθεὶς ἔχειν θησαυροὺς σοφίας καὶ γνώσεως, καὶ προμηνύσας·
Ἔσονται ἐν ὑμῖν αἱρέσεις καὶ σχίσματα.

Lactantius, Div. Instit. IV, 30 (Migne, PL, VI, 540)

ante omnia scire nos convenit, et ipsum et legatos eius praedixisse, quod plurimae sectae et haereses haberent existere.

All three of these passages are very close to Dial. 35:3b; however, two of them have the word order αἱρέσεις καὶ σχίσματα whereas Dial. 35:3b reads σχίσματα καὶ αἱρέσεις. The appearance of this saying in Justin, Didymus, Lactantius, and the Didascalia leaves little doubt that this logion, whether an authentic saying of Jesus or not, circulated as such in the early church.[3] It appears, therefore, that we are dealing with a logion attributed to Jesus at an early date; and although it was not preserved in the gospel material, the saying has been preserved independently by Justin, Didymus Lactantius, and the Syriac Didascalia.[4] But whether this patristic saying was actually based on I Cor. 11:18f. or whether Paul actually knew such a saying of Jesus is uncertain;

---

[1] πρῶτον μὲν γὰρ συνερχομένων ὑμῶν ἐν ἐκκλησίᾳ ἀκούω σχίσματα ἐν ὑμῖν ὑπάρχειν, καὶ μέρος τι πιστεύω. δεῖ γὰρ καὶ αἱρέσεις ἐν ὑμῖν εἶναι, ἵνα καὶ οἱ δόκιμοι φανεροὶ γένωνται ἐν ὑμῖν.

[2] See also Bousset, p. 96. There is a German translation of the Syriac Didascalia by Hans Achelis and Johannes Flemming, Die Ältesten Quellen des Orientalischen Kirchenrechts, Zweites Buch: Die Syrische Didaskalia (Leipzig, 1904), p. 118; this text reads in translation: "Es werden Häresien und Spaltungen entstehen."

[3] Lactantius does not attribute these words to Jesus; however, the phrase does occur in a didactic section, and it is possible that Lactantius is here making an indirect reference to this saying of Jesus, although not referring to it as such.

[4] Wright does not take these patristic parallels into account when he maintains (p. 84) that this text is probably an "allusive quotation on the part of Justin." If, as Wright maintains, Justin's passage is a mere allusion to I Cor. 11:18 f., then it is difficult to account for the appearance of the saying in these three patristic writings in forms very close to the text of Dial. 35:3b. Furthermore, the use of Paul's epistles by Justin is another uncertain factor.

indeed, it is quite probable that Paul's text is completely unrelated to this *logion*, because the text of I Cor. 11:18f. makes no reference to a saying of Jesus. It appears more likely that this saying had its origin in the early church at a time, when the problem of heresy was becoming serious; perhaps this saying had its origin in the vocabulary of anti-heretical literature.

3. *The Third Logion*

Dial. 35:3c	Mt. 7:15
Προσέχετε	Προσέχετε
ἀπὸ τῶν ψευδοπροφητῶν,	ἀπὸ τῶν ψευδοπροφητῶν,
οἵτινες ἐλεύσονται πρὸς	οἵτινες ἔρχονται πρὸς
ὑμᾶς, ἔξωθεν ἐνδεδυμένοι	ὑμᾶς ἐν ἐνδύμασι
δέρματα προβάτων,	προβάτων,
ἔσωθεν δέ	ἔσωθεν δέ
εἰσι λύκοι ἅρπαγες.	εἰσιν λύκοι ἅρπαγες.

This third saying is very similar to the saying in *Dial.* 35:3a, and the two have perhaps been brought into harmony by either Justin or by his source in two instances. (1) The opening words of *Dial.* 35:3c (προσέχετε ἀπὸ τῶν ψευδοπροφητῶν, οἵτινες ἐλεύσονται πρὸς ὑμᾶς) are almost identical to the text of Mt. 7:15, the only difference being in the use of ἐλεύσονται in *Dial.* 35:3c, where Mt. 7:15 reads ἔρχονται; but this variation in the verb is probably the result of assimilation to *Dial.* 35:3a (πολλοὶ ἐλεύσονται ἐπὶ τῷ ὀνόματί μου), where ἐλεύσονται occurs in a similar context. (2) The second half of *Dial.* 35:3c (ἔξωθεν . . . ἅρπαγες) is identical to *Dial.* 35:3a, and it has already been argued in the section that analyzes *Dial.* 35:3a with its parallel *Apol.* 16:13 that this reading is based on Mt. 7:15 and is actually an improvement of the style of Matthew's text (see above, pp. 45f).

4. *The Fourth Logion*

Dial. 35:3d	Mt. 24:11	Mt. 24:24	Mk. 13:22
Ἀναστήσονται	καὶ	ἐγερθήσονται	ἐγερθήσονται
πολλοὶ	πολλοὶ	γὰρ	δὲ
ψευδόχριστοι	ψευσοπροφῆται	ψευδόχριστοι	ψευδόχριστοι
καὶ		καὶ	καὶ
ψευδοαπόστολοι,	ἐγερθήσονται	ψευδοπροφῆται,	ψευδοπροφῆται
		καὶ δώσουσιν	καὶ ποιήσουσιν
		σημεῖα μεγάλα	σημεῖα
		καὶ τέρατα,	καὶ τέρατα

καὶ πολλοὺς   καὶ πλανήσουσιν   ὥστε πλανῆσαι,   πρὸς τὸ ἀποπλανᾶν
τῶν πιστῶν

                                   εἰ δυνατόν,   εἰ δυνατόν,
πλανήσουσιν.   πολλούς.   καὶ τοὺς   τοὺς
                                     ἐκλεκτούς.   ἐκλεκτούς.

The Gospel of Matthew apparently contains two versions of this saying: (1) Mt. 24:24, which was based on Mk. 13:22, and (2) Mt. 24:11, which was probably derived from Matthew's peculiar source M. The verb ἀναστήσονται of *Dial.* 35:3d occurs in none of the gospel parallels, all of which have ἐγερθήσονται; but either Justin or his source apparently preferred the verb ἀνίστημι to its near-synonym ἐγείρω.[1] Justin's πολλοὶ has its only parallel in Mt. 24:11, and ψευδόχριστοι has parallels in Mt. 24:24 and Mk. 13:22. The phrase καὶ ψευδοαπόστολοι in *Dial.* 35:3d has no gospel parallel; however, ψευδοπροφῆται does appear in this instance in Mt. 24:24 and Mk. 13:22. It is quite probable that either Justin or his source changed this reading ψευδοπροφῆται to ψευδοαπόστολοι, because Justin's Gentile audience would more likely confront people who claimed to be apostles of Jesus rather than people who would claim to be Christian prophets.[2] The word ψευδαπόστολοι occurs only once in the New Testament (2 Cor. 11:13) in the context of Paul's discussion about rival apostles, and here it probably refers to those who represent themselves as apostles of Christ without having divine authorization. In the subapostolic age there were actually itinerant ministers called apostles (*Did.* 11:4, 6), and it is probably this order to which Justin is referring when he issues his warning against "false prophets."

Justin's final phrase καὶ πολλοὺς τῶν πιστῶν πλανήσουσιν finds its closest parallel in Mt. 24:11 (καὶ πλανήσουσιν πολλούς), but it is perhaps significant that Mt. 24:5 and Mk. 13:6 have the order καὶ πολλοὺς πλανήσουσιν.[3] Either Justin or his source has apparently added τῶν πιστῶν to the gospel material here, perhaps to define more precisely the indefinite

---

[1] The appearance of ἀναστήσονται in several later manuscripts of Mt. 24:11 (OWΣ 4. 262. 273) is probably the result of influence from the same tradition underlying its use in *Dial.* 35:3d, although it should be noted that the word order of *Dial.* 35:3d is different from that of Mt. 24:11.

[2] See Bauer, pp. 197 f., 143 ff.; James Hastings, *Dictionary of the Apostolic Church*, Vol. I (New York, 1916), pp. 82-84; Karl Rengstorf, "ἀπόστολος," *Theologisches Wörterbuch zum Neuen Testament*, Vol. I, pp. 421-448.

[3] Several manuscripts of Mt. 24:11 (Sinaiticus L 33. 157. 348. 477. 713. 892. 1093. 1279. 1473. 1579 hr 1. 2. Syr. hier. Aeth. Arm.) also have the order πολλοὺς πλανήσουσιν, but this reading is, like *Dial.* 35:3d, probably the result of influence from Mt. 24:5 (and/or Mk. 13:6).

πολλούς of the gospel parallel, because the specific problem in Justin's time was the misdirection of Christians.[1]

Although not identical to the text of *Dial.* 35:3d, there is evidence from the patristic literature to support the kind of reading found in *Dial.* 35:3d:

Apostolic Constitutions 6, 13 (Migne, *PG*, I, 945)
Ἀναστήσονται γὰρ ψευδόχριστοι καὶ ψευδοπροφῆται, καὶ πλανήσουσι πολλούς.

Both *Dial.* 35:3d and *Apost. Const.* 6, 13 read ἀναστήσονται; and *Apost. Const.* has καὶ ψευδοπροφῆται, which, I have argued, was probably changed by Justin or his source to ψευδοαπόστολοι. Indeed, both *Dial.* 35:3d and *Apost. Const.* 6, 13 are probably based on a tradition that was based on Mt. 24:11 and Mt. 24:24 with the influence of the word order of Mt. 24:5 (and/or Mk. 13:6).

5. *Results*

That Justin used as his source for *Dial.* 35:3 a written text that had already combined these four *logia* is substantiated if the text of *Dial.* 35:3 is compared with *Apost. Const.* 6, 13:

Dial. 35:3	*Apost. Const.* 6, 13
a) Πολλοὶ ἐλεύσονται	Ἐλεύσονται, λέγων,
ἐπὶ τῷ ὀνόματί μου,	πρὸς ὑμᾶς ἄνθρωποι
ἔξωθεν ἐνδεδυμένοι	ἐν ἐνδύμασι
δέρματα προβάτων,	προβάτων·
ἔσωθεν δέ εἰσι	ἔσωθεν δέ εἰσι
λύκοι ἅρπαγες.	λύκοι ἅρπαγες·
	ἀπὸ τῶν καρπῶν αὐτῶν
	ἐπιγνώσεσθε αὐτούς.
καὶ·	
b) Ἔσονται σχίσματα	See Syriac *Didascalia* [2]
καὶ αἱρέσεις.	
καί·	

---

[1] Wright, on the other hand, maintains (p. 56) that τῶν πιστῶν is "an interpolation of high apologetic importance in the scheme of Justin's defense."

[2] There is in the *Apostolic Constitutions* no parallel to this saying, but it should be remembered that the *Didascalia* (VI, 5), which served as the main source for the first six books of the *Apostolic Constitutions*, has a parallel to this saying (see above, p. 101).

c) Προσέχετε ἀπὸ   Προσέχετε ἀπ'
τῶν ψευδοπροφητῶν,   αὐτῶν.
οἵτινες ἐλεύσονται
πρὸς ὑμᾶς,
ἔξωθεν ἐνδεδυμένοι
δέρματα προβάτων,
ἔσωθεν δέ εἰσι
λύκοι ἅρπαγες.
καί·

d) Ἀναστήσονται   Ἀναστήσονται γὰρ
πολλοὶ ψευδόχριστοι   ψευδόχριστοι
καὶ ψευδοαπόστολοι,   καὶ ψευδοπροφῆται,
καὶ πολλοὺς   καὶ πλανήσουσι
τῶν πιστῶν
πλανήσουσιν.   πολλούς.

Dial. 35:3a, which is based on a harmony of Mt. 24:5 and Mt. 7:15, (16, 19), is paralleled in *Apost. Const.* 6, 13 in a form close to that which, I have argued, underlies *Dial.* 35:3a and its parallel *Apol.* 16:13.[1] *Apost. Const.* 6, 13 has, however, no parallel to the *logion* in *Dial.* 35:3b, although it is interesting that the *Didascalia* (VI, 5), the source for the *Apostolic Constitutions*, does have a parallel to this saying of *Dial.* 35:3b. The *logion* in *Dial.* 35:3c is certainly reflected in *Apost. Const.* 6, 13 in the words προσέχετε ἀπ' αὐτῶν. Quite probably the author of the *Apostolic Constitutions* (or the author of the *Didascalia*) here used as his source a text close to the one used by Justin and deliberately neglected to produce in full the saying because of its closeness to the first *logion*. Instead he chose to paraphrase the source with the words προσέχετε ἀπ' αὐτῶν, still retaining the essential meaning of the text.

Most striking of all is the fact, like *Dial.* 35:3d, *Apost. Const.* 6, 13 resumes with material based on Mt. 24:11 (καὶ πλανήσουσι πολλούς) and Mt. 24:24 (ψευδόχριστοι καὶ ψευδοπροφῆται). The striking concurrence of these two patristic writings can hardly be accidental; yet it is certain that there is no literary dependence between Justin and the author of

---

[1] Although *Dial.* 35:3 a reproduces only that material combining Mt. 24:5 and Mt. 7:15, I have argued that *Apol.* 16:13 demonstrates that Justin's source probably continued with Mt. 7:16, 19 in this section (see above, pp. 44-47). This view is supported, at least in part, by *Apost. Const.* 6, 13, which parallels material of Mt. 24:5 (ἐλεύσονται) and Mt. 7:15 (πρὸς ὑμᾶς . . . ἐν ἐνδύμασι προβάτων· ἔσωθεν δέ εἰσι λύκοι ἅρπαγες), Mt. 7:16 (ἀπὸ τῶν καρπῶν αὐτῶν ἐπιγνώσεσθε αὐτούς), but not Mt. 7:19.

the *Apostolic Constitutions*. It seems rather that both authors used a single source or tradition that had already combined these features. The argument would be even more convincing if the *Didascalia* already contained the same collection of sayings.

Although *Dial.* 35:3 contains several sayings based on the text of our canonical gospels, this collection of sayings is different in character from the collection in *Apol.* 15-17. It has already been shown that *Apol.* 15-17 is a post-synoptic harmony of Matthew, Mark, and Luke based on the Sermon on the Mount with related material from the synoptic parallels and from other parts of Matthew. *Dial.* 35:3, on the other hand, shows no harmonistic tendencies, although it does combine elements from different parts of Matthew; and one of the four sayings in *Dial.* 35:3 has no gospel parallel, a feature never observed in *Apol.* 15-17. What we have in *Dial.* 35:3 is perhaps not a harmony such as that underlying *Apol.* 15-17, but part of a sayings collection used by early Christians as a *vade mecum* against heresies, and it appears that this manual of Justin's school or a manual related to it was known to the author of the *Apostolic Constitutions* and perhaps also to Didymus, Lactantius, and the author of the *Didascalia*.

CHAPTER FOUR

THE MISCELLANEOUS SYNOPTIC SAYINGS

In addition to those sayings that occur in sources that have with some degree of probability already been defined and described (the sources underlying *Apol.* 15-17 and *Dial.* 35:3), there are several *logia* that can less definitely be assigned to written sources and some *logia* that appear in Justin's text as single sayings without any hint of the context from which they might have been extracted.

A. APOLOGY 19

There are in *Apol.* 19 two sayings that are joined by the conjunction καί, a feature already observed several times in passages in which Justin was quoting from written sources.[1] These two *logia* are introduced by the quotation formula in *Apol.* 19:6:

κρεῖττον δὲ πιστεύειν καὶ τὰ τῇ ἑαυτῶν φύσει καὶ ἀνθρώποις ἀδύνατα, ἢ ὁμοίως τοῖς ἄλλοις ἀπιστεῖν παρειλήφαμεν, ἐπειδὴ καὶ τὸν ἡμέτερον διδάσκαλον Ἰησοῦν Χριστὸν ἔγνωμεν εἰπόντα·

1. *Apology* 19:6

Apol. 19:6	Mt. 19:26	Mk. 10:27	Lk. 18:27
Τὰ	παρὰ	παρὰ	τὰ
ἀδύνατα	ἀνθρώποις	ἀνθρώποις	ἀδύνατα
παρὰ	τοῦτο		παρὰ
ἀνθρώποις	ἀδύνατόν	ἀδύνατον,	ἀνθρώποις
	ἐστιν,		
		ἀλλ' οὐ	
		παρὰ θεῷ·	
		πάντα γὰρ	
δυνατὰ	παρὰ δὲ θεῷ	δυνατὰ	δυνατὰ
παρὰ θεῷ.	πάντα δυνατά.	παρὰ τῷ θεῷ.	παρὰ τῷ θεῷ ἐστιν.

A comparison of *Apol.* 19:6 with its gospel parallels reveals that this passage is based either on Lk. 18:27, which is in turn derived from Mk. 10:27, or on a source that is later than Luke and based on Lk. 18:27. There are only two differences between *Apol.* 19:6 and Lk. 18:27, and

---

[1] See above, pp. 96, 97, 100.

both of these differences are minor: (1) *Apol.* 19:6 does not have τῷ before θεῷ, and (2) *Apol.* 19:6 does not contain the final ἐστιν of Lk. 18:27. The omission of τῷ by either Justin or his source is apparently a minor improvement upon the Greek of Lk. 18:27, because the article is generally omitted before θεός after a preposition;[1] and the omission of the verb ἐστιν is perhaps for the purpose of bringing the two parts of the saying into stylistic balance and thereby creating a gnomic expression:

Apol. 19:6a Τὰ ἀδύνατα παρὰ ἀνθρώποις
Apol. 19:6b   δύνατα παρὰ θεῷ.

2. *Apology* 19:7

Apol. 19:7	Mt. 10:28	Lk. 12:4, 5	2 Clem. 5:4 [2]	Ps. Clem. Hom. XVII 5, 2 [3]
			Μὴ φοβείσθωσαν τὰ ἀρνία τοὺς λύκους μετὰ τὸ ἀποθανεῖν αὐτά·	
	καὶ		καὶ ὑμεῖς	
Μὴ φοβεῖσθε τοὺς ἀναιροῦντας	μὴ φοβεῖσθε ἀπὸ τῶν ἀποκτεν- νόντων	[4]μὴ φοβηθῆτε ἀπὸ τῶν ἀποκτεν- νόντων	μὴ φοβεῖσθε τοὺς ἀποκτέν- νοντας	μὴ φοβηθῆτε ἀπὸ τοῦ ἀποκτέν- νοντος
ὑμᾶς καὶ μετὰ ταῦτα	τὸ σῶμα,	τὸ σῶμα καὶ μετὰ ταῦτα	ὑμᾶς καὶ	τὸ σῶμα,
	τὴν δὲ ψυχὴν		μηδὲν ὑμῖν	τῇ δὲ ψυχῇ
μὴ δυναμένους	μὴ δυναμένων	μὴ ἐχόντων περισσότερόν	δυναμένους	μὴ δυναμένου
τι		τι		τι

---

[1] Blass-Debrunner-Funk, 254.
[2] Lake, Vol. I, p. 134.
[3] Rehm, *GCS*, p. 231.

ποιῆσαι, (εἶπε,)	ἀποκτεῖναι·	ποιῆσαι. ⁵ὑποδείξω δὲ ὑμῖν τίνα φοβηθῆτε·	ποιεῖν, ἀλλὰ	ποιῆσαι·
φοβήθητε δὲ	φοβεῖσθε δὲ μᾶλλον	φοβήθητε	φοβεῖσθε	φοβήθητε δὲ
τὸν μετὰ τὸ ἀποθανεῖν	τὸν	τὸν μετὰ τὸ ἀποκτεῖναι	τὸν μετὰ τὸ ἀποθανεῖν ὑμᾶς	τὸν
δυνάμενον	δυνάμενον	ἔχοντα ἐξουσίαν	ἔχοντα ἐξουσίαν	δυνάμενον
καὶ ψυχὴν καὶ σῶμα	καὶ ψυχὴν καὶ σῶμα ἀπολέσαι	ἐμβαλεῖν	ψυχῆς καὶ σώματος τοῦ βαλεῖν	καὶ σῶμα καὶ ψυχὴν
εἰς γέενναν	ἐν γεέννῃ.	εἰς τὴν γέενναν.	εἰς γέενναν πυρός.	εἰς τὴν γέενναν τοῦ πυρὸς βαλεῖν.
ἐμβαλεῖν.				

An examination of the above table indicates clearly that *Apol.* 19:7 reflects material found in both Mt. 10:28 and Lk. 12:4, 5. μὴ φοβεῖσθε in *Apol.* 19:7 is identical to Mt. 10:28, but the Lukan parallel reads μὴ φοβηθῆτε. The words καὶ μετὰ ταῦτα μὴ δυναμένους τι ποιῆσαι reflect material from both Matthew and Luke: καὶ μετὰ ταῦτα is identical to the text of Lk. 12:4, but μὴ δυναμένους in *Apol.* 19:7 is closer to Mt. 10:28 (μὴ δυναμένων) than to Lk. 12:4 (μὴ ἐχόντων), and the phrase τι ποιῆσαι again agrees with the text of Lk. 12:4. That Justin's reading is later than the synoptic gospels and not based on the text of Q is proved by the fact that Justin's opening words μὴ φοβεῖσθε τοὺς ἀναιροῦντας ὑμᾶς are quite different from the text of Q, which can be reconstructed by comparing Mt. 10:28 with Lk. 12:4 and which must have read μὴ φοβεῖσθε (φοβηθῆτε) ἀπὸ τῶν ἀποκτεννόντων τὸ σῶμα.

The second part of *Apol.* 19:7 reveals additional harmonization. φοβήθητε in *Apol.* 19:7 is identical to Lk. 12:5, whereas the Matthaean parallel reads φοβεῖσθε.[1] τὸν μετὰ τὸ ἀποθανεῖν δυνάμενον in *Apol.* 19:7 parallels the phrases τὸν μετὰ τὸ ἀποκτεῖναι of Lk. 12:5 and (τὸν) δυνάμενον

---

[1] However, Mt 10:28 Koine DΘ also reads φοβηθῆτε probably by assimilation to the text of Lk. 12:5.

of Mt. 10:28. Further, Justin's καὶ ψυχὴν καὶ σῶμα is found in Mt. 10:28 but not in the Lukan parallel, whereas εἰς γέενναν ἐμβαλεῖν of *Apol.* 19:7 is closer to ἐμβαλεῖν εἰς τὴν γέενναν of Lk. 12:5 than to the Matthaean parallel (ἀπολέσαι ἐν γεέννῃ).[1]

This evidence leaves little doubt that Justin either used as his source for *Apol.* 19:7 a harmony combining elements from Mt. 10:28 and Lk. 12:4, 5 or that he himself combined these elements from Matthew and Luke. Massaux argues that Justin himself combined Mt. 10:28 and Lk. 12:4, 5;[2] however, the parallel material in 2 *Clement* and in the Pseudoclementine *Homilies* indicates rather that this harmony was not composed by Justin but that it was in use before Justin composed his *Apology*.

Although neither 2 *Clem.* 5:4 nor Pseudoclementine *Homilies* XVII, 5, 2 is identical to the text of *Apol.* 19:7 (see chart above), they both support readings of *Apol.* 19:7 against Mt. 10:28 and Lk. 12:4, 5, and both of them reflect some of the harmonistic tendencies already seen in *Apol.* 19:7. (1) The form τοὺς ἀναιροῦντας ὑμᾶς of *Apol.* 19:7 is closer in case construction to τοὺς ἀποκτέννοντας ὑμᾶς of 2 *Clement* than to ἀπὸ τῶν ἀποκτεννόντων in the gospel parallels, even though 2 *Clement* uses the same verb as the gospel texts. (2) δυναμένους ποιεῖν in 2 *Clement* reflects the same harmonization of Matthew and Luke found in the phrase δυναμένους τι ποιῆσαι in *Apol.* 19:7. (3) The phrase τὸν μετὰ τὸ ἀποθανεῖν in 2 *Clement* is identical to the text of *Apol.* 19:7, whereas Lk. 12:5 reads τὸν μετὰ τὸ ἀποκτεῖναι, and Mt. 10:28 has no parallel. (4) Pseudoclementine *Homilies* XVII, 5 reads μὴ δυναμένου τι ποιῆσαι, which reflects the same harmonistic tendency found in *Apol.* 19:7 (μὴ δυναμένους τι ποιῆσαι) and in 2 *Clem.* 5:4 (δυναμένους ποιεῖν).

Justin's τοὺς ἀναιροῦντας ὑμᾶς is secondary as compared with τοὺς ἀποκτέννοντας ὑμᾶς of 2 *Clement*, which is in turn secondary to the text of Matthew and Luke (ἀπὸ τῶν ἀποκτεννόντων τὸ σῶμα). καὶ μηδὲν ὑμῖν δυναμένους ποιεῖν of 2 *Clement* is, on the other hand, secondary to καὶ μετὰ ταῦτα μὴ δυναμένους τι ποιῆσαι of *Apol.* 19:7, which, I have already shown, reveals features of harmonization of Matthew and Luke. However, there is no reason to conclude here that a single written source could not be responsible for these readings in 2 *Clement* and *Apol.* 19:7. Only one fact seems to stand in the way of assuming that 2 *Clem.* 5:4 and *Apol.* 19:7 are dependent on a single harmony of Mt. 10:28 and Lk. 12:4,

---

[1] Mt. 10:28 (D it.pler. vg.pler.) reads εἰς γέενναν (in gehennan); however, the verb ἀπολέσαι in the Matthaean version leaves little doubt that it is Lk. 12:5 that is closer to *Apol.* 19:7 in this phrase.

[2] *Influence de l'Evangile*, p. 494.

5: whereas Justin reads δυνάμενον in agreement with Matthew, 2 *Clement* agrees with Luke's reading ἔχοντα ἐξουσίαν. However, Köster suggests that the presence of δύναμαι in this place in *Apol.* 19:7 (and Pseudo-clementine *Homilies* XVII, 5, 2) instead of an original ἔχοντα ἐξουσίαν could be the result of the use of δύναμαι earlier in this saying.[1] It is, therefore, quite possible that Justin and 2 *Clement* are here based on the same harmony of Matthew and Luke.

There is no evidence to indicate that *Apol.* 19:6 and *Apol.* 19:7 appeared together in a written source in spite of the fact that they are joined together in Justin's text. On the contrary, if both Justin and 2 *Clement* are based on a single written gospel harmony here, then the context of 2 *Clem.* 5:2-4 would seem to indicate that the two sayings in Justin's text are not from a single source.[2] Rather, Justin has probably himself joined these two sayings in *Apology* 19 and introduced them by a single quotation formula (*Apol.* 19:6), perhaps in agreement with the form employed in *Apol.* 15-17.

B. DIALOGUE 17

There are in *Dialogue* 17 two sayings that in Justin's text concern the money-changers in the temple, *Dial.* 17:3 and *Dial.* 17:4. I shall first examine each of these passages separately and then try to determine the relationship between the two *logia*.

1. *Dialogue* 17:3

Dial. 17:3	Mt. 21:13	Mk. 11:17	Lk. 19:46
		καὶ ἐδίδασκεν	
βοῶν	καὶ λέγει	καὶ ἔλεγεν	λέγων
παρ' ὑμῖν·	αὐτοῖς·	αὐτοῖς·	αὐτοῖς·
Γέγραπται·	γέγραπται·	οὐ γέγραπται	γέγραπται·
		ὅτι	καὶ ἔσται
Ὁ οἶκός μου	ὁ οἶκός μου	ὁ οἶκός μου	ὁ οἶκός μου
οἶκος	οἶκος	οἶκος	οἶκος
προσευχῆς	προσευχῆς	προσευχῆς	προσευχῆς·
ἐστιν,	κληθήσεται,	κληθήσεται	
		πᾶσιν τοῖς	
		ἔθνεσιν;	

[1] *Synoptische Überlieferung*, p. 97. That this may be the case with *Apol.* 19:7 is possible, but I cannot believe that τὸν δυνάμενον of Ps. Clem. *Hom.* is not derived from τὸν δυνάμενον of Mt. 10:28.

[2] See Köster, *Synoptische Überlieferung*, pp. 94-99.

ὑμεῖς δὲ	ὑμεῖς δὲ	ὑμεῖς δὲ	ὑμεῖς δὲ
πεποιήκατε	αὐτὸν	πεποιήκατε	αὐτὸν
αὐτὸν	ποιεῖτε	αὐτὸν	ἐποιήσατε
σπήλαιον	σπήλαιον	σπήλαιον	σπήλαιον
λῃστῶν	λῃστῶν.	λῃστῶν.	λῃστῶν.

That this quotation from *Dial.* 17:3 is based on the reading of the synoptic gospels and not on the Old Testament text of Jer. 7:11 is evident when the wording of the Septuagint of Jer. 7:11 is examined: μὴ σπήλαιον λῃστῶν ὁ οἶκός μου, οὗ ἐπικέκληται τὸ ὄνομά μου ἐπ' αὐτῷ ἐκεῖ, ἐνώπιον ὑμῶν;

Justin agrees basically with the text of Matthew, Mark, and Luke against the Septuagint, although some divergence from the synoptics is evident. Matthew (γέγραπται· ὁ οἶκός μου οἶκος προσευχῆς κληθήσεται) and Luke (γέγραπται· καὶ ἔσται ὁ οἶκός μου οἶκος προσευχῆς) have the closest parallels to Justin's text, whereas Mark's version is in the form of a question and is longer than the versions of Matthew, Luke, and Justin (οὐ γέγραπται ὅτι ὁ οἶκός μου οἶκος προσευχῆς κληθήσεται πᾶσιν τοῖς ἔθνεσιν;).

The second half of *Dial.* 17:3 (ὑμεῖς δὲ πεποιήκατε αὐτὸν σπήλαιον λῃστῶν), on the other hand, finds its only parallel in Mk. 11:17, which is identical to the reading of Justin. We should, therefore, conclude that either Justin or his source harmonized Mk. 11:17b with material from either Mt. 21:13a or Lk. 19:46a, the ἐστιν at the end of *Apol.* 17:3a apparently being an individual change made by Justin. That such a harmonistic text of this verse probably did not originate with Justin himself is supported by the following patristic text, which shows harmonization of Mt. 21:13a and Mk. 11:17b very similar to that found in *Dial.* 17:3:

> Origen, *Commentary in Matthew* 16, 23 (Klostermann, X, *GCS*, p. 556)
> γέγραπται· ὁ οἶκός μου οἶκος προσευχῆς κληθήσεται, ὑμεῖς δὲ αὐτὸν πεποιήκατε σπήλαιον λῃστῶν.

This text contains the γέγραπται· ὁ οἶκός μου οἶκος προσευχῆς κληθήσεται of Mt. 21:13a and *Dial.* 17:3 (changed by Justin to ἐστιν) and the ὑμεῖς δὲ αὐτὸν πεποιήκατε σπήλαιον λῃστῶν of Mk. 11:17b and *Dial.* 17:3 except for the order πεποιήκατε αὐτὸν in Mark and Justin.

2. *Dialogue* 17:4

Following the saying in *Dial.* 17:3 there is a formula which seems to serve both as an inverted conclusion to *Dial.* 17:3 and as an introduction to the saying in *Dial.* 17:4, and this formula is apparently based on the text of Mt. 21:12 rather than on the parallel in Mk. 11:15 as the following table indicates:

Dial. 17:3	Mt. 21:12	Mk. 11:15
καὶ τὰς τραπέζας	καὶ τὰς τραπέζας	καὶ τὰς τραπέζας
τῶν ἐν τῷ ναῷ	τῶν	τῶν
κολλυβιστῶν	κολλυβιστῶν	κολλυβιστῶν
		καὶ τὰς καθέδρας
		τῶν πωλούντων
		τὰς περιστερὰς
κατέστρεψε.	κατέστρεψεν	κατέστρεψεν,
	καὶ τὰς καθέδρας	
	τῶν πωλούντων	
	τὰς περιστεράς·	

The dependence on Matthew rather than on Mark is not certain, but the apparent preference for the Matthaean word order suggests that Justin is here dependent on Mt. 21:12. In Matthew this formula is used to introduce the saying in Mt. 21:13 (= *Dial.* 17:3, see above), but in Justin's text the formula introduces not the saying in *Dial.* 17:3 as one would expect but serves rather as an inverted conclusion to this saying and as an introduction to the following saying, *Dial.* 17:4, which in the Matthaean and Lukan parallels has nothing to do with the incident of the money-changers in the temple but which is based rather on a harmony of Mt. 23:13, 16, 23, (24,) 27 and Lk. 11:42, 52 (see above, pp. 33-37).

The saying in *Dial.* 17:4 is introduced with the formula καὶ ἐβόα, which has no parallel in the synoptic gospels and which is certainly to be attributed to Justin himself. It is clear from this analysis that either Justin or his source has carefully harmonized Matthew, Mark, and Luke in composing both the narrative and the sayings material that appears in *Dial.* 17:3, 4, and the simple addition of καὶ ἐβόα by Justin can easily be accounted for when it is realized that the context of Justin's text demands such a formula for a smooth transition to the following sayings material.

C. DIALOGUE 76:4-6

Dial. 76:4-6 contains four *logia* that are regarded by Justin as teachings of Jesus about God's plans for good and evil men:

Dial. 76:3-6

³ἃ γὰρ μεγάλα ἐβεβούλευτο ὁ πατὴρ εἴς τε πάντας τοὺς εὐαρέστους

γενομένους αὐτῷ καὶ γενησομένους ἀνθρώπους, καὶ τοὺς ἀποστάντας τῆς
βουλῆς αὐτοῦ ὁμοίως ἀνθρώπους ἢ ἀγγέλους, οὗτος μόνος ἀπαρακαλύπτως
ἐδίδαξεν, εἰπών· ⁴"Ηξουσιν ἀπὸ ἀνατολῶν καὶ δυσμῶν, καὶ ἀνακλιθήσονται
μετὰ Ἀβραὰμ καὶ Ἰσαὰκ καὶ Ἰακὼβ ἐν τῇ βασιλείᾳ τῶν οὐρανῶν· οἱ
δὲ υἱοὶ τῆς βασιλείας ἐκβληθήσονται εἰς τὸ σκότος τὸ ἐξώτερον. ⁵καί·
Πολλοὶ ἐροῦσί μοι τῇ ἡμέρᾳ ἐκείνῃ· Κύριε, κύριε, οὐ τῷ σῷ ὀνόματι
ἐφάγομεν καὶ ἐπίομεν καὶ προεφητεύσαμεν καὶ δαιμόνια ἐξεβάλομεν; καὶ
ἐρῶ αὐτοῖς· Ἀναχωρεῖτε ἀπ' ἐμοῦ. καὶ ἐν ἄλλοις λόγοις, οἷς καταδικάζειν
τοὺς ἀναξίους μὴ σῴζεσθαι μέλλει, ἔφη ἐρεῖν· Ὑπάγετε εἰς τὸ σκότος
τὸ ἐξώτερον, ὃ ἡτοίμασεν ὁ πατὴρ τῷ σατανᾷ καὶ τοῖς ἀγγέλοις αὐτοῦ.
⁶καὶ πάλιν ἐν ἑτέροις λόγοις ἔφη· Δίδωμι ὑμῖν ἐξουσίαν καταπατεῖν
ἐπάνω ὄφεων καὶ σκορπίων καὶ σκολοπενδρῶν καὶ ἐπάνω πάσης δυνάμεως
τοῦ ἐχροῦ.

I shall proceed now to an analysis of each of these sayings and then
try to determine the relationship, if any, among the four *logia*.

1. *Dialogue* 76:4

I have already analyzed this quotation (see above, pp. 28-30) and
concluded that Justin used a written post-synoptic source based on
Mt. 8:11, 12 harmonized with Lk. 13:29.

2. *Dialogue* 76:5a

As his source for the saying in *Dial.* 76:5a Justin used a harmony of
Mt. 7:22, 23 and Lk. 13:26, 27, and this source was known in similar
form to Origen, Pamphilius, and 2 *Clement* (see above, pp. 22-25).

3. *Dialogue* 76:5b

Dial. 76:5b	Ps. Clem. *Hom.* 19, 2 [1]	Mt. 25:30, 41
	καὶ ἄλλη που	
	εἰπεῖν ὑπέσχετο	³⁰ καὶ τὸν
ἔφη ἐρεῖν·	τοῖς ἀσεβέσιν·	ἀχρεῖον δοῦλον
Ὑπάγετε εἰς	Ὑπάγετε εἰς	ἐκβάλετε εἰς
τὸ σκότος	τὸ σκότος	τὸ σκότος
τὸ ἐξώτερον,	τὸ ἐξώτερον,	τὸ ἐξώτερον·
		ἐκεῖ ἔσται
		ὁ κλαυθμὸς

---

[1] Rehm, *GCS*, p. 254.

καὶ ὁ βρυγμὸς
τῶν ὀδόντων.
⁴¹τότε ἐρεῖ
καὶ τοῖς
ἐξ εὐωνύμων·
πορεύεσθε ἀπ' ἐμοῦ
κατηραμένοι εἰς τὸ
πῦρ τὸ αἰώνιον

ὁ ἡτοίμασεν	ὁ ἡτοίμασεν	τὸ ἡτοιμασμένον
ὁ πατὴρ	ὁ πατὴρ	
τῷ σατανᾷ καὶ	τῷ διαβόλῳ καὶ	τῷ διαβόλῳ καὶ
τοῖς ἀγγέλοις	τοῖς ἀγγέλοις	τοῖς ἀγγέλοις
αὐτοῦ.	αὐτοῦ.	αὐτοῦ.

A comparison of *Dial.* 76:5b with its closest gospel parallels reveals that Justin's text is different in context from Mt. 25:30, 41; whereas Mt. 25:30 is spoken by the master in the parable of the talents and the saying in Mt. 25:41 is spoken by the king in the so-called parable of the last judgment, the saying in *Dial.* 76:5b is attributed directly to Jesus. Furthermore, Ps. Clem. *Hom.* 19, 2, which is identical to *Dial.* 76:5b except for its use of διαβόλῳ where Justin has σατανᾷ, like Justin attributes the saying to Jesus.

The opening words of *Dial.* 76:5b (ὑπάγετε εἰς τὸ σκότος τὸ ἐξώτερον) find their closest gospel parallel in Mt. 25:30 (ἐκβάλετε εἰς τὸ σκότος τὸ ἐξώτερον), the only difference being in the use of the verb ὑπάγετε in Justin's text where Matthew has ἐκβάλετε. The change from ἐκβάλλω to ὑπάγω is apparently the result of the omission of the object τὸν ἀχρεῖον δοῦλον in Justin's text; the transitive verb ἐκβάλλω is unsuitable in the saying as recorded in *Dial.* 76:5b (and Ps. Clem. *Hom.* 19, 2) and has apparently been changed by either Justin or his source to the intransitive verb ὑπάγω.

The remainder of *Dial.* 76:5b (ὁ ἡτοίμασεν ὁ πατὴρ τῷ σατανᾷ καὶ τοῖς ἀγγέλοις αὐτοῦ) is parallel to the second part of Mt. 25:41 (τὸ ἡτοιμασμένον τῷ διαβόλῳ καὶ τοῖς ἀγγέλοις αὐτοῦ), which has been joined by either Justin or his source to the related material of Mt. 25:30 (εἰς τὸ σκότος τὸ ἐξώτερον of Mt. 25:30 probably suggested εἰς τὸ πῦρ τὸ αἰώνιον of Mt. 25:41). The combining of the two passages has apparently resulted in the syntactical change of adding ὁ πατὴρ as the subject of the active verb ἡτοίμασεν.[1] The appearance of σατανᾷ in *Dial.* 76:5b for διαβόλῳ in

---

[1] This change has apparently affected many later manuscripts, which agree in

Matthew is for several reasons probably a change made by Justin himself
and not the reading of his source: (1) the manuscript witnesses that are
probably dependent on the same tradition as Justin (see p. 115 n. 1)
preserve Matthew's διαβόλῳ; (2) Pseudoclementine *Homilies* reads
διαβόλῳ; and (3) although Justin uses both διάβολος and σατανᾶς in his
writings, it is possible that he has a certain preference for σατανᾶς. He
recognizes the common use of both words:

Apol. 28:1

    καλεῖται καὶ σατανᾶς καὶ διάβολος

But he says that Jesus himself used the word σατανᾶς:

Dial. 103:5

    ἢ λέοντα τὸν ὠρυόμενον ἐπ' αὐτὸν ἔλεγε τὸν διάβολον, ὃν Μωυσῆς μὲν
    ὄφιν καλεῖ, ἐν δὲ τῷ Ἰὼβ καὶ τῷ Ζαχαρίᾳ διάβολος κέκληται, καὶ ὑπὸ τοῦ
    Ἰησοῦ σατανᾶς προσηγόρευται.

That the author of Ps. Clem. *Hom.* 19, 2 did not use *Dial.* 76:5b as
his source is evident from his use of διαβόλῳ (= Mt. 25:41) instead of
Justin's σατανᾷ. Although we might allow him liberty in quoting his
source, it would be a strange coincidence if in altering the reading σατανᾷ
in his text, the author of the Pseudoclementine *Homilies* should have
used the original διαβόλῳ of Mt. 25:41. It is much more likely that *Dial.*
76:5b and Ps. Clem. *Hom.* 19, 2 used a common source that read διαβόλῳ
in agreement with Mt. 25:41 and that Justin altered this reading to
σατανᾷ, whereas the author of Ps. Clem. *Hom.* 19, 2 retained the reading
of his source.[1]

    4. *Dialogue* 76:6

Dial. 76:6	Lk. 10:19
Δίδωμι ὑμῖν	ἰδοὺ δέδωκα ὑμῖν
ἐξουσίαν καταπατεῖν	τὴν ἐξουσίαν τοῦ πατεῖν
ἐπάνω ὄφεων	ἐπάνω ὄφεων
καὶ σκορπίων	καὶ σκορπίων,
καὶ σκολοπενδρῶν	

Mt. 25:41 with Justin's reading ὃ ἡτοίμασεν ὁ πατὴρ κ.τ.λ. (D fam. 1 [exc. 118].
1582. 22. a b c d ff[1.2]. g[1] r[1.2]. aur. vg. [1 MS.]). All of these manuscripts, however,
preserve Matthew's διαβόλῳ and not Justin's σατανᾷ. Cf. also Hippol. *De Christo
et Antichristo* 65; Iren. *Contra Haer.* IV, 33, 11; IV, 40, 2; and Cyprian, *Test.* II, 30.
    [1] Bousset also argues (p. 97) that Justin and the author of the Pseudoclementine
Homilies used an extra-canonical source for this saying.

καὶ ἐπάνω πάσης   καὶ ἐπὶ πᾶσαν
δυνάμεως τοῦ ἐχθροῦ.   τὴν δύναμιν τοῦ ἐχθροῦ,
                         καὶ οὐδὲν ὑμᾶς
                         οὐ μὴ ἀδικήσει.

Dial. 76:6 finds its only gospel parallel in Lk. 10:19, and there are no patristic parallels that shed light upon the history of transmission of this saying. That either Lk. 10:19 or a text related to Lk. 10:19 is the source of *Dial.* 76:6 is certain; however, there are between the two passages some differences that require explanation: (1) the absence of ἰδοὺ and τὴν at the beginning of the passage may be a stylistic change made by either Justin or his source; [1] (2) the use of the future δίδωμι in *Dial.* 76:6 for the perfect δέδωκα in Luke is perhaps an attempt either by Justin or his source to recover by the use of the verb tense the scene when the authority was originally given by Jesus rather than merely recording the event as something in the past, as would be the case with the perfect form of the verb; [2] (3) the substitution of καταπατεῖν in *Dial.* 76:6 for τοῦ πατεῖν in Lk. 10:19 may also be a stylistic change made either by Justin or his source; [3] (4) the presence of καὶ σκολοπενδρῶν in *Dial.* 76:6 is most difficult to explain, because the word occurs nowhere in the New Testament and may be an addition made by Justin or his source; [4] (5) the alteration of Luke's ἐπὶ πᾶσαν τὴν δύναμιν to ἐπάνω πάσης δυνάμεως can be explained as an attempt to parallel the preceding ἐπάνω ὄφεων κ.τ.λ. and is certainly an improvement on the style of Lk. 10:19. It is, therefore, apparent that either Justin or his source modified the text of Lk. 10:19 making stylistic changes and improvements in the text.

5. *Conclusion*

The sayings in *Dial.* 76:4 and *Dial.* 76:5a are joined in Justin's text by the simple connective καί, which in *Apol.* 15:1-4 (see above, pp. 96-97),

---

[1] Plummer remarks (p. 279) that the use of the article with ἐξουσία is very unusual in the New Testament and completely lacking in the gospels except for this verse.

[2] AC³DWᵃΓΔΛΠ unc.⁷ al.pler. c of Lk. 10:19 also read δίδωμι and may have been influenced by the same tradition that underlies the text of *Apol.* 76:6.

[3] In the only other instance in which δίδοναι ἐξουσίαν occurs with the infinitive in the New Testament we do not find the τοῦ of Luke. Rather the form preserved by Justin without τοῦ seems to be more common (Jn. 1:12 and Rev. 13:5).

[4] Alfred Resch argues that σκολοπενδρῶν is derived from extra-canonical material, but he gives no evidence for this position (*Ausserkanonische Paralleltexte* [Leipzig, 1893-1897], Vol. II, p. 194).

Apol. 15:10-17 (see above, pp. 97-98), *Dial.* 35:3 (see above, pp. 100-106) indicates a close relationship among the passages involved. The results of my analysis of *Dial.* 76:4 and *Dial.* 76:5a indicate a similarly close relationship between these two verses in Justin's text:

Dial. 76:4   harmony of Mt. 8:11, 12 & Lk. 13:29
Dial. 76:5a harmony of Mt. 7:22, 23 & Lk. 13:26, 27

Obviously Justin's text is here following the context of Luke 13 with harmonization from the respective Matthaean parallels.

Between the sayings in *Dial.* 76:5a and *Dial.* 76:5b and between the sayings in *Dial.* 76:5b and *Dial.* 76:6, Justin has inserted longer introductory formulas, and the relationship among the synoptic sources of these passages is likewise remote:

Dial. 76:5b is derived from a source based on Mt. 25:30, 41 and known
    to the author of the Pseudo-clementine *Homilies.*
Dial. 76:6 is based on Lk. 10:19.

It appears that Justin has collected in *Dial.* 76:4-6 four *logia* that are concerned with the theme of God's plan for good and evil men.

D. The Narrative Exposition of Psalm 21 (*Dial.* 98-106)

In his still unpublished study of the synoptic narrative in Justin's writings Köster distinguishes in *Dial.* 98-106 a section devoted to the exposition of Psalm 21.[1] Within the limits of this section there are ten instances in which Justin quotes words of Jesus (*Dial.* 99:1, 2; 100:1, 3; 101:2; 103:6, 8; 105:5, 6; 107:1 [2]); however, these words of Jesus are not technically "sayings": they belong rather to the narrative material in scriptural proof and may have been extracted by Justin from a special source. I shall, nevertheless, proceed to a discussion of the individual sayings in this section to determine some of the features of the source on which this material is based.

1. *The sayings previously discussed*

Of the ten times that Justin quotes words of Jesus in this section, I have already analyzed six of these in the chapter devoted to the sayings that occur more than once in Justin's writings. A summary of the con-

---

[1] *Septuaginta und Synoptischer Erzählungsstoff*, pp. 189-192.
[2] Although *Dial.* 107:1 falls outside the limits defined by Köster (*Dial.* 98-106), it appears to me that *Dial.* 107:1 is part of the section on the exposition of Psalm 21; and in private consultation with me Prof. Köster has recognized the probability of my position.

clusions reached with regard to these sayings appears in the following table:

Dial. 99:2 (see above, pp. 32-33)
based on Mt. 26:39 with influence perhaps from Mk. 14:36 for the word order

Dial. 100:1 (see above, pp. 25-28)
based on either Mt. 11:27 or Lk. 10:22

Dial. 100:3 (see above, pp. 30-32)
based on a post-synoptic combination of Lk. 9:22 (or Mk. 8:31) and Lk. 24:7

Dial. 101:2 (see above, pp. 17-20)
based on Mk. 10:18 and/or Lk. 18:19 in harmony with Mt. 19:17, plus an ending known to other fathers

Dial. 103:6 (see above, pp. 37-43)
combines Mt. 4:10 and Mt. 16:23

Dial. 103:8 (see above, pp. 32-33)
related to *Dial.* 99:2 (see above on this page) perhaps quoted from memory

2. *Dialogue* 99:1

Dial. 99:1	Mt. 27:46b	Mk. 15:34b
Ὁ Θεός,	θεέ μου	ὁ Θεός μου
ὁ Θεός,	θεέ μου,	ὁ Θεός μου,
ἵνα τί	ἱνατί	εἰς τί
ἐγκατέλιπές με;	με ἐγκατέλιπες;	ἐγκατέλιπές με;

The text of *Dial.* 99:1 reveals harmonization of Mt. 27:46b and Mk. 15:34b. The cry ὁ Θεός, ὁ Θεός in *Dial.* 99:1 is closer to Mk. 15:34b (ὁ Θεός μου, ὁ Θεός μου) than to Mt. 27:46b (θεέ μου, θεέ μου), but ἵνα τί of *Dial.* 99:1 is based on the reading of Mt. 27:46b (ἱνατί),[1] where Mk. 15:34b has εἰς τί.[2] Justin's final phrase ἐγκατέλιπές με returns to the text of Mk. 15:34b (ἐγκατέλιπές με), where Mt. 27:46 has the reverse order (με ἐγκατέλιπες). That Justin's text is based on a harmony of Matthew and

---

[1] There is no difference between ἵνα τί and ἱνατί because there was no spacing between words in most Greek manuscripts of this period (Blass-Debrunner-Funk, 12 (3) and 299 (4)).

[2] Mk. 15:34b reads ἵνατι in 237. 349. 713. 1424. 14; however, these manuscripts are all much later than Justin and merely reveal the same harmonization of Mt. 27:46 b and Mk. 15:34b found in *Dial.* 99:1.

Mark here is certain, because Mt. 27:46b is based on Mk. 15:34b, which it has altered; yet *Dial.* 99:1 contains features of both gospels in this saying. That Justin himself did not harmonize these texts but used rather a written source that had these harmonistic features is supported by the presence of the same harmonistic features in Eusebius: [1]

Demonstr. evang. X, 8, 8 (Heikel, VI, *GCS*, p. 472)

ὁ θεὸς ὁ θεός μου ἵνατι ἐγκατέλιπές με;

Eusebius claims to be quoting Matthew here, but what he was probably quoting was a text of Mt. 27:46b harmonized with material from Mk. 15:34b.[2]

3. *Dialogue* 105:5

Dial. 105:5	Lk. 23:46
Πάτερ, εἰς χεῖράς σου	πάτερ, εἰς χεῖράς σου
παρατίθεμαι τὸ πνεῦμά μου.	παρατίθεμαι τὸ πνεῦμά μου.

The exact agreement between *Dial.* 105:5 and Lk. 23:46 leaves no doubt that either Justin or his source was here based on Luke. Matthew and Mark do not have a parallel to the passage.

4. *Dialogue* 105:6

Dial. 105:6	Mt. 5:20
	λέγω γὰρ ὑμῖν ὅτι
Ἐὰν μὴ περισσεύσῃ	ἐὰν μὴ περισσεύσῃ
ὑμῶν ἡ δικαιοσύνη	ὑμῶν ἡ δικαιοσύνη
πλεῖον τῶν γραμματέων	πλεῖον τῶν γραμματέων
καὶ Φαρισαίων	καὶ Φαρισαίων,
οὐ μὴ εἰσέλθητε	οὐ μὴ εἰσέλθητε
εἰς τὴν βασιλείαν	εἰς τὴν βασιλείαν
τῶν οὐρανῶν.	τῶν οὐρανῶν.

The exact agreement of *Dial.* 105:6 with the text of Mt. 5:20 leaves little doubt that either Justin or his source was here dependent on Matthew.

---

[1] This agreement between Justin and Eusebius also refutes the view of Baldus (p. 43) that Justin was here quoting from memory.

[2] The only difference between *Dial.* 99:1 and Eusebius' text is the absence of μου in Justin's version, a difference that does not affect the results of my analysis.

5. *Dialogue* 107:1

Dial. 107:1	Mt. 16:4	Mk. 8:12	Mt. 12:39	Lk. 11:29
Γενεὰ	γενεὰ	τί ἡ γενεὰ	γενεὰ	ἡ γενεὰ
πονηρὰ	πονηρὰ	αὕτη	πονηρὰ	αὕτη
καὶ	καὶ	ζητεῖ	καὶ	γενεὰ πονηρά
μοιχαλὶς	μοιχαλὶς		μοιχαλὶς	ἐστιν·
σημεῖον	σημεῖον	σημεῖον;	σημεῖον	σημεῖον
ἐπιζητεῖ,	ἐπιζητεῖ,	ἀμὴν	ἐπιζητεῖ,	ζητεῖ,
καὶ	καὶ	λέγω	καὶ	καὶ
σημεῖον	σημεῖον	ὑμῖν,	σημεῖον	σημεῖον
οὐ	οὐ	εἰ	οὐ	οὐ
δοθήσεται	δοθήσεται	δοθήσεται	δοθήσεται	δοθήσεται
αὐτοῖς	αὐτῇ	τῇ γενεᾷ	αὐτῇ	αὐτῇ
εἰ μὴ τὸ	εἰ μὴ τὸ	ταύτῃ	εἰ μὴ τὸ	εἰ μὴ τὸ
σημεῖον	σημεῖον	σημεῖον.	σημεῖον	σημεῖον
Ἰωνᾶ.	Ἰωνᾶ.		Ἰωνᾶ	Ἰωνᾶ.
			τοῦ	
			προφήτου.	

Two versions of this saying are found in the synoptic tradition: (1) the version of Q preserved in Mt. 12:39 and Lk. 11:29 and (2) the version of Mk. 8:12 used as the source for Mt. 16:4.[1] The text of *Dial.* 107:1 is identical to Mt. 16:4 and Mt. 12:39, except for the use of the plural αὐτοῖς in *Dial.* 107:1 for the singular αὐτῇ in both Mt. 16:4 and Mt. 12:39 and the addition in Mt. 12:39 of τοῦ προφήτου, which is not found in either *Dial.* 107:1 or in Mt. 16:4; however, this minor difference does not exclude the possibility that either Justin or his source used Mt. 12:39 as the basis for this saying. *Dial.* 107:1 is, however, closest to Mt. 16:4, and it is probable that Justin is dependent upon this verse in Matthew for this saying in *Dial.* 107:1.

E. Sayings That Appear in Narrative Contexts

There are in *Dial.* 49:5 and *Dial.* 51:3 two sayings of Jesus that occur in Justin's text in a narrative context that concerns John the Baptist. Apparently these sayings were quoted by Justin from narrative material rather than from a sayings collection; nevertheless, I shall analyze in detail each of these sayings in its narrative context.

---

[1] See Vincent Taylor, *The Gospel According to Saint Mark* (London, 1955), p. 363. The question of synoptic sources is here complicated by the fact that in Matthew the versions of Mark and Q are identical except for the addition of τοῦ προφήτου in Mt. 12:39; however, this uncertainty does not affect my discussion.

1. *Dialogue* 49:5

Dial. 49:5	Mt. 17:10-13	Mk. 9:11-13
διὸ καὶ	¹⁰καὶ ἐπηρώτησαν	¹¹καὶ ἐπηρώτων
ὁ ἡμέτερος	αὐτὸν οἱ μαθηταὶ	αὐτὸν
Χριστὸς	λέγοντες·	λέγοντες
εἰρήκει	τί οὖν	ὅτι
ἐπὶ γῆς τότε	οἱ γραμματεῖς	λέγουσιν
τοῖς λέγουσι	λέγουσιν	οἱ γραμματεῖς
πρὸ τοῦ Χριστοῦ	ὅτι	ὅτι
'Ηλίαν δεῖν	'Ηλίαν δεῖ	'Ηλίαν δεῖ
ἐλθεῖν·	ἐλθεῖν	ἐλθεῖν
	πρῶτον;	πρῶτον;
	¹¹ὁ δὲ ἀποκριθεὶς	¹²ὁ δὲ ἔφη
	εἶπεν·	αὐτοῖς·
'Ηλίας μὲν	'Ηλίας μὲν	'Ηλίας μὲν
ἐλεύσεται καὶ	ἔρχεται καὶ	ἐλθὼν πρῶτον
ἀποκαταστήσει	ἀποκαταστήσει	ἀποκαθιστάνει
πάντα·	πάντα·	πάντα·
		καὶ πῶς γέγραπται
		ἐπὶ τὸν υἱὸν
		τοῦ ἀνθρώπου,
		ἵνα πολλὰ παθῇ
		καὶ ἐξουδενηθῇ;
λέγω δὲ	¹²λέγω δὲ	¹³ἀλλὰ λέγω
ὑμῖν ὅτι	ὑμῖν ὅτι	ὑμῖν ὅτι καὶ
'Ηλίας ἤδη ἦλθε,	'Ηλίας ἤδη ἦλθεν,	'Ηλίας ἐλήλυθεν,
καὶ οὐκ	καὶ οὐκ	
ἐπέγνωσαν αὐτόν,	ἐπέγνωσαν αὐτόν,	
ἀλλ' ἐποίησαν	ἀλλ' ἐποίησαν	καὶ ἐποίησαν
αὐτῷ	ἐν αὐτῷ	αὐτῷ
ὅσα ἠθέλησαν	ὅσα ἠθέλησαν.	ὅσα ἤθελον,
		καθὼς γέγραπται
		ἐπ' αὐτόν.
	οὕτως καὶ ὁ υἱὸς	
	τοῦ ἀνθρώπου	
καὶ γέγραπται	μέλλει πάσχειν	
ὅτι	ἀπ' αὐτῶν.	
Τότε συνῆκαν	¹³τότε συνῆκαν	
οἱ μαθηταὶ	οἱ μαθηταὶ	

ὅτι περὶ	ὅτι περὶ
Ἰωάννου	Ἰωάννου
τοῦ βαπτιστοῦ	τοῦ βαπτιστοῦ
εἶπεν αὐτοῖς.	εἶπεν αὐτοῖς.

The introductory narrative material of *Dial.* 49:5 is vaguely reminiscent of Mt. 17:10 and Mk. 9:11, but it appears that Justin or his source exercised considerable freedom in composing this introduction, because its relationship to the gospel parallels is hardly more than allusive.

With respect to the saying itself there are only two differences between the text of *Dial.* 49:5 and that of Mt. 17:11, 12, and both differences can be explained as stylistic changes made by Justin: (1) *Dial.* 49:5 reads ἐλεύσεται for Matthew's ἔρχεται; however, we have already observed a similar preference in the case of *Dial.* 35:3c where Justin's text has ἐλεύσονται for ἔρχονται of Mt. 7:15 (see above, p. 102); and (2) the absence of ἐν before αὐτῷ in *Dial.* 49:5 is apparently an attempt by Justin or his source to suppress a Semitism.[1]

Following the saying itself Justin has more narrative material, which is in this instance identical to the text of Mt. 17:13. Inasmuch as Mt. 17:10-13 used as its source Mk. 9:11-13, there can be little doubt that Matthew's text and not a presynoptic source was ultimately the basis of Justin's reading. Indeed, this investigation leads us to the conclusion that Justin used either the text of Mt. 17:10-13 or a post-synoptic narrative source based on this Matthaean narrative.

2. *Dialogue* 51:3

The narrative introduction in *Dial.* 51:3 has no close gospel parallel and is, therefore, probably a composition of Justin himself:

εἰρήκει δὲ περὶ τοῦ μηκέτι γενήσεσθαι ἐν τῷ γένει ὑμῶν προφήτην καὶ περὶ τοῦ ἐπιγνῶναι ὅτι ἡ πάλαι κηρυσσομένη ὑπὸ τοῦ θεοῦ καινὴ διαθήκη διαταχθήσεσθαι ἤδη τότε παρῆν, τοῦτ᾿ ἔστιν αὐτὸς ὢν ὁ Χριστός, οὕτως.

However, the saying itself has close parallels in Matthew and Luke:

Dial. 51:3	Mt. 11:12-15	Lk. 16:16
Ὁ νόμος καὶ		Ὁ νόμος καὶ
οἱ προφῆται	[12]ἀπὸ δὲ τῶν	οἱ προφῆται

---

[1] Lohmeyer, p. 269. This suppression of the Semitism finds widespread support in the manuscript witnesses of Mt. 17:12 (Sinaiticus DFUW 047. 13. 28. 213. 477. 517. 660. 700. 1010. 1279. 1293. 1424. 1555. 1604. 2145. al. cf. ei it.pler. Syr.[hl.text.hier.] Cop.[bo·] Arm. Geo).

μέχρι Ἰωάννου	ἡμερῶν Ἰωάννου	μέχρι Ἰωάννου·
τοῦ βαπτιστοῦ·	τοῦ βαπτιστοῦ	
ἐξ ὅτου	ἕως ἄρτι	ἀπὸ τότε
ἡ βασιλεία	ἡ βασιλεία	ἡ βασιλεία
τῶν οὐρανῶν	τῶν οὐρανῶν	τοῦ θεοῦ
		εὐαγγελίζεται
		καὶ πᾶς εἰς αὐτὴν
βιάζεται,	βιάζεται,	βιάζεται.
καὶ βιασταὶ	καὶ βιασταὶ	
ἁρπάζουσιν αὐτήν.	ἁρπάζουσιν αὐτήν.	
	¹³πάντες γὰρ	
	οἱ προφῆται	
	καὶ ὁ νόμος	
	ἕως Ἰωάννου	
	ἐπροφήτευσαν·	
καὶ εἰ θέλετε	¹⁴καὶ εἰ θέλετε	
δέξασθαι,	δέξασθαι,	
αὐτός ἐστιν	αὐτός ἐστιν	
Ἡλίας ὁ μέλλων	Ἡλίας ὁ μέλλων	
ἔρχεσθαι.	ἔρχεσθαι.	
ὁ ἔχων ὦτα	¹⁵ ὁ ἔχων ὦτα	
ἀκούειν		
ἀκοτέτω	ἀκοτέτω	

This material in Mt. 11:12-15 and Lk. 16:16 has its origin in Q, which both Matthew and Luke adapted for their own respective needs.[1] Creed argues that "from a literary point of view the version given here [Lk. 16:16] may be confidently pronounced secondary. Luke probably felt the obscurity [of Q, which is more closely preserved in Matthew] and has given a clear but different meaning to the words."[2]

The opening words of *Dial.* 51:3 ὁ νόμος καὶ οἱ προφῆται μέχρι Ἰωάννου are identical to the first half of Lk. 16:16, but from this point on the text of *Dial.* 51:3 follows closely the text of Mt. 11:12-15. The mention of John in Lk. 16:16a was a convenient point at which to move from the Lukan reading (μέχρι Ἰωάννου) to the Matthaean parallel (Ἰωάννου τοῦ βαπτιστοῦ).

The use of ἐξ ὅτου in *Dial.* 51:3 is different from both ἕως ἄρτι of Mt. 11:12 and ἀπὸ τότε of Lk. 16:16, although it is synonymous with the

---

Lukan phrase. It is clear, however, that Justin could not have followed the Matthaean reading ἕως ἄρτι, which presupposes the ἀπὸ δὲ κ.τ.λ. at the beginning of Mt. 11:12. Rather this change to ἐξ ὅτου in Justin's text was required by Justin's progression from Lk. 16:16a to Mt. 11:12b.

That Justin has no exact parallel to Mt. 11:13 is not surprising, because the contents of this verse have already been included at the beginning of *Dial.* 51:3 from the Lukan parallel (Lk. 16:16), but *Dial.* 51:3 returns to the order of Matthew, reproducing exactly the reading of Mt. 11:14, 15, except for the addition of ἀκούειν in *Dial.* 51:3 perhaps from Lk. 8:8 or Lk. 14:35.[1]

This investigation leads us to the conclusion that for the saying in *Dial.* 51:3 Justin or his source harmonized Lk. 16:16a with Mt. 11:12b-15, but from the evidence available it is impossible to determine whether this harmonization was produced by Justin himself or was derived by him from a harmonistic source.

F. The Saying Quoted from Memory (*Dial.* 122:1)

Dial. 122:1	Mt. 23:15
	Οὐαὶ ὑμῖν, γραμματεῖς
	καὶ Φαρισαῖοι ὑποκριταί,
	ὅτι περιάγετε τὴν θάλασσαν
	καὶ τὴν ξηρὰν ποιῆσαι ἕνα
	προσήλυτον, καὶ ὅταν
	γένηται, ποιεῖτε αὐτὸν
νῦν δὲ διπλότερον	υἱὸν γεέννης
υἱοὶ γεέηης,	διπλότερον ὑμῶν.
ὡς αὐτὸς εἶπε,	
γίνεσθε.	

The context of this passage in *Dial.* 122:1 indicates that Justin was probably only alluding to this saying of Jesus in Mt. 23:15, and a comparison of the two passages shows that this is indeed the case. Justin was here apparently quoting from memory, and there is no reason to believe from the context of this verse that Justin was trying to quote exactly the words of Jesus.

---

[1] In Mk. 4:9, 23; (7:16) ἀκούειν also appears, but the wording is slightly different from that of Luke's text. Only in Matthew does this saying appear consistently without the word ἀκούειν (11:15; 13:9, 43).

G. Remaining Synoptic Sayings

There still remain to be discussed two sayings that have parallels in the synoptic gospels, *Dial.* 81:4 and *Dial.* 125:1.

1. *Dialogue* 81:4

Dial. 81:4	Mt. 22:30	Mk. 12:25	Lk. 20:35, 36
			35οἱ δὲ καταξιωθέντες τοῦ αἰῶνος ἐκείνου τυχεῖν
	ἐν γὰρ τῇ ἀναστάσει	ὅταν γὰρ ἐκ νεκρῶν ἀναστῶσιν,	καὶ τῆς ἀναστάσεως τῆς ἐκ νεκρῶν
Οὔτε	οὔτε	οὔτε	οὔτε
γαμήσουσιν	γαμοῦσιν	γαμοῦσιν	γαμοῦσιν
οὔτε	οὔτε	οὔτε	οὔτε
γαμηθήσονται,	γαμίζονται,	γαμίζονται,	γαμίζονται·
ἀλλὰ	ἀλλ' ὡς	ἀλλ' εἰσὶν ὡς	36οὐδὲ γὰρ ἀποθανεῖν ἔτι δύνανται,
ἰσάγγελοι	ἄγγελοι	ἄγγελοι	ἰσάγγελοι
ἔσονται,	ἐν τῷ	ἐν τοῖς	γάρ εἰσιν,
τέκνα	οὐρανῷ	οὐρανοῖς.	καὶ υἱοί
τοῦ θεοῦ	εἰσιν.		εἰσιν θεοῦ
τῆς			τῆς
ἀναστάσεως			ἀναστάσεως
ὄντες.			υἱοὶ ὄντες.

The text of *Dial.* 81:4 is not identical to the text of any of the synoptic gospels, nor are there any patristic texts that duplicate the peculiarities of Justin's reading. The opening words of *Dial.* 81:4 οὔτε γαμήσουσιν οὔτε γαμηθήσονται are different from the reading of the synoptic gospels, all of which agree in reading οὔτε γαμοῦσιν οὔτε γαμίζονται. The ἀλλὰ of *Dial.* 81:4 finds its parallel in Mt. 22:30 (ἀλλ') and Mk. 12:25 (ἀλλ') but not in Luke, which continues οὐδὲ γὰρ ἀποθανεῖν ἔτι δύναται. Justin's ἰσάγγελοι is identical to Lk. 20:36, whereas Mt. 22:30 and Mk. 12:25 both have ὡς ἄγγελοι; however, the context here follows either Mt. 22:30 or Mk. 12:25, omitting the Lukan phrase οὐδὲ γὰρ ἀποθανεῖν ἔτι δύναται. The future form of the verb in *Dial.* 81:4 (ἔσονται) finds no parallel in the synoptic gospels, all of which have the present εἰσιν; however, this change to the future is in agreement with the future forms γαμήσουσιν and γαμηθήσονται in *Dial.* 81:4 and is demanded by the syntax. The verb ἔσονται of *Dial.* 81:4 comes at the end of its phrase (ἀλλὰ ἰσάγγελοι ἔσονται) as is the case with the εἰσιν in Mt. 22:30 (ἀλλ' ὡς ἄγγελοι ἐν τῷ οὐρανῷ εἰσιν), whereas the εἰσιν in Mk. 12:25 occurs at the beginning (ἀλλ' εἰσὶν ὡς ἄγγελοι ἐν τοῖς οὐρανοῖς). This word order in Justin's text might indicate that either Justin or his source was here harmonizing Luke with Matthew rather than with Mark.

The remainder of the text of *Dial.* 81:4 (τέκνα τοῦ θεοῦ τῆς ἀναστάσεως ὄντες) finds its only gospel parallel in Lk. 20:36 (καὶ υἱοί εἰσιν θεοῦ τῆς ἀναστάσεως υἱοὶ ὄντες), which either Justin or his source has condensed and altered lightly in meaning: whereas in Lk. 20:36 τῆς ἀναστάσεως modified υἱοί, in *Dial.* 81:4 τῆς ἀναστάσεως modifies τοῦ θεοῦ.

That Justin himself either harmonized Mt. 22:30 (or perhaps Mk. 12:25) with Lk. 20:36 or used a post-synoptic harmony of these verses is certain. Matthew and Luke have both based their text on Mk. 12:25, which Luke altered considerably in adapting it to his context. This consideration excludes the possibility of the use by Justin or any source other than a post-synoptic harmony.

2. *Dialogue* 125:1

Dial. 125:1	Mt. 13:3b-8	Mk. 4:3-8	Lk. 8:5-8
		[3]ἀκούετε.	
a) Ἐξῆλθεν	[3]Ἰδοὺ ἐξῆλθεν	ἰδοὺ ἐξῆλθεν	[5]ἐξῆλθεν
ὁ σπείρων	ὁ σπείρων	ὁ σπείρων	ὁ σπείρων
τοῦ σπεῖραι	τοῦ σπείρειν.	σπεῖραι.	τοῦ σπεῖραι
τὸν σπόρον·			τὸν σπόρον
			αὐτοῦ·
	[4]καὶ ἐν τῷ	[4]καὶ ἐγένετο	καὶ ἐν τῷ
	σπείρειν	ἐν τῷ	σπείρειν
	αὐτὸν	σπείρειν	αὐτὸν
b) καὶ ὃ μὲν	ἃ μὲν	ὃ μὲν	ὃ μὲν
ἔπεσεν	ἔπεσεν	ἔπεσεν	ἔπεσεν
εἰς τὴν	παρὰ τὴν	παρὰ τὴν	παρὰ τὴν
ὁδόν,	ὁδόν,	ὁδόν,	ὁδὸν
	καὶ ἐλθόντα	καὶ ἦλθεν	καὶ κατεπατήθη,
	τὰ πετεινὰ	τὰ πετεινὰ	καὶ τὰ πετεινὰ
		καὶ	τοῦ οὐρανοῦ
	κατέφαγεν	κατέφαγεν	κατέφαγεν
	αὐτά.	αὐτό.	αὐτό.

d) ὃ δὲ ἐπὶ τὰ πετρώδη,	⁵ἀλλὰ δὲ ἔπεσεν ἐπὶ τὰ πετρώδη ὅπου οὐκ εἶχεν γῆν πολλήν, καὶ εὐθέως ἐξανέτειλεν διὰ τὸ μὴ ἔχειν βάθος γῆς· ⁶ἡλίου δὲ ἀνατείλαντος ἐκαυματίσθη, καὶ διὰ τὸ μὴ ἔχειν ῥίζαν ἐξηράνθη.	⁵καὶ ἄλλο ἔπεσεν ἐπὶ τὸ πετρῶδες ὅπου οὐκ εἶχεν γῆν πολλήν, καὶ εὐθὺς ἐξανέτειλεν διὰ τὸ μὴ ἔχειν βάθος γῆς· ⁶καὶ ὅτε ἀνέτειλεν ὁ ἥλιος ἐκαυματίσθη, καὶ διὰ τὸ μὴ ἔχειν ῥίζαν ἐξηράνθη.	⁶καὶ ἕτερον κατέπεσεν ἐπὶ τὴν πέτραν, καὶ φυὲν ἐξηράνθη διὰ τὸ μὴ ἔχειν ἰκμάδα.
c) ὃ δὲ εἰς τὰς ἀκάνθας,	⁷ἄλλα δὲ ἔπεσεν ἐπὶ τὰς ἀκάνθας, καὶ ἀνέβησαν αἱ ἄκανθαι καὶ ἀπέπνιξαν αὐτά.	⁷καὶ ἄλλο ἔπεσεν εἰς τὰς ἀκάνθας, καὶ ἀνέβησαν αἱ ἄκανθαι καὶ συνέπνιξαν αὐτό, καὶ καρπὸν οὐκ ἔδωκεν.	⁷καὶ ἕτερον ἔπεσεν ἐν μέσῳ τῶν ἀκανθῶν καὶ συμφυεῖσαι αἱ ἄκανθαι ἀνέπνιξαν αὐτό.
e) ὃ δὲ ἐπὶ τὴν γῆν τὴν καλήν.	⁸ἀλλὰ δὲ ἔπεσεν ἐπὶ τὴν γῆν τὴν καλὴν καὶ ἐδίδου καρπόν, ὃ μὲν ἑκατόν, ὃ δὲ ἑξήκοντα,	⁸καὶ ἄλλα ἔπεσεν εἰς τὴν γῆν τὴν καλὴν καὶ ἐδίδου καρπὸν ἀναβαίνοντα καὶ αὐξανόμενα, καὶ ἔφερεν εἰς τριάκοντα καὶ ἐν ἑξήκοντα	⁸καὶ ἕτερον ἔπεσεν εἰς τὴν γῆν τὴν ἀγαθὴν καὶ φυὲν ἐποίησεν καρπὸν

ὃ δὲ   καὶ ἐν

τριάκοντα.   ἑκατόν.   ἑκατονταπλασίονα.

The parable of the sower was first contained in Mark, which is the source of its appearance in Matthew and Luke, both of whom made alterations in adapting the Markan text to their own gospels. In comparing the version in *Dial.* 125:1 with the synoptic parallels, it is obvious that Justin's text is shorter, but it is important to determine whether this text is an abridgement of the gospel material or a form older than any of our gospels.

The opening phrase of *Dial.* 125:1 (ἐξῆλθεν ὁ σπείρων τοῦ σπεῖραι τὸν σπόρον) has its closest parallel in Lk. 8:5 (ἐξῆλθεν ὁ σπείρων τοῦ σπεῖραι τὸν σπόρον αὐτοῦ). Both Mt. 13:3 and Mk. 4:3 begin ἰδοὺ ἐξῆλθεν, and Mk. 4:3 does not have τοῦ before σπεῖραι; and although many manuscripts of both Mt. 13:3 and Mk. 4:3 add τὸν σπόρον (αὐτοῦ) to this verse, these witnesses are all late and leave little doubt that Justin is here dependent on Lk. 8:5.[1]

The phrase καὶ ὃ μὲν ἔπεσεν εἰς τὴν ὁδόν of *Dial.* 125:1 has the ὃ μὲν of Mk. 4:4 and Lk. 8:5, whereas Mt. 13:4 has ἃ μὲν; however, all three synoptic gospels read παρὰ τὴν ὁδόν, whereas *Dial.* 125:1 reads εἰς τὴν ὁδόν, indicating a different emphasis in the direction or destination of the fall.

At this point *Dial.* 125:1 departs from the order of the gospels and continues ὃ δὲ εἰς τὰς ἀκάνθας, a reading found in Mk. 4:7, whereas Matthew has ἐπὶ τὰς ἀκάνθας, and Luke has ἐν μέσῳ τῶν ἀκανθῶν.[2]

Dial. 125:1d is closest to Mt. 13:5, both of which read ἐπὶ τὰ πετρώδη, while Mk. 4:5 reads ἐπὶ τὸ πετρῶδες and Lk. 8:6 reads ἐπὶ τὴν πέτραν.[3]

The concluding section of *Dial.* 125:1 ὃ δὲ ἐπὶ τὴν γῆν τὴν καλήν is closest to Mt. 13:8, which also reads ἐπὶ τὴν γῆν τὴν καλήν. Mk. 4:8, on the other hand, has εἰς τὴν γῆν τὴν καλήν,[4] and Lk. 8:8 has εἰς τὴν γῆν τὴν ἀγαθήν.

---

[1] Mt. 13:3 + τὸν σπόρον 485 Syr.ˢ·
+ τὸν σπόρον αὐτοῦ 28. 71. 477. 1012. ff¹ h vg.pauc.

Mk. 4:3 + τὸν σπόρον αὐτοῦ F 10. 29. 71. 125. 157. 179. 218. 220. 433. 471. 569. 1071. g².
These witnesses are obviously the result of assimilation to Lk. 8:5.

[2] D fam. 13. 174. 230. 826. 828. 983. 1689 of Mt. 13:7 also read εἰς τὰς ἀκάνθας in agreement with Justin and probably reveal dependence on a tradition similar to that underlying *Dial.* 125:1.

[3] The appearance of ἐπὶ τὰ πετρώδη in many manuscripts of Mk. 4:5 and Lk. 8:6 is probably the result of harmonization of these manuscripts to the reading of Mt. 13:5 (Sinaiticus DWΘ fam. 1. 33. 517. 565. 569 of Mk. 4:5; and Z 131 of Lk. 8:6).

[4] The appearance of ἐπὶ τὴν γῆν in many manuscripts of Mk. 4:8 is probably only the result of harmonization of this text to the reading of Mt. 13:8 (CΣ fam. 1. 124. 28. 36. 40. 106. 237. 259. 349. 565. 159. Syr. ˢ·ᵖᵉˢʰ·ʰˡ·).

The results of this investigation leave no doubt that Justin based his text upon our canonical gospels and not on a pre-synoptic source, because *Dial.* 125:1 reveals features peculiar to each of the three synoptic gospels. Apparently Justin has harmonized the parallel texts of the parable of the sower and has condensed the material considerably for use in his *Dialogue*.

H. CONCLUSIONS

A review of the conclusions reached in this chapter confirms the conclusions already drawn in the preceding chapters: (1) Justin did not quote the sayings of Jesus from memory, but he used one or more written sources, of which at least some parts had been written before Justin wrote his *Apology* and his *Dialogue* (*Apol.* 19:7; *Dial.* 76:5a; 76:5b); (2) Justin's text shows features of harmonization of Matthew and Luke (*Apol.* 19:7; *Dial.* 17:4; 51:3; 76:4; 76:5a; 81:4); (3) Justin's text occasionally reveals harmonization of Mark with the other synoptic gospels (*Dial.* 17:3; 99:1; 125:1); (4) different parts of the same gospel were sometimes combined into a single saying of Jesus (*Dial.* 100:3; 103:6); (5) Justin occasionally quotes from a single gospel, either Matthew or Luke but never Mark (*Apol.* 19:6; *Dial.* 49:5; 76:6; 105:5; 105:6; 107:1 [122:1]); and (6) many manuscript witnesses preserve a textual tradition that reveals the influence of readings similar to those found in Justin's text.

Each of these conclusions confirms the results of the previous chapters; however, there is also evidence in this chapter either that Justin himself was inclined to group the sayings of Jesus according to subject matter or context or else that he derived these sayings from sources in which they had already been so grouped.

I have in this chapter indicated certain sections that contain several sayings (*Apol.* 19, *Dial.* 17, *Dial.* 76:4-6, *Dial.* 98-106, and the narrative section concerning John the Baptist [*Dial.* 49:5 and *Dial.* 51:3]); however, it is impossible to determine with certainty whether Justin himself was the author of these collections and groupings or whether the sayings had already been so grouped in his source. But what is certain is that throughout the *Dialogue* and the *Apology* the sayings of Jesus tend to be grouped into small units rather than to appear as isolated sayings, and that these units at least in part reflect an order derived from the comparison of gospel parallels.

CHAPTER FIVE

THE NON-SYNOPTIC SAYINGS

There are in Justin's writings three sayings of Jesus that do not have parallels in any of the synoptic gospels. Indeed, two of them, *Dial.* 35:3b and *Dial.* 47:5, have no parallels in any of the gospel material; and the third saying, *Apol.* 61:4, has no synoptic parallel, but it does have a parallel in the gospel of John.

A. Dialogue 35:3b

Ἔσονται σχίσματα καὶ αἱρέσεις

I have already indicated above (see pp. 101f.) that this saying is part of a sayings collection used by early Christians as a vade mecum against heresies and that this manual of Justin's school or a manual related to it was known to the author of the *Apostolic Constitutions* and perhaps also to Didymus, Lactantius, and the author of the *Didascalia*.

B. Dialogue 47:5 [1]

διὸ καὶ ἡμέτερος κύριος Ἰησοῦς Χριστὸς εἶπεν· Ἐν οἷς ἂν ὑμᾶς καταλάβω, ἐν τούτοις καὶ κρινῶ.

The saying in *Dial.* 47:5 has no gospel parallels, nor does it appear anywhere else in the patristic literature as a saying of Jesus. There are, however, several writings in the early church that are either quoting or referring [2] to the same saying that Justin here attributes to Jesus, but

---

[1] The following argument has already been presented in substantially the same form elsewhere. See Arthur J. Bellinzoni, Jr., "The Source of the Agraphon in Justin Martyr's Dialogue with Trypho 47:5," *Vigiliae Christianae*, 17 (1963), pp. 65-70.

[2] There are two Latin sources that do not quote this saying directly, but they are almost certainly alluding to the same saying:
Cyprian, *De Mortalitate* 17 (Migne, *PL*, IV, 616)
   Qualem te invenit Dominus cum vocat, talem pariter et iudicat.
Athanasius, *Vita S. Antonii* (Migne, *PL*, LXXIII, 136)
   in quo quemque invenerit, in eo sit judicaturus, quod prophetica per Ezechielem voce testatur.
The context of Cyprian does not reveal who spoke this saying, but Athanasius, like Johannes Climacus, attributes it to Ezekiel.

none of them regards the *logion* as a dominical saying. Rather the saying is attributed to God (sometimes as quoted through one or more of his prophets, sometimes specifically Ezekiel):

Clem. Alex., *Quis Dives Salvetur* 40, 1 f. (Stählin, Vol. 3, p. 186)

τῶν μὲν οὖν προγεγενημένων θεὸς δίδωσιν ἄφεσιν, τῶν δὲ ἐπιόντων αὐτὸς ἕκαστος ἑαυτῷ. καὶ τοῦτ' ἔστι μεταγνῶναι τὸ καταγνῶναι τῶν παρῳχημένων καὶ αἰτήσασθαι τούτων ἀμνηστίαν παρὰ πατρός, ὃς μόνος τῶν ἁπάντων οἷός τέ ἐστιν ἄπρακτα ποιῆσαι τὰ πεπραγμένα ἐλέῳ τῷ παρ' αὐτοῦ καὶ δρόσῳ πνεύματος ἀπαλείψας τὰ προημαρτημένα. "ἐφ' οἷς γὰρ ἂν εὕρω ὑμᾶς," φησίν, "ἐπὶ τούτοις καὶ κρινῶ."

Pseudo-Athanasius, *Quaest. ad Antiochum*, Quaest. 36 (Migne, *PG*, XXVIII, 617)

ἀκούσας τοῦ Θεοῦ διὰ τοῦ προφήτου εἰπόντος, ὅτι "'Εν ᾧ εὕρω σε, ἐν ἐκείνῳ κρινῶ σε."

Vita S. Johannici (quoted from Ropes, pp. 137 f.)

ἐν ᾧ γὰρ εὕρω σε τόπῳ (2 of 4 manuscripts read τρόπῳ), φησὶ ὁ Θεὸς διὰ τῶν προφητῶν, ἐν αὐτῷ καὶ κρινῶ σε.

Johannes Climacus, *Scala Paradisi* 7 (Migne, *PG*, LXXXVIII, 812)

Οἴ μοι, οἴ μοι, ποῦ ἦν τότε ἡ τοῦ 'Ιεζεκιὴλ φωνή, ἵνα εἴπῃ πρὸς αὐτούς, ὅτι 'Εν ᾧ εὕρω σε, ἐν αὐτῷ καὶ κρινῶ σε, εἶπεν ὁ Θεός.

Vita S. Johannici attributes the saying to God as spoken through the prophets (plural); Pseudo-Athanasius attributes it to God as spoken through the prophet (singular); and Johannes Climacus and Athanasius (*Vita S. Antonii* 15) proceed to identify Ezekiel as the prophet who has delivered this saying from God. These positions are in no way mutually exclusive; indeed, they are complementary. Clement's text contains no reference to prophets and merely attributes the saying to God. Only Justin attributes the saying to Jesus; and inasmuch as Justin is the earliest of the fathers to quote this saying, we can be certain that he is not the source of the saying in the later literature. Otherwise, it is difficult to understand how the dominical origin for this saying could have been unanimously replaced by its attribution to God (as spoken through his prophet Ezekiel).[1] I shall now move on to a comparison of the several

---

[1] Jeremias, therefore, concludes that "this saying came from the apocryphal Book of Ezekiel and was mistakenly attributed to Jesus by Justin." Resch agrees (*Agrapha*, pp. 322-325). Such a position is only conjectural and must remain beyond the scope of my investigation, but it is important to notice the agreement of Jeremias and Resch with my conclusion that the saying had its origin before Justin.

versions of this saying with the text of *Dial.* 47:5 in the hope that this study will lead to definite conclusions about the history of the transmission of this saying.

Dial. 47:5	Clem. Alex., Quis Dives Salvetur [40]	Ps. Athan., Quaest. ad Antiochum, Quaest. 36	*Vita S. Johannici*	Johannes Climacus, Scala Paradisi 7
ἐν οἷς	ἐφ' οἷς γὰρ	ἐν ᾧ	ἐν ᾧ γὰρ	ἐν ᾧ
ἂν ὑμᾶς	ἂν εὕρω	εὕρω	εὕρω	εὕρω
καταλάβω,	ὑμᾶς,	σε,	σε τόπῳ	σε
ἐν τούτοις	ἐπὶ τούτοις	ἐν ἐκείνῳ	ἐν αὐτῷ	ἐν αὐτῷ
καὶ κρινῶ.	καὶ κρινῶ.	καὶ κρινῶ	καὶ κρινῶ	καὶ κρινῶ
		σε.	σε.	σε.

I have already argued above that although *Dial.* 47:5 is the earliest source for this saying, the other fathers cannot have derived the saying from Justin, because Justin alone of all the fathers attributes this saying to Jesus, whereas the other witnesses unanimously agree in attributing the saying to God (through his prophet Ezekiel). And an examination of the saying itself supports this position. Pseudo-Athanasius, *Vita S. Johannici*, and Johannes Climacus agree basically in the following reading: ἐν ᾧ (γὰρ) εὕρω σε, ἐν αὐτῷ (ἐκείνῳ) καὶ κρινῶ σε. Their agreement against Justin (ἐν οἷς ἂν ὑμᾶς καταλάβω, ἐν τούτοις καὶ κρινῶ) certainly eliminates the possibility of the use of *Dial.* 47:5 as their source.

Ropes maintains [1] that these fathers may have been dependent on Clement of Alexandria, but this view is equally preposterous, because these three later sources agree in several instances against Clement: (1) they all read ἐν ᾧ for Clement's ἐφ' οἷς; (2) they all agree in using the singular σε instead of Clement's plural form ὑμᾶς; (3) they all use the singular ἐν αὐτῷ (ἐκείνῳ), where Clement reads ἐπὶ τούτοις; and (4) all three agree against Clement in reading σε after κρινῶ. Indeed, it seems that Pseudo-Athanasius, *Vita S. Johannici*, and Johannes Climacus are all dependent on a text that possibly read ἐν ᾧ εὕρω σε, ἐν αὐτῷ καὶ κρινῶ σε and that attributed the saying to Ezekiel or a prophet.

Dial. 47:5, on the other hand, agrees more closely with Clement of Alexandria, and it seems that Justin and Clement are dependent upon a tradition other than that underlying these three later patristic texts. ἐν οἷς and ἐν τούτοις in *Dial.* 47:5 and ἐφ' οἷς and ἐπὶ τούτοις in *Quis Dives*

[1] p. 138.

Salvetur 40 both read the plural form, differing only in their use of the preposition.[1] Also both Clement and Justin agree in their use of ἄν and the plural ὑμᾶς, although Justin has καταλάβω where Clement reads εὕρω.[2]

We might, therefore, reasonably conclude that a common source underlies Justin and Clement in their reading of this saying and that this source perhaps read: ἐν οἷς ἄν εὕρω ὑμᾶς, ἐν τούτοις καὶ κρινῶ. And upon this basic source both Justin and Clement made certain stylistic changes to adapt this text to their own context and needs.

We are still confronted with the problem why only Justin attributed this saying to Jesus, and I should now like to suggest a possible explanation. Justin introduces the saying with the words διὸ καὶ ὁ ἡμέτερος κύριος Ἰησοῦς Χριστὸς εἶπεν. Perhaps Justin's source contained the saying introduced by the words διὸ καὶ ὁ κύριος λέγει, and Justin either mistakenly understood ὁ κύριος to refer to Jesus and consequently inserted Ἰησοῦς Χριστὸς for clarity or else deliberately made the change, a practice not uncommon in the early church.[3]

The results of this investigation lead to the conclusion that Justin used as his source for *Dial.* 47:5 a written tradition known probably in the same form to Clement of Alexandria, and it appears that this saying was attributed in this source not to Ezekiel or one of the prophets but to God. In adapting this *logion* from his source, Justin apparently transformed what was a saying of God into a saying of Jesus by interpreting ὁ κύριος as a reference to Jesus and consequently changing his introductory formula to ὁ ἡμέτερος κύριος Ἰησοῦς Χριστὸς. Apparently the same saying in a slightly different form was known to Pseudo-Athanasius, Johannes Climacus, and the author of *Vita S. Johannici* from a source in which the saying was attributed to Ezekiel.

C. APOLOGY 61:4

There is in the writings of Justin a single *logion* that is apparently related in some way to a saying of Jesus in the Gospel of John; it is,

---

[1] The ἐν in Pseudo-Athanasius, *Vita S. Johannici*, and Johannes Climacus supports the reading of Justin (ἐν) against Clement (ἐπί).

[2] The use of εὕρω in Pseudo-Athanasius, *Vita S. Johannici*, and Johannes Climacus supports the reading of Clement (εὕρω) against Justin (καταλάβω). It should be noted that καταλαμβάνω contains the element of planned surprise, whereas εὑρίσκω has the connotation of accident (see Bauer, pp. 816 f., 642 ff. and Liddell-Scott, pp. 897, 729 f.). The reading of *Dial.* 47:5 is, therefore, possibly a change made by Justin to emphasize the suddenness and surprise of God's judgment.

[3] See Bauer, pp. 907-911; Kittel, Vol. III, pp. 1038-1095; and any standard dictionary or word study on the use of κύριος in the New Testament and in early Christian literature.

however, important to determine whether Justin is dependent on the gospel text or on the tradition that underlies the Johannine version of this saying. Although Resch recognizes the influence of only Jn. 3:5 in Justin's text,[1] it has generally been maintained that the entire section Jn. 3:3-5 is important for a study of *Apol.* 61:4.[2] Indeed, both Jn. 3:3 and Jn. 3:5 have parallels to Justin's saying and are relevant in determining what John's source must have read.

Apol. 61:4	Jn. 3:3	Jn. 3:5
καὶ γὰρ ὁ	ἀπεκρίθη Ἰησοῦς	ἀπεκρίθη Ἰησοῦς·
Χριστὸς εἶπεν·	καὶ εἶπεν αὐτῷ·	
	ἀμὴν ἀμὴν	ἀμὴν ἀμὴν
	λέγω σοι,	λέγω σοι,
Ἂν μὴ	ἐὰν μή τις	ἐὰν μή τις
ἀναγεννηθῆτε,	γεννηθῇ ἄνωθεν,	γεννηθῇ.
		ἐξ ὕδατος
		καὶ πνεύματος,
οὐ μὴ	οὐ δύναται	οὐ δύναται
εἰσέλθητε εἰς	ἰδεῖν	εἰσελθεῖν εἰς
τὴν βασιλείαν	τὴν βασιλείαν	τὴν βασιλείαν
τῶν οὐρανῶν.	τοῦ θεοῦ.	τοῦ θεοῦ.

It is quite certain that this saying refers in both Justin's *Apology* and in the Gospel of John to Christian baptism.[3] Although both Jn. 3:3 and 3:5 introduce the baptismal saying with the words ἀμὴν ἀμὴν λέγω σοι, Justin has no parallel for this phrase; however, the fact that this phrase is so peculiarly Johannine in character is sufficient evidence that the words, at least in this form, probably did not occur in John's source.[4]

The saying in *Apol.* 61:4 begins with the words ἂν μὴ ἀναγεννηθῆτε, apparently a direct address in the second person plural to the catechumens. John, on the other hand, presents two different versions of the

---

[1] *Agrapha*, p. 162. Resch actually argues that Justin's text is a harmony of Jn. 3:5 and Mt. 28:19.

[2] John S. Romanides, "Justin Martyr and the Fourth Gospel," *The Greek Orthodox Theological Review*, IV, 2 (1958-1959), pp. 115-134; Massaux, *Influence de l'Evangile*, p. 508; Bousset, p. 117.

[3] Rudolf Bultmann, *Das Evangelium des Johannes* (Göttingen, 1957), p. 98; Helmut Köster, "Geschichte und Kultus im Johannes-evangelium und bei Ignatius von Antiochien," *Zeitschrift für Theologie und Kirche*, 54 (1957), p. 63.

[4] ἀμὴν ἀμὴν λέγω σοι occurs elsewhere in Jn. 3:11; 13:38; 21:18; and ἀμὴν ἀμὴν λέγω ὑμῖν occurs in Jn. 1:52; 5:19, 24, 25; 6:26, 32, 47, 53; 8:34, 51, 58; 10:1, 7; 12:24; 13:16, 20, 21; 14:12; 16:20, 23.

saying in 3:3 and 3:5, although in both instances the reference is impersonal (τις). An examination of John's context reveals that ἄνωθεν γεννηθῆναι of Jn. 3:3 is probably purposely ambiguous, meaning both *born from above* and *born again*,[1] because Nicodemus misunderstands the saying in this form and needs the explanation of Jn. 3:5 (ἐὰν μή τις γεννηθῇ ἐξ ὕδατος καὶ πνεύματος). Although Bultmann regards ἐξ ὕδατος as a later addition to the gospel to secure the reference to Christian baptism,[2] Köster has clearly shown that the reference to baptism in Jn. 3:3 is certain even apart from this reference to water.[3] Köster argues that the reference to baptism is evident in verse 3 in the phrase ἄνωθεν γεννηθῆναι, which is fashioned after the terms ἀναγέννησις (1 Pet. 1:3, 23) and παλιγγεννησία (Tit. 3:6) both of which are technical terms for baptism.[4] In addition, Romanides notes that the verb ἀναγεννάω is often used by Justin in his description of Christian baptism and may, therefore, have been a technical term used at the time of Justin to describe the baptismal rite.[5] It is certainly true that ἀναγεννάω was a technical term, but 1 Peter proves that such a use dates much earlier than the writing of Justin's *Apology*.

The suggestion that οὐ δύναται ἰδεῖν τὴν βασιλείαν τοῦ θεοῦ is a secondary reading and that οὐ μὴ εἰσέλθητε εἰς τὴν βασιλείαν τῶν οὐρανῶν of *Apol.* 61:4 is the older version is supported by the fact that Justin elsewhere uses the verb ὁράω in this sense (3:36 ὁ δὲ ἀπειθῶν τῷ υἱῷ οὐκ ὄψεται ζωήν), whereas the synoptic gospels prefer the phrase εἰσελθεῖν εἰς τὴν βασιλείαν τῶν οὐρανῶν (or τοῦ θεοῦ) (Mt. 5:20; 7:21; 18:3; 19:23 f.; Mk. 9:47; 10:15, 23 ff.; Lk. 18:17, 25). Thus, εἰσελθεῖν εἰς τὴν βασιλείαν in Jn. 3:5 seems to be closer to John's source than ἰδεῖν τὴν βασιλείαν in Jn. 3:3.

It is impossible to determine at this point whether βασιλεία τῶν οὐρανῶν of *Apol.* 61:4 or βασιλεία τοῦ θεοῦ of Jn. 3:3, 5 is original; however, an examination of the patristic parallels below supports the primacy of Justin's reading and leaves little doubt that John has himself substituted the phrase βασιλεία τοῦ θεοῦ. This analysis of *Apol.* 61:4 and Jn. 3:3-5 points to the conclusion that Justin has independently preserved a

---

[1] So too Bauer, pp. 152 f.; C. H. Dodd, *The Interpretation of the Fourth Gospel* (Cambridge, 1955), p. 303, n. 2; see also Bultmann, *Das Evangelium des Johannes*, p. 95, n. 2; R. H. Strachan, *The Fourth Gospel Its Significance and Environment* (London, 1960), p. 131; C. K. Barrett, *The Gospel According to St John* (New York, 1956), p. 171.

[2] *Das Evangelium des Johannes*, p. 98.

[3] "Geschichte und Kultus," p. 63.

[4] *Ibid.*; cf. Bauer, p. 102.

[5] p. 127

liturgical baptismal text in a form older than that found in John and that John's text is probably based on the same or on a similar tradition.[1] This position is supported by an examination of the following patristic witnesses, all of whom preserve a similar baptismal text:

Hippolytus, *Elenchos* VIII, 10 (Wendland, III, *GCS*, p. 230)

ἐὰν μή τις γεννηθῇ ἐξ ὕδατος καὶ πνεύματος, οὐκ εἰσελεύσεται εἰς τὴν βασιλείαν τῶν οὐρανῶν.

Apostolic Constitutions 6:15 (Migne, *PG*, I, 948)

Ἐὰν μή τις βαπτισθῇ ἐξ ὕδατος καὶ Πνεύματος, οὐ μὴ εἰσέλθῃ εἰς τὴν βασιλείαν τῶν οὐρανῶν.

Pseudoclementine *Homilies* 11, 26 (Rehm, *GCS*, p. 167)

Ἀμὴν ὑμῖν λέγω, ἐὰν μὴ ἀναγεννηθῆτε ὕδατι ζῶντι, εἰς ὄνομα πατρός, υἱοῦ, ἁγίου πνεύματος, οὐ μὴ εἰσέλθητε εἰς τὴν βασιλείαν τῶν οὐρανῶν.

Pseudoclementine *Recognitions* 6, 9 (Migne, *PG*, I, 1332)

Amen dico bovis, nisi quis denuo renatus fuerit ex aqua, non introibit in regna coelorum.

Each of these texts has in common with *Apol.* 61:4 features that indicate clearly that Justin is independent of the Johannine tradition, and in addition certain features of these texts can clearly be labeled as secondary. Hippolytus has probably preserved a very old form of this baptismal tradition except for the use of the future εἰσελεύσεται, which is apparently secondary. The form of *Apostolic Constitutions* is probably original except for the use of the verb βαπτισθῇ. Pseudoclementine *Homilies* has the form ὕδατι ζῶντι instead of ἐξ ὕδατος καὶ πνεύματος, and this text also has the addition of the trinitarian formula (εἰς ὄνομα πατρός, υἱοῦ, ἁγίου πνεύματος). However, Pseudoclementine *Homilies* has in common with *Apol.* 61:4 ἀναγεννηθῆτε and εἰσέλθητε εἰς τὴν βασιλείαν τῶν οὐρανῶν and the trinitarian formula,[3] perhaps indicating that the version of this saying in *Apol.* 61:4 is a fairly accurate reproduction of a traditional liturgical formula used in Justin's church in Rome. Pseudo-clementine *Recognitions*, like *Homilies*, has the addition amen dico vobis, perhaps indicating that this introduction was often attached to the

---

[1] So too Köster, "Geschichte und Kultus," p. 63.

[2] The saying itself in *Apol.* 61:4 does not contain the trinitarian formula, but there is positive indication of baptism in the name of the Trinity in the immediate context in *Apol.* 61:3 (ἐπ' ὀνόματος γὰρ τοῦ πατρὸς τῶν ὅλων καὶ δεσπότου θεοῦ καὶ τοῦ σωτῆρος ἡμῶν Ἰησοῦ Χριστοῦ καὶ πνεύματος ἁγίου τὸ ἐν τῷ ὕδατι τότε λουτρὸν ποιοῦνται).

saying and was merely modified by John to the Johannine version with a double ἀμήν; and all of these patristic texts agree with Justin's βασιλείαν τῶν οὐρανῶν against John's βασιλεία τοῦ θεοῦ.

None of these patristic witnesses produces this saying in exactly the same form as that found in *Apol.* 61:4, but they all confirm the opinion reached earlier in this section that Justin is in no way dependent on Jn. 3:3-5 but is in fact dependent on a traditional baptismal saying probably derived by Justin from the baptismal liturgy.[1] It should also be noted, in conclusion, that *Apol.* 61:4 is the only instance where Justin quotes a pre-gospel tradition.

D. Conclusions

The discussion in this chapter points to the conclusion that when Justin is not quoting from our synoptic gospels or from a post-synoptic harmony, he is quoting from traditional sources, such as liturgical texts or early Christian handbooks known in similar form to other fathers in the early church. But certainly there is no need, on the basis of an analysis of these three sayings, to conclude that Justin is dependent on one or more extra-canonical gospels.[2]

---

[1] There is certainly no basis for the position of Romanides (pp. 131, 133) that Justin was quoting from the fourth gospel and at the same time confusing the vocabulary of Jn. 3:3-5 with Mt. 18:3, especially when we realize that Mt. 18:3 occurs in a context completely different from Justin's context of baptismal rebirth. See also Dodd, *Interpretation*, p. 304 and C. H. Dodd, *Historical Tradition in the Fourth Gospel* (Cambridge, 1963), pp. 158 f.

[2] The words of institution recorded by Justin in *Apol.* 66:3 are also from traditional liturgical forms older than the versions found in our synoptic gospels, but a detailed study of this material is beyond the scope of my present investigation.

CHAPTER SIX

CONCLUSION

Now that each of the sayings of Jesus in the writings of Justin Martyr has been studied in detail with reference to the parallels in the canonical gospels and in the patristic literature, it is possible to summarize the results of this investigation and then indicate Justin's place in the development of the gospel tradition. However, I should like, first of all, to comment on the conclusions reached in previous discussions of this subject.

It has been clearly shown that there is no basis whatever for the position of Semisch and Zahn that Justin's deviations from the canonical gospels are the result of a failure of memory in his attempt to quote from the gospels; indeed, Justin is probably quoting from written sources except in the case of *Dial.* 122:1, where he appears to be quoting from memory. I have also demonstrated that Bousset's thesis that Justin is dependent on pre-synoptic material is without any foundation. Not only is there absolutely no evidence to indicate the use of a pre-synoptic source, but there is overwhelming evidence for the use of post-synoptic material.

The thesis of Westcott, Baldus, and Massaux that Justin used as his source nothing other than the canonical gospels is likewise unsound. Although Justin's sources were based almost entirely on the canonical gospels, there is a considerable amount of evidence that indicates that Justin's sources were not always the canonical gospels themselves but rather post-canonical sources based on the synoptic gospels.

There is also no evidence to support the position that Justin is dependent on one or more non-canonical gospels. The argument of Credner and Hilgenfeld that Justin was dependent on the *Gospel of Peter* has been undermined by the subsequent discovery of the *Gospel of Peter* as well as by the present investigation of the sayings of Jesus. Not only are there no parallels between Justin's text and the *Gospel of Peter*, but there is a definite difference in their versions of Jesus' words from the cross:

Dial. 99:1 ὁ θεός, ὁ θεός, ἵνα τί ἐγκατέλιπές με;

Gosp. Pet. ἡ δύναμίς μου, ἡ δύναμις, κατέλιψάς με.[1]

---

[1] H. B. Swete, ΕΥΑΓΓΕΛΙΟΝ ΚΑΤΑ ΠΕΤΡΟΝ, *The Akhîm Fragment of the Apocryphal Gospel of St. Peter* (London, 1893), pp. 9-10.

Furthermore, with the exception of three sayings, all of the sayings of Jesus in Justin's writings are ultimately based on sayings in the synoptic gospels; and I have already argued in the last chapter that these three non-synoptic sayings can be explained without appealing to the use of extra-canonical gospels.

It has been maintained by von Engelhardt, Sanday, and Lippelt that Justin used as his source a post-synoptic harmony of Matthew, Mark, and Luke. This position comes closest to the results reached in my investigation, although it should be stated that it is an oversimplification of the matter to assert merely that Justin's source was a harmony of the synoptic gospels.

Indeed, I shall assemble here the cumulative evidence of my investigation and try to define more specifically the source of Justin's sayings of Jesus: (1) it has been clearly demonstrated that Justin used more than a single source; (2) Justin generally used as his source written documents except for *Dial.* 122:1, where he was probably quoting from memory, and *Apol.* 61:4, where he was quoting from a liturgical tradition; (3) Justin's written sources harmonized parallel material from Matthew, Mark, and Luke; (4) in the case of Matthew and Luke, related material from different parts of a single gospel were often combined into a single saying; (5) Justin's sources often derived material from a single gospel (either Matthew or Luke, never Mark or John); (6) Justin's quotations of the sayings of Jesus show absolutely no dependence on the Gospel of John; (7) the harmonistic texts used by Justin as his source for the sayings of Jesus are part of a tradition that had great influence on the later manuscript tradition of Matthew, Mark, and Luke; (8) the sayings of Jesus are found in Justin's writings in a few groups of several collected sayings, and rarely do sayings occur singly in Justin's text.

Two of these groups of sayings are probably based on written sources in which the sayings had already been collected and arranged in substantially the same form as that found in Justin's text. (1) *Apol.* 15-17 is probably based on a primitive Christian catechism in use in Justin's school in Rome, and it is likely that this same catechism or a similar catechism was known to Clement of Alexandria, Origen, and to the author of the Pseudoclementine *Homilies.* This catechism was based primarily on the text of the Sermon on the Mount with the addition of related material from Mark and Luke and from other parts of Matthew. (2) The four sayings in *Dial.* 35:3 are apparently derived from an early Christian *vade mecum* of sayings against heresies, and it is likely that this manual or a similar manual for use against heresies was known to the author of the *Apostolic Constitutions* and perhaps also to Didymus, Lactantius, and the author of the *Didascalia*.

In addition to these two written sources there are several other instances in which sayings of Jesus occur in Justin's writings in groups, but it is possible, perhaps probable, that Justin himself is responsible for these groupings and that these sayings were not so grouped in his source: (1) *Apol.* 19:6, 7 (2 sayings); (2) *Dial.* 17:3, 4 (2 sayings); (3) *Dial.* 76:4-6 (4 sayings); (4) the narrative exposition of Psalm 21 in *Dial.* 98-106 (10 sayings); and (5) the narrative about John the Baptist (2 sayings, *Dial.* 49:5; 51:3).

It has never been questioned that Justin was one of the leading figures in the catechetical school of Rome in the second century, but the influence of this school tradition on Justin's writings and on other Christian schools of the second century has never been fully understood. There is evidence in Justin's writings for the use in the school at Rome of catechisms, manuals for instruction against heresies, harmonistic texts of the synoptic gospels; and apparently some of the same material was in use in the school of Alexandria a few decades after Justin's death, perhaps indicating a definite link between the Roman and Alexandrian schools. The role of Justin himself in the formation of this school tradition is largely unanswered by my investigation of the sayings of Jesus, but it is reasonable to assume that Justin, as a prominent teacher in the school of Rome, took an active part in the creation and formation of that school's tradition. In fact, it seems reasonable to conclude that the catechisms and church manuals used in Justin's school at Rome were the compositions of Justin and his pupils. Justin and his pupils apparently used the synoptic gospels as their primary source and composed church catechisms and *vade mecums* by harmonizing material from the synoptic gospels as described above. It was the composition of such harmonies which gave rise in time to the corruption of gospel manuscripts through systematic harmonization of parallel passages. It must, however, be emphasized that there is absolutely no evidence that Justin ever composed a complete harmony of the synoptic gospels; his harmonies were of a limited scope and were apparently composed for didactic purposes. Whether the thought of a full gospel harmony ever occurred to Justin can only be conjectured, but he apparently never undertook to compose such a work.

Justin's writings have many features in common with 2 *Clement*, which was probably written before Justin wrote the *Apology* and the *Dialogue*; however, Justin and 2 *Clement* have none of the striking similarities found when Justin's text is compared with the writings of

Clement of Alexandria, Origen, or the Pseudoclementine *Homilies*, all of which reveal a literary dependence upon some of the tradition used by Justin. Rather 2 *Clement* merely indicates that there were in use before Justin's period written gospel harmonies, which served as models for the harmonies used and perhaps composed by Justin. Justin's similarities to 2 *Clement* are no more than would be expected when two different harmonies of the synoptic gospels are compared; identical harmonistic patterns are certain to occur to some extent, and examples of such agreement have been shown.

A final comment should be made concerning Tatian. It has long been known that Tatian was a pupil of Justin and that after Justin's death Tatian composed a harmony of the four canonical gospels, the *Diatessaron*. It is now apparent that the concept of a gospel harmony did not originate with Tatian; indeed he was a pupil in a school in which gospel harmonies were apparently commonplace. What is new in Tatian's *Diatessaron* and what is not found in Justin's writings is a full gospel harmony rather than one of limited scope and the incorporation into the gospel harmony of the Gospel of John.

BIBLIOGRAPHY

1. Primary Sources

Butterworth, George William. *Clement of Alexandria*. The Loeb Classical Library. London, 1919.

Goodspeed, Edgar J. *Die ältesten Apologeten*. Göttingen, 1914.

Hartel, William. *S. Thasci Caecili Cypriani Opera Omnia*. 3 Volumes. Vienna, 1868-1871.

Heikel, Ivar A. *Eusebius Werke*. Vol. VI. Die Griechischen Christlichen Schriftsteller. Leipzig, 1913.

Holl, Karl. *Epiphanius*. Die Griechischen Christlichen Schriftsteller. 3 Volumes. Leipzig, 1915-1933.

Huck, Albert. *Synopse der drei ersten Evangelien neu bearbeitet von Hans Lietzmann*. 10th edition. Tübingen, 1950.

Klostermann, Erich. *Apocrypha II*. Kleine Texte. Edited by Hans Lietzmann. Volume 8. 3rd edition. Berlin, 1929.

Klostermann, Erich. *Origenes Werke*. Volume X. Die Griechischen Christlichen Schriftsteller. Leipzig, 1935.

Koetschau, Paul. *Origenes Werke*. Volumes I and II. Die Griechischen Christlichen Schriftsteller. Leipzig, 1899.

Lake, Kirsopp. *The Apostolic Fathers*. 2 Volumes. The Loeb Classical Library. Cambridge, Massachusetts, 1948-1952.

Lommatzsch, C. H. E. *Origenis Opera Omnia*. 25 Volumes. Berlin, 1831-1848.

Migne, Jacques Paul. *Patrologia Graeca*. Paris, 1857-1866.

——. *Patrologia Latina*. Paris, 1844-1865.

Nestle, Eberhard. *Novum Testamentum Graece*. 25th edition. Stuttgart, 1963.

Otto, Johannes Carl Theodor Eques de. *Iustini Philosophi et Martyris Opera Quae Feruntur Omnia*. 3 Volumes. 3rd edition, Jena. 1876.

Preuschen, Erwin. *Origenes Werke*. Volume IV. Die Griechischen Christlichen Schriftsteller. Leipzig, 1903.

Rehm, Bernhard. *Die Pseudoklementinen. I Homilien*. Die Griechischen Christlichen Schriftsteller. Berlin, 1953.

Scheidweiler, Felix. *Theodoretus*. Die Griechischen Christlichen Schriftsteller. Berlin, 1954.

Stählin, Otto. *Clemens Alexandrinus*. 3 Volumes. Die Griechischen Christlichen Schriftsteller. Leipzig, 1906-1909.

Swete, Henry Barclay. *The Old Testament in Greek*. Cambridge, 1887.

van de Sande Bakhuyzen, W. H. *Der Dialog des Adamantius*. Die Griechischen Christlichen Schriftsteller. Leipzig, 1901.

Wendland, Paul. *Hippolytus Werke*. Volume III. Die Griechischen Christlichen Schriftsteller. Leipzig, 1916.

Zangemeister, Karl. *Orosius, Paulus*. Vienna, 1882.

2. Secondary Sources

Achelis, Hans and Flemming, Johannes. *Die ältesten Quellen des orientalischen Kirchenrechts, Zweites Buch: Die Syrische Didaskalia*. Leipzig, 1904.

Allen, Willoughby C. *A Critical and Exegetical Commentary on the Gospel According to S. Matthew*. Edinburgh, 1951.

Altaner, Berthold. *Patrologie*. 3rd edition. Freiburg, 1951.

Arendt, Wilhelm. "Kritische Untersuchungen über die Schriften Justins des Märtyrers," *Theologische Quartalschrift* (1834), pp. 256-295.

Baldus, Aloys. *Das Verhältnis Justins des Märtyrers zu unsern synoptischen Evangelien*. Münster, 1895.

Barrett, C. K. *The Gospel According to St. John*. New York, 1956.

Barthélemy, D. "Redécouverte d'un chaînon manquant de l'histoire de la Septante," *Revue Biblique*, LX (1953), pp. 18-29.

Bell, H. Idris and Skeat, T. C. *Fragments of an Unknown Gospel and Other Early Christian Papyri*. London, 1935.

Bellinzoni, Arthur J., Jr. "The Source of the Agraphon in Justin Martyr's Dialogue with Trypho 47: 5," *Vigiliae Christianae*, XVII, 2 (1963), pp. 65-70.

Bousset, Wilhelm. *Die Evangeliencitate Justins des Märtyrers in ihrem Wert für die Evangelienkritik*. Göttingen, 1891.

Buckley, E. R. "Justin Martyr's Quotations from the Synoptic Tradition," *Journal of Theological Studies*, XXXVI (1935), pp. 173-176.

Bultmann, Rudolf. *Das Evagelium des Johannes*. Göttingen, 1957.

——. *The History of the Synoptic Tradition*. New York, 1963.

Carrington, Philip. *The Primitive Christian Catechism*. Cambridge, 1940.

von Christs, Wilhelm. *Geschichte der Griechischen Litteratur*. 5th edition. Part II, second half. Munich, 1913.

Credner, Carl August. *Beiträge zur Einleitung in die biblischen Schriften*. Halle, 1832.

——. *Geschichte des neutestamentlichen Kanons*. Berlin, 1860.

Creed, John Martin. *The Gospel According to St. Luke*. London, 1953.

Davies. W. D. *The Setting of the Sermon on the Mount*. Cambridge, 1964.

Dibelius, Martin. *Der Brief des Jakobus*. Göttingen, 1957.

——. *Die Formgeschichte des Evangeliums*. 3rd edition. Tübingen, 1959.

——. *Geschichte der urchristlichen Literatur*. Berlin, 1926.

Dodd, C. H. *Historical Tradition in the Fourth Gospel*. Cambridge, 1963.

——. *The Interpretation of the Fourth Gospel*. Cambridge, 1955.

Dräseke, Johannes. "Zu den unter des Justinus Namen überlieferten christologischen Bruchstücken," *Jahrbücher für protestantische Theologie*, X (1884), pp. 347-352.

von Engelhardt, Moritz. *Das Christenthum Justins des Märtyrers*. Erlangen, 1878.

Fonck, Leopold. "Die Echtheit von Justins Dialog gegen Trypho," *Biblica*, II (1921), pp. 342-347.

Glover, Richard. "The Didache's Quotations and the Synoptic Gospels," *New Testament Studies*, V (1958-1959), pp. 12-39.

Goodspeed, Edgar J. *A History of Early Christian Literature*. Chicago, 1942.

Grant, Robert M. *The Secret Sayings of Jesus*. London, 1960.

Grenfell, B. P. and Hunt, A. S. ΛΟΓΙΑ ΙΗΣΟΥ, *Sayings of Our Lord*. New York, 1897.

——. *New Sayings of Jesus and Fragment of a Lost Gospel from Oxyrhynchus*. London, 1904.

Harnack, Adolf. *Geschichte der altchristlichen Litteratur*. Leipzig, 1893.

Hauck, Friedrich, "μοιχεύω, μοιχάω, κ.τ.λ." *Theologisches Wörterbuch zum Neuen Testament*. Edited by Gerhard Kittel. Volume IV. Stuttgart, 1957.

Hilgenfeld, Adolf. *Kritische Untersuchungen über die Evangelien Justin's, der Clementinischen Homilien und Marcion's*. Halle, 1850.

——. "Die Überlieferung über die griechischen Apologeten des Christenthums im zweiten Jahrhundert und ihr neuester Censor," *Zeitschrift für wissenschaftliche Theologie*, XXVI (1883), pp. 1-45.

Jeremias, Joachim. *Unknown Sayings of Jesus*. Translated by Reginald Fuller. London, 1957.

Katz, P. "Septuagintal studies in the mid-century. Their links with the past and their present tendencies," *The Background of the New Testament and Its Eschatology*. Edited by W. D. Davies and David Daube. Cambridge, 1956, pp. 176-208.

Knopf, Rudolf. *Die Lehre der zwölf Apostel*. Tübingen, 1920.

Köster, Helmut. "Geschichte und Kultus im Johannesevangelium und bei Ignatius von Antiochien," *Zeitschrift für Theologie und Kirche*, LIV (1957), pp. 56-69.

Köster, Helmut. *Septuaginta und Synoptischer Erzählungsstoff im Schriftbeweis Justins des Märtyrers*. Habilitationsschrift. Heidelberg, 1956.

Köster, Helmut. *Synoptische Überlieferung bei den Apostolischen Vätern*. Berlin, 1957.

Krüger, Gustav. "Zu Justin," *Zeitschrift für die neutestamentliche Wissenschaft*, VII (1906), pp. 138 f.

Lietzmann, Hans. "Justinus der Märtyrer," *Pauly-Wissowa Real-Encyclopädie der classischen Altertumswissenschaft*. Volume X. Stuttgart, 1919.

Lippelt, Ernst. Quae Fuerint Justini Martyris ΑΠΟΜΝΗΜΟΝΕΥΜΑΤΑ *Quaeque Ratione Cum Forma Evangeliorum Syro-Latina Cohaeserint*. Halle, 1901.

Lohmeyer, Ernst. *Das Evangelium des Matthäus*. Göttingen, 1958.

Massaux, Edouard. *Influence de l'Évangile de saint Matthieu sur la Littérature chrétienne avant Irénée*. Louvain, 1950.

——. "Le Texte du Sermon sur la Montagne de Matthieu Utilisé par Saint Justin," *Ephemerides Theologicae Lovanienses*, XXVIII (1952), pp. 411-448.

Maurer, Christian. "Petrusevangelium," *Neutestamentliche Apokryphen in deutscher Übersetzung*. Volume I. Edited by Edgar Hennecke and Wilhelm Schneemelcher. Tübingen, 1959.

M'Neile, Alan Hugh. *The Gospel According to St. Matthew*. London, 1955.

Piper, Otto A. "The Nature of the Gospel According to Justin Martyr," *The Journal of Religion*, XLI, 3 (July 1961), pp. 155-168.

Plummer, Alfred. *A Critical and Exegetical Commentary on the Gospel According to S. Luke*. Edinburgh, 1956.

Preuschen, Erwin, "Die Echtheit von Justin's Dialog gegen Trypho," *Zeitschrift für die neutestamentliche Wissenschaft* (1919-1920), pp. 102-127.

Quasten, Johannes. *Patrology*. Westminster, Maryland, 1950.

Redlich, E. Basil. *Form Criticism Its Value and Limitations*. London, 1939.

Rengstorf, Karl. "ἀπόστολος," *Theologisches Wörterbuch zum Neuen Testament*. Edited by Gerhard Kittel. Stuttgart, 1933, Volume I, pp. 406-447.

Resch, Alfred. *Agrapha*. Leipzig, 1906.

——. *Ausserkanonische Paralleltexte*. 3 Volumes. Leipzig, 1893-1897.

Romanides, John S. "Justin Martyr and the Fourth Gospel," *The Greek Orthodox Theological Review*, IV, 2 (1958-1959), pp. 115-134.

Ropes, James Hardy. *Die Sprüche Jesu*. Texte und Untersuchungen. XIV, 2. Leipzig, 1896.

Sanday, William. *The Gospels in the Second Century*. London, 1876.

Seeberg, Alfred. *Der Katechismus der Urchristenheit*. Leipzig, 1903.

Selwyn, Edward G. *The First Epistle of Peter*. London, 1946.

Semisch, Karl. *Die apostolischen Denkwürdigkeiten des Märtyrers Justinus*. Hamburg, 1848.

Strachan, R. H. *The Fourth Gospel Its Significance and Environment*. London, 1960.

Swete, H. B. ΕΥΑΓΓΕΛΙΟΝ ΚΑΤΑ ΠΕΤΡΟΝ, *The Akhmîm Fragment of the Apocryphal Gospel of Peter*. London, 1893.

Taylor, Vincent. *The Formation of the Gospel Tradition*. London, 1957.

——. *The Gospel According to Saint Mark*. London, 1955.

Thoma, A. "Justins literarisches Verhältnis zu Paulus und zum Johannisevangelium," *Zeitschrift für wissenschaftliche Theologie*, XVIII (1875), pp. 383-412, 490-565.

Titus, Eric Lane. "The Motivations of Changes Made in the New Testament by Justin Martyr and Clement of Alexandria: A Study in the Origin of New Testament Variation." Unpublished Ph. D. dissertation, University of Chicago, 1942.

Volkmar, Gustav. *Über Justin den Märtyrer und sein Verhältniss zu unsern Evangelien.* Zurich, 1853.

Westcott, Brooke Foss. *A General Survey of the History of the Canon of the New Testament.* London, 1870.

White, Hugh G. Evelyn. *The Sayings of Jesus from Oxyrhynchus.* Cambridge, 1920.

Windisch, Hans. *Der Barnabasbrief.* Tübingen, 1920.

Wright, Leon E. *Alterations of the Words of Jesus as Quoted in the Literature of the Second Century.* Cambridge, Massachusetts, 1952.

Zahn, Theodor. *Geschichte des neutestamentlichen Kanons.* Volume I, Part 2. Erlangen, 1888.

3. Reference Works

Bauer, Walter. *Griechisch-Deutsches Wörterbuch zu den Schriften des Neuen Testaments und der übrigen urchristlichen Literatur.* 5th edition. Berlin, 1958.

Blass, F. and Debrunner, A. *A Greek Grammar of the New Testament and Other Early Christian Literature.* Translated and revised by Robert Funk. Chicago, 1961.

Goodspeed, Edgar J. *Index Apologeticus.* Leipzig, 1912.

——. *Index Patristicus.* Leipzig, 1907.

Hastings, James. *Dictionary of the Apostolic Church.* 2 Volumes. New York, 1916.

Kittel, Gerhard. *Theologisches Wörterbuch zum Neuen Testament.* 7 Volumes. Stuttgart, 1933-1964.

Lampe, G. W. H. *A Patristic Greek Lexicon.* Oxford, 1961.

Legg, S. C. E. *Novum Testamentum Graece. Evangelium Secundum Marcum.* Oxford, 1935.

——. *Novum Testamentum Graece. Evangelium Secundum Matthaeum.* Oxford, 1940.

Liddell, Henry George and Scott, Robert. *A Greek-English Lexicon.* Oxford, 1953.

Moule, C. F. D. *An Idiom Book of New Testament Greek.* Cambridge, 1953.

Moulton, W. F. and Geden, A. S. *A Concordance to the Greek Testament.* Edinburgh, 1957.

von Soden, Hermann Freiherr. *Griechisches Neues Testament.* Göttingen, 1913.

Tischendorf, Constantinus. *Novum Testamentum Graece.* 8th edition. Leipzig, 1869.

INDICES

I. OLD TESTAMENT REFERENCES

II. NEW TESTAMENT REFERENCES

III. REFERENCES TO EXTRA-CANONICAL CHRISTIAN WRITINGS

IV. INDEX OF AUTHORS